PENGUIN BOOKS

COMMUNES USA

Richard Fairfield was born in Gardner, Maine, in 1937. His extremely varied education included work in Japanese, psychology, English literature, creative writing, and Mandarin Chinese, which he learned in connection with his military service. After establishing and operating his own insurance agency, he went on to study religion at Tufts University, Medford, Massachusetts, and to serve as student minister in two Massachusetts churches. He received his Bachelor of Divinity degree at Starr King School for the Ministry in Berkeley, California. In the fall of 1970, he visited communes in England, France, Holland, Denmark, Germany, and Switzerland. Fairfield edits and publishes *The Modern Utopian,* which he founded in 1966 to report on the developing communal movement in the United States.

COMMUNES USA

A PERSONAL TOUR

RICHARD FAIRFIELD,

1937

PENGUIN BOOKS INC · BALTIMORE, MD.

Penguin Books Inc
7110 Ambassador Road
Baltimore, Maryland 21207

First published 1972
Copyright © Alternatives Foundation 1971

Library of Congress Catalog Card number: 71–185040

Set in Linofilm Bodoni
Printed in the United States of America
by Kingsport Press Inc., Kingsport, Tenn. 37662
Typography by Martin Connell

TO MY PARENTS—GEORGE AND DAISY FAIRFIELD

10046

ACKNOWLEDGMENTS

The author gratefully acknowledges the following persons who provided their photographs: Walt Odets for photographs on pages 39, 42, 48, 102, 109, 112, 115, 120, 124, 130, 194, 199, 202, 206, 209, 212, 214, 217, 229, 306, 323, 325, 354, 363, 375; Sylvia Clarke Hamilton on pages ii, 234, 237, 239, 245, 247, 253, 255, 261, 266, 269, 271, 273, 276, 279, 310, 328, 371; the author on pages 61, 63, 79, 89, 99, 171, 335, 341; Buddy Mays on pages 167, 175, 181; F. Gieger on page 26; Barry Korar on page 140; and Clintell C. Porter on page 135.

Thanks also to Edmund Helminsky who conducted the interviews with Bob Carey of the Oregon Family, Steve Durky of the Lama Foundation, Max Finstein of New Buffalo and for the group session at the Lama Foundation.

CONTENTS

Introduction   1

Chapter One: A Brief Historical Survey of Utopian Communities   9

Chapter Two: Marxist/Anarchist Ideological Communes   19
    The Morgans of Yellow Springs
    The Homer L. Morris Fund
    The School of Living
    Cold Mountain Farm

Chapter Three: Scientific Ideology/Walden Two   55
    Walden House
    Twin Oaks Takes Root
    The Growth of Twin Oaks

Chapter Four: Modern Religious Communes   101
    The Oregon Family
    The Lama Foundation
    The One World Family
    The City of Light
    The Ananda Cooperative Community
    The Himalayan Academy

Chapter Five: Hip Communes of Rural America   163
    The Lower Farm
    Hippies and Hassles in the Taos Area
    New Buffalo
    Drop City
    Liberty
    Magic Farm
    Olompali Ranch
    Gorda Mountain
    Morning Star Ranch
    Sheep Ridge Ranch
    Tolstoy Farm

Chapter Six: Group Marriage Communes   291
    Harrad West
    The CRO Research Organization
    The Family

Chapter Seven: Service Communities   331
    Camphill Village
    The Catholic Worker Farm
    Synanon
    Gould Farm
    Ammon Hennacy

Chapter Eight: Youth Communes   347
    Yellow Submarine
    Greenfeel

Chapter Nine: Commentary/Views   359
    The Way to Oneness
    Ideals
    Matter over Mind
    Plotting the i in Self-Direction

Appendices   375

Bibliographies   385

INTRODUCTION

DEFINITIONS

A commune, a collective, a cooperative, an intentional community, an experimental community — each of these is an arrangement of three or more persons among whom the primary bond is some form of sharing rather than blood or legal ties. The degree of sharing is as varied as the arrangements made, ranging from perhaps simply owning land in common to holding all things common (as was the practice of the early Christians*).

Each of the terms given above has a specific, narrowly defined meaning that is related in general to the degree of sharing involved. For instance, there is more sharing in a commune than a collective and more sharing in a collective than a cooperative. The cooperative community is the most conservative form: co-op families maintain their traditional structure, with separate homes and jobs, but they share land, recreational space, and tending the common gardens. The commune is the most radical form: it includes sharing housing, economic activities and income, child-rearing, and perhaps even sex in the form of an extended family. The two other terms encountered are "intentional community" and "experimental community." The first phrase is an older and more general term for a planned Utopian ideal community, one in which the end, and the means for attaining that end, is clearly outlined in advance. "Experimental community" is a more recent term referring to a more flexible organization, one open to change and ad-hoc planning.

* See the Bible, *Acts*, 2, 45.

So much for narrow definitions. Using the language loosely, however, one term is as good as another; take your pick. I often use "commune." I like the word. It's easier to write and say than "community" and "cooperative." If the Establishment media still wish to identify communes with dirty-hippie-drug-addicted-sex-orgy-crash-pads, that is their prerogative. But such a label dates the media's understanding, going back to a few bad guys in the bad days of the Haight-Ashbury/East Village psychedelic revolution, just before the massive hippie exodus from the cities.

TYPES

There are many possible ways—none of them are very accurate—of categorizing the types of communes that exist. Most communes defy definition because they are constantly changing and growing. Nevertheless, oversimplification can be valid when introducing unfamiliar material to a reader. I've divided this book into sections which classify communes as religious, ideological, hip, group marriage, service and youth.

Religious groups have traditionally been rural and agricultural Christian communities. Today, with the exception of the holdovers from that tradition (e.g. Amish, Hutterite, Bruderhof), religious communes are usually a mixture of Christian and Eastern, messianic and yoga. Ideological groups tend to have the same fervor as religious ones but that fervor is concentrated on a secular rationalistic philosophy such as Marxism or Skinnerian behavioral psychology. Hip communes are those which have received much of their initial inspiration from the use of drugs such as LSD, mescaline and peyote. They have a more experiential and mystical quality in contrast to the rational and intellectual quality of the ideological groups. Yet they do not identify themselves, as a rule, as "religious." Group marriage communes have as their primary goal the working out of new family and interpersonal relations. Service communities are created in order to provide a total work-recreational environment for disadvantaged individuals. Youth communes, which do not fall into the hip or ideological categories, are those which are usually composed of college graduates or dropouts who wish simply to share the advantages of group living.

THE RECENT GROWTH OF COMMUNES

The last two years (1969–1970) have seen drastic changes in the commune movement throughout the United States. From a few urban groups, crash pads, and a handful of intellectual utopians and Christian conservative communes, the movement has grown very rapidly so that there are now over 2,000 communes.* (This figure does not include the several thousand urban co-ops and collectives that have also arisen.)

Most of these groups neither seek publicity nor view themselves as part of any movement. They have little evangelical desire to turn the world on to the glories of communal living and are content to be left alone in order to solve their own problems and build their own alternatives. One anonymous community gives this advice to those interested in starting a commune:

Publicity is the death of a community. If you last for two years, you will find you have dozens of visitors a week, often coming in such crowds as to make you feel like an animal on display. . . . it would probably be a good idea to refrain from giving yourselves a name. You will be harder to talk about without a handle.**

Although I understand very well the problem of visitors, I am not sympathetic with this particular community's

---

*The New York Times, December 17, 1970.

**How to Make a Commune, a pamphlet published in January 1971 by Alternatives Foundation, PO Drawer A, Diamond Heights Station, San Francisco, California, 94131.

means of solving the problem. Several communes welcome publicity and visitors without consequently feeling that they are on display. This is because they have established a workable procedure for handling guests. They don't just let passers-by overrun their homes. They care enough about what they are doing to want others to know about it and not to allow others to disrupt it. Communes that receive no publicity get few visitors, so they do not have to deal with this situation. But they lose the opportunity for new blood and vitality that publicity can bring.

THE TRUTH ABOUT COMMUNES

The innundation of communes by visitors is convincing evidence of America's growing interest in the communal life style. Much is now being written about communes, with some writers adopting a scholarly perspective and others a descriptive or factual one. I aspire to neither, for I believe that truth, whether about communes or anything else, is personal and subjective.

No matter how objective-sounding and scholarly a finished work is, it must still have been filtered through a subjective human agency. Certain information has been selected for presentation, other details have been left out; the total picture can never be rendered. Whatever we read or see on television, for example, is only a portion of the truth. The "eyewitness news" is the news as viewed through two (perhaps four or six) particular eyes; it is never the whole news. Impersonal, objective truth — truth with a capital T — will forever elude us (if indeed it exists anywhere). Even Divine Revelation must be communicated to and through the subjective human psyche; so it will do no good to claim direct inspiration.

No commune mentioned in this book need take offense at what I say about it, for on my next visit I might change my impression entirely. After all, it is not really the commune I am writing about, but myself. And it is only the collective egotism of others that may criticize the subjective writer for inaccuracies or omissions. So, dear reader, credit only your naïveté if one day you actually encounter one of the communes described herein and exclaim: "That Dick Fairfield is full of shit; this commune is nothing like the way he described it." Note also that this is dated information. The commune movement has matured a great deal since much of this material was written. And even I've changed some — don't expect me to agree tomorrow with everything I've said today.

THE TRUTH ABOUT ME

I've been involved in the experimental/intentional community movement since early 1966 when I read a lot of books about 19th century utopias and a few modern utopian novels such as *Walden Two, Island,* and *Stranger in a Strange Land.*

In September 1966, after a summer of research on current happenings, I began a magazine about communes. The magazine is called *The Modern Utopian.* Originally it dealt with such radical social-change issues as ending the war and legalizing abortion as well as with communes. But little was then happening on the community scene. Now the magazine is concerned with alternative life styles almost exclusively. Subscriptions have quadrupled, although the magazine still has a very small circulation (5,000), mostly among college students and professors, semi-dropouts and dissatisfied middle-class professionals.

During the first few years of the magazine's existence, I visited only a few communes. Articles were written by other people as I was too busy attending graduate school and keeping the magazine afloat. I didn't believe that people (including myself) should visit a commune without prior knowledge of it and without the serious intention of joining if they find what they like. Since I had no intention of joining, I visited only a few communes. I did actually start a commune of sorts. It is still going, although I am no longer a part of it and I don't agree with its point of view. I have also been active in helping other people begin communes.

After finishing graduate school, I spent several months as a Unitarian minister but found little challenge or inspiration in organized religion. Instead, I decided to work full-time at exploring alternative life styles (see details on Alternatives Foundation in Appendix). Penguin Books approached me to write a paperback book about communes. This sparked my interest in visiting communes and telling their story as I saw it, not only for readers of Penguins but also for the increasing number of readers of *The Modern Utopian*.

ON THE ROAD

I have written elsewhere that "My advice to people interested in communal living is 'Do it where you are! You don't find it by . . . traveling half way around the world.'" Not following my own advice, and armed with the rationalization that I was writing a book, my companion Consuelo Sandoval and I traveled 12,000 miles from our home in San Francisco in an old 1962 Plymouth station-wagon that already had 80,000 miles under its belt, polluting the atmosphere and our lungs as we went. The back window was broken and whenever the wind blew just right, we got a good whiff of what ordinarily only Mother Nature and tailgaters have to endure.

Apart from having a general curiosity about the communal life style, most people visit communes for one or more of three basic reasons:

1. They want someone or something "out there" to turn them on and for this they are not even charged admission. (People in communes should think about that; they don't need to farm or get food stamps — they should simply charge admission for all the tourists and curious passers-by.)

2. Visitors want a hip place to stay for awhile before returning to their ordinary world of reality — mom and dad's place or the prestigious job and color TV. (The commune thereby becomes the new summer camp without curfew or regulation.)

3. They are writing a book, doing research for a term paper or a PhD dissertation — perhaps for some liberal institution that provides funds for the study of deviant behavior. (Most of this writing turns out to be more academic bullshit, more misinformation, and more of an excuse for talking and reading and thinking about communal living rather than having to face the practical reality of doing it.)

And now Consuelo and I were driving around the big old USA to "investigate" communes and thus contribute our bit to the moral decay of a society that would rather talk than do.

Richard Fairfield and Consuelo Sandoval

CHAPTER ONE

A BRIEF HISTORICAL SURVEY
OF UTOPIAN COMMUNITIES

The Historical Background

As I HAVE SAID, this book is not intended to be any kind of so-called scholarly work. However, just to let you know that a 1962 Plymouth station wagon hasn't been my only research tool, that I have read books on the history of utopian communities, and that I have even done an entire course on one 19th century community,* I include the following brief overview of utopian communities. And for those of you who want to read more, there is, in the Appendix, a lengthy bibliography of musty old books on the subject you can find in any good library.

The history of man's quest for the ideal state stretches back some 2,000 years or more, during which many people have experienced dissatisfaction with the society in which they have lived. Many have dreamed of a better world for mankind—an orderly, fruitful existence free from chaos, misery, poverty, and other all too common social evils. Some of these dreamers have translated their visions into plans, pamphlets and books, such as Sir Thomas More and his classic *Utopia* (1516). But only a few men have managed to translate such visionary dreams and writings into action, albeit in the form of the temporary ideal community rather than the permanent ideal state. Nevertheless these people have been the founders and members of the numerous religious and secular communities that have evolved and flourished at many different times and places during the past two millennia. It is such communities that have, in the history of thought, fostered the view that the basic goodness of human nature (as opposed to the corruption of human society) is encouraged by a truly cooperative way of life.

---

* At Crane Theological School, Tufts University, I set up a self-study course on the Oneida Community under the guidance of a wise history professor (a rarity).

Why has this social phenomenon of the ideal community persisted throughout history; that is, why have men repeatedly established communities apart from society as a whole? Dr. H. Darin-Drabkin lists seven basic reasons:*

1. Man is a cooperative animal in whom there exists a strong urge for social behavior and cooperation.

2. People have always wished for equality and for a society based on justice.

3. Economic hardships compel people to live together.

4. Human migration cuts off people from traditional forms of economic, social and cultural enterprise.

5. Communal life helps combat threats of physical extinction and lack of security.

6. Cooperative and collective communities can help to modernize an undeveloped country in a hurry, as has happened in the Soviet Union and Israel.

7. Communal life can be a way for the individual to overcome social class barriers and other such societal disadvantages.

A unique religious ideology, shared only by a chosen few, is often a strong additional motivation for establishing a community.

EARLY COMMUNAL ACTIVITIES IN EUROPE

Possibly the earliest communal society was that of the Essenes, who lived along the shores of the Dead Sea in Palestine from the 2d century B.C. to the 2d century A.D. A pious Judaic sect, it consisted solely of celibate men; women, celibate or otherwise, were not allowed membership.

Although each Essene pursued his own separate occupation, all property was held in common. The members

*The Other Society, pp. 15–17.

lived in separate dwellings scattered throughout various towns and villages, yet they shared and consumed the products of their labor collectively. This emphasis on collective consumption, coupled with independent productive methods was a common feature of the communes of antiquity, as well as those of the Middle Ages.

With the development of Christianity, utopian aspirations (to use the phrase retroactively) became even more otherworldly; the dream of establishing a perfect society on earth tended to be replaced by the belief in the return of the Savior and a new spiritual kingdom. Early Christians formed religious communities, sold their riches, and lived with all things in common, while awaiting the Second Coming of their Lord and Master.

The Master never returned. By the 4th or 5th century Christians had transferred their communal emphasis to the monastic orders that enforced celibacy and solitude. During the early Middle Ages, the utopian ideal degenerated to become little more than the hope for a future existence, in a far-off heaven in the presence of God. The vision of earthly utopias faded but it never entirely vanished.

Between the 11th and 17th centuries communal living was a feature of a number of minority religious sects throughout Europe. Often faced with persecution, the adherents of each sect tended to band together, sharing their beliefs, property, and lives. These sects included the Bogomils in Bulgaria, the Cathars in France, the Lollards in England, and the Waldenses and Anabaptists in various parts of central and western Europe. Religious ideology was, naturally, the basis for these communal sects and was the people's strength and support. The Anabaptists were the most radical and the most democratic of the sects that separated themselves from traditional society. They uncompromisingly opposed government restrictions on the individual. They refused to fight in wars or pay taxes or submit to any outside religious authority. They believed in direct inspiration from God as their guide to behavior, Biblical interpretation and religious practices. They were as a result the most persecuted of sects. Even Martin Luther cried out for the Church authorities to "stab, crush and strangle" these deviant utopians.

COMMUNITARIANISM IN THE UNITED STATES

With the growth of the New World colonies, many members of persecuted European sects fled to America. Some of these people, having had communal experience in Europe, settled in communities of a religious nature apart from the general colonial society. A number of these groups prospered. The Ephratans, for example, were so successful that they actually abandoned their mills and workshops to escape prosperity's corrupting influence (unlike some groups that elected to give up communitarianism in favor of prosperity). Later the Shaker communities, founded by Ann Lee, flourished and prospered in spite of their strict codes of celibacy and their austere communal living conditions. Other early US communes were not so fortunate, suffering much hardship and deprivation before disappearing.

The 19th century marked the heyday of communitarianism in the United States. Not only religious but also secular visionaries attempted to establish the perfect society on earth. This new breed of secular utopians was created largely by the growth of cities with their sweatshops, child labor, and increasing unemployment problems under a ruthlessly competitive economic system. For the secularists the primary motive was to gain a greater measure of economic and social security. This was considered achievable through some form of socialistic organization. The secular communities accordingly stressed collective production of goods, as well as collective consumption. This means economic cooperation and equality. Owen,

Wright, Fourier, Brisbane, Ripley, Cabet—pioneering utopians all—each set out to establish a new social order at the community level. Trade-unionist and socialist ideology were, at that time, becoming an active part of the political and economic scene, thereby lending some support to the communal movement.

While religious communities were prolific, they too maintained a strong emphasis on socio-economic reform. The Oneida Community founded by John Humphrey Noyes is an excellent example of a religion-based, 19th-century community that succeeded so well economically that its manufacturing operations are still maintained profitably today.

In general, communal life in 19th century America was superior to industrial and agricultural life in most of the country. A contemporary journalist, Charles Nordhoff, visited the major communities, and then summarized his impressions as follows:*

1. The communal members are utilitarians. (Too much so, Nordhoff observed, for they did not even care for flowers.)

2. They do not toil severely.

3. They are all very clean.

4. They are known for their honesty.

5. They are humane and charitable.

6. Their lives are full of devices for personal ease and comfort.

7. They all live well, according to different tastes; food is abundant and cooked well.

8. They are usually healthy.

9. They are the most long-lived people of our population.

10. They are temperate in the use of liquor; drunkenness is unknown.

11. They try to keep out of debt and they avoid all speculative and haphazard enterprises.

*The Communistic Societies of the United States, pp. 399–406.

12. They are prosperous and either marry young or remain celibate.

13. They engage in a wholesome variety of occupations and an infinite variety of both healthful work and amusement.

14. They have ingenious ways of securing harmony and of eliminating — without violence — improper or rather uncongenial members of the group.

And to this summary Nordhoff added the following comment:*

It [communal life] provides a greater variety of employment for each individual and this increases the dexterity and broadens the faculties of men. It offers a wider range of wholesome enjoyment and also greater restraints against debasing pleasures. It gives independence and inculcates prudence and frugality. It demands self-sacrifice and restrains selfishness and greed; and thus increases the happiness which comes from the moral side of human nature. Finally, it relieves the individual's life from a great mass of (carking) cares, from the necessity of oversevere and exhausting toil, from the dread of misfortune or exposure in old age.

A modern writer, Mark Holloway, in assessing the US utopian communities, has made the following general comment about them:**

[these communities] . . . produced a high standard of living and workmanship, were pioneers in Negro and feminine emancipation, in democratic government, in eugenics, in the primitive psychoanalysis of mutual criticism, and in education and social reform. They were a benefit to their neighbours and also to the nation; and they showed by example that associative effort of this type can be highly satisfactory.

* Ibid., p. 406.
** *Heavens on Earth*, 2d ed., p. 228.

By the early part of the 20th century, most if not all of the major community experiments in the United States had been abandoned or were in serious decline. Nevertheless, several 19th century groups did survive; among them were the Shakers, Inspirationists (Amana Society) and the Oneida Community. Because of their celibacy and lack of converts, though, the Shakers declined in numbers to less than 100 by 1940 and to few if any by 1960. The Inspirationists still exist today as a cooperative society with a stable population of about 1,400, although their traditional way of communal living has been changed considerably (and deliberately) since the early 1930s. So too the famous Oneida Community is still in existence, but as an economic enterprise rather than as a communal experiment.

Among the 19th century communities that have survived are various Christian farming communes in the United States and also Canada. Most of these are Hutterite groups. In addition, there are a few communities that, although founded in the 20th century, are firmly rooted in the ideas and ideals of the 19th century and earlier times. The Bruderhof — Society of Brothers — is one of these.

The fact that religious communities have outlived secular ones is not surprising since ideological convictions can be a strong cohesive force among people. Robert V. Hine has reported the following:[*]

The average life of religious colonies in California has been over twenty years, while that of the secular colonies has been well under ten. Most analysts of utopian experiments from Charles Nordhoff to Arthur Bestor, Jr. have observed this discrepancy between the life spans of the sectarian and the secular and, therefore, have concluded

[*]*California's Utopian Communities*, pp. 169–170.

that religious fervor is one of the ingredients requisite to colony longevity.

Another writer, Victor Calverton, has listed six principal causes for the failure of communal experiments.*

1. A lack of a division of labor—too much diversification and not enough specialization in an attempt to be self-contained, completely self-reliant communities.

2. A lack of capital for initial investment and expansion.

3. A conflict between the agrarian and the industrial way of life, with the former usually being emphasized although the latter was more profitable.

4. An innate human disposition against *excessive* cooperation; communities tended to emphasize unity at the expense of diversity, freedom, and individual initiative.

5. Hostility from the general public and unfavorable publicity from the press.

6. A low-quality membership. Most communities neither carefully screened their members nor provided a probationary or training period; thus, undesirable types (lazy, argumentative, hostile) became part of these groups.

Summing up, it can be said that the majority of the traditional utopian communities that flourished in the 19th century believed in and practiced communal ownership of the land and buildings, complete sharing of all basic necessities, communal dining, preventive medicine with free medical care for all, equal rights for women, no servant labor, a progressive educational program, simplicity of dress, cooperative purchase and production of goods, equal sharing of labor, community child care by trained nurses and teachers, and an alteration of the traditional code of sexual behavior either by liberalization or severe restriction.

These characteristics have been shared, to a greater or lesser degree, by communal groups ranging across

Where Angels Dared to Tread.

17

time from the pre-Christian Essenes to the present-day pioneers of the Israeli Kibbutzim. And the influence of these and other communal ideas—whether practiced, preached, or both—on the general society cannot be adequately measured. Some of them that were once ridiculed by outsiders are commonly accepted today. Others, still denigrated, may well be accepted tomorrow.

It is time now to leave the library and head for the open road—the road that leads to America's contemporary communes, and self-discovery.

CHAPTER TWO

MARXIST/ANARCHIST
IDEOLOGICAL COMMUNES

THE MORGANS OF YELLOW SPRINGS

YELLOW SPRINGS, a scenic village in the rich farmlands of west-central Ohio, can be selectively identified as the seat of progressive Antioch College, the former headquarters of the American Humanist Association, and the home of two organizations associated with Arthur and Griscom Morgan.

Community Services, Inc. is an organization set up by Arthur Morgan, who is perhaps best-known as the author of *Nowhere is Somewhere* (the story of the sources of the ideas in Thomas More's classic *Utopia*). However, I don't want to write much here about Community Services, Inc., because, frankly, it has never really interested me. Furthermore, its main function in recent years has been to give financial, moral and physical support to a new community in India named Mitraniketan — a role that places it somewhat outside the realm of communal activities within the United States.

Neither do I want to take up time and space in discussing The Vale Community, for which Griscom Morgan (Arthur's son) serves as spokesman. Suffice it to say that, in its own words, "The Vale Community numbers five member families and more than that number of residents and associates living with them, particularly college students. It has a school for the early years. It is a complex and spontaneous fellowship."

My aim here is not really to be dismissive of the Morgans and their endeavors, but rather to temporarily shift the focus away from individual communes to consideration of the ongoing changeover in the US community movement.

Griscom Morgan is extremely knowledgeable about the old-line community movement. Over the years he has cooperated with Community Services in publishing an occasional issue of the *Intentional Community Newsletter*. It was from just such an issue that I first learned of a dozen or more old-line socialist and Christian communities back in 1966, when I began my survey of contemporary communes. Although the newsletter was useful to me, I hardly had any illusions about it. The publication was poorly typed, badly edited, and imperfectly mimeographed; it had limited distribution. Even when I first read it, I felt that the ideas it expressed were very much out of touch with the newly developing movement.

I met Griscom Morgan at the first annual Walden Two Convention, which was held near Ann Arbor, Michigan, in the summer of 1966. This convention marked a turning point in the development of interest in communes in America. Prior to this time, only die-hard socialists from the 30s maintained an active interest in utopian communities. Now, turned on by the rising popularity of such books as Skinner's *Walden Two*, Huxley's *Island*, and Heinlein's *Stranger in a Strange Land*, many middle-class suburbanites and college students were beginning to think seriously about an alternative life style.

The psychedelic revolution had also begun to receive widespread popularity, as people apparently took Tim Leary's advice to "Turn on, Tune in, Drop out." It took another year for the drug culture to produce the widespread effect of impelling the hippies to drop out into communal living groups. Alienated, acid-tripping hippies and dissatisfied middle-class intellectuals began forming and/or joining communities separately from each other.

Today the middle-class suburbanites intent on dropping out are recognizing their need to rely less on their heads, while the dropped-out longhairs have matured in their use of psychedelics. But the old-line utopians, together with most of the mainstream older generation, retain their deep-rooted fear of drugs and their ingrained distrust of any way of life that lacks structure, organized philosophy, and a clear-cut and rational ideology.

Considering not only the current mood of the national counter-culture, but also the specific situation at Yellow Springs (think of Antioch College and all those fresh young minds and hearts), one would certainly expect that the Morgans, irrespective of how old they are, would be more in tune with the younger generation. It is not that they have no direct contact with young people. Indeed, I believe that some young people have been recruited to work on the Morgans' revived IC newsletter, now called *Community Comments*. But *Community Comments*, despite being well-typed and printed by offset, clings to abstract generalizations about the glories of small community and the ugliness of modern industrial technology; it still smacks of the same old Marxist jargon. (Perhaps, being publisher of a paper myself, I am too critical of other papers in the commune movement. Numerous friends of mine, who have talked with Griscom Morgan more recently than I, have been greatly impressed with him.)

THE HOMER L. MORRIS FUND:

A LITTLE HELP TO FRIENDS

One of the still-blooming flowers of the old-time IC movement is the much-needed Homer L. Morris Fund, which was established in the early 1950s. Griscom Morgan has been secretary of the fund for many years. The fund's purpose is to provide short-term loans at a reasonable rate of interest to help communities finance various undertakings — precisely the kinds of loans that orthodox banks and loan agencies would either provide only at exorbitant rates of interest or not consider at all. (The fund is named for a man who devoted a lifetime of service to such causes as intentional communities; he also participated in the development of the American Friends Service Committee's Pencraft Community project and played a key role in developing work camps for the AFSC.)

Since its inception, the fund has helped more than a dozen communities not only to weather their financial crises but also to continue their growth and development until either other credit sources were willing to help or until difficult conditions were alleviated. Most of the loans are short-term because of the fund's limited capital resources. In some cases, though, a loan has been extended from year to year with the understanding that if the funds were needed for emergency loans or for helping new communities, the longer-term borrower would pay back the loan on short notice.

One dramatic instance of the value of the HLM Fund occurred a few years ago when the Koinonia Community in Georgia was faced with major difficulties. The community, which has black members as well as frequent black visitors, was viciously attacked by local racists; its buildings were shot up and its candy-factory was bombed. Subsequently, commercial suppliers and outlets succumbed to boycott pressures and local banks refused to lend the community money for needed repairs. The HLM Fund was one of several organizations that came to the community's aid.

The fund's general policies are worked out by its members and board of directors at an annual meeting. The qualifications for membership are not rigid — only that the prospective member be an individual interested in intentional communities or, better yet, that he or she be a representative of an existing community or a person closely associated with intentional communities.

In general, it is the fund's loan committee that decides whether or not loan applications are approved. To qualify for a loan from the HLM Fund, a community must consist of at least three families with a significant degree of sharing together. (This, though, does not mean that there must be pooling of all income or holding of all property in common.)

The fund places a limit of $3,000 on loans granted to any one community and requires reasonable assurance that the community will repay the loan within the agreed-upon period. There are no religious, political, or life-style requirements involved in obtaining a loan from the fund, but it should be realized that the views and biases of those who serve on the loan committee obviously play a part in determining the kinds of groups that will receive loans. More information can be obtained about it by writing directly to Griscom Morgan c/o The Vale, Yellow Springs, Ohio.

THE SCHOOL OF LIVING

The School of Living was originally begun in 1936 and has had an interesting if checkered history. Started in New York, maintained in Ohio, reborn in Maryland—it has been more firmly rooted in a set of ideas than in one place. And it owes much to the vision and tenacity of a woman named Mildred Loomis. Its inception, though, had its origins in the thought of Ralph Borsodi.

BEGINNINGS AND BAYARD LANE

In 1921 Ralph Borsodi, an economist and New York City advertising and marketing consultant, moved to upstate New York and subsequently experimented with developing a self-sufficient homestead there. He and his family built a big stone house of native rock, cultivated a garden, began a small orchard, and raised chickens, pigs, and goats. Planning ahead, they even constructed two small cottages for the Borsodi sons when they got married. Ralph Borsodi later wrote a book in which he described his experiences with homesteading and tried to show how this approach to living was a constructive alternative and antidote to modern technological civilization.*

This Ugly Civilization (Harpers, 1928). This and *National Advertising vs. Prosperity* are the best known of the several books that Borsodi wrote during the 1920s and 1930s.

24

In the 30s, during the Depression, when the federal government was desperately trying to help the unemployed find gainful work, Borsodi was invited to Ohio to help establish the Dayton Homesteading Experiment. A million dollars was earmarked for this project by the federal government. Agreeable to government funding, but opposed to what he began to feel was intrusive governmental supervision, Borsodi left the project, which soon lost most of its direction and momentum.

Borsodi then decided to develop the homesteading movement on his own, independent of government subsidies and control. So he moved back to New York, where he founded the School of Living in 1936, as an organization to help educate people to live on the land. As part of his plans for the School of Living, he and some friends bought 32 acres of land in Suffern, where they set up a community called Bayard Lane. They also established the Independence Foundation, with a low-interest credit plan and a group-landholding plan that made it easy for people to become members of the homestead community. Eventually 16 families built houses and took up residence at Bayard Lane. The School of Living held many seminars and informal lectures centering around the ideas of Ralph Borsodi.*

LANE'S END HOMESTEAD

Borsodi's assistant, a former teacher and social worker named Mildred Loomis, became totally convinced that his approach was a way out of the ever-increasing urban rat race in American society. When the School of Living closed down at Bayard Lane during World War II, Mildred Loomis, and her husband John Loomis moved to Brookville, a village in western Ohio, where they started

*Ralph Borsodi now lives in New Hampshire, continues to write and lecture, and has recently helped to reactivate the Independence Foundation as a wordwide rural renewal program.

and developed Lane's End Homestead. At Lane's End they lived almost entirely off the land, keeping their income below taxable level and producing up to 95 percent of their own food supply (including all of their meat, grain, vegetables, fruit, honey, and dairy products).

After the war, however, Mildred Loomis resumed the task of carrying out the educational function of the School of Living, encouraging people to go back to the land, start homesteads, become self-sufficient. She published a monthly newspaper called *The Green Revolution*, which gained nationwide distribution. And with the help of friends, she began publishing a scholarly journal, *A Way Out* (originally titled *Balanced Living*).

Meanwhile, the homestead was growing, for over the years Mildred Loomis had built a dedicated following of many hundreds of readers, some of whom had become active supporters. Inevitably it became necessary to erect a second building at Lane's End. In addition to accommodating assistants and apprentices, the new structure came to be utilized as a meeting place and library.

James Iden Smith, Mildred Loomis, Paul Keane

THE MOVE TO MARYLAND

By the 1960s Mildred and her friends and followers at Lane's End were thinking seriously about expanding the School of Living and developing a full-blown community. Then, in 1965, a 37 acre plot of land and five buildings (including a large, 100-year-old stone mill) became available in rural Maryland. Financial support came in the form of $1,000 investment shares, which made it possible to buy the Maryland property.

Frequent workbees were held to renovate the mill building and make its seven-room wing habitable. By August 1966, the Maryland property—called Heathcote—was sufficiently ready for the group's first annual workshop on major problems of living. Thereafter under Mildred's direction, at least one family lived in the mill building year-round in order to supervise the activities of the center. Weekend seminars were initiated, to be held once a month from April through September.

The School of Living at Heathcote soon became a success, thanks in large part to the guidance and concern of Mildred Loomis. John continued to maintain Lane's End while Mildred traveled back and forth between Ohio and Maryland. Although still dogmatically enamored of Ralph Borsodi and his "17 Major Problems of Living," Mildred remained sensitive to the new community movement emerging in the 60s. She showed sympathy and encouragement to the young dropouts and hippies, seeing in the young the only hope for the rural revival toward which she had so fervently worked for so many years. Such an attitude, combined with a searching mind, gave the School of Living the kind of leadership it needed to avoid both stagnation and irrelevance (the twin banes of so many communities rooted in the 30s).

MY DAYS AT HEATHCOTE

It so happened that I had an opportunity to meet Mildred

Loomis and see Heathcote for myself, this coming about as a result of my activities on *The Modern Utopian.* Herb Roseman, onetime editor of *A Way Out* and a member of the School of Living's board of directors, had been corresponding with a mutual friend, Jerald Baker. Jerry was an early promoter of Walden Two ideas* and had provided me with the initial mailing list which helped start *The Modern Utopian* magazine. Jerry suggested a merger of *A Way Out* and TMU. Roseman was impressed with TMU's readability, appeal to youth and treatment of a broad range of social issues. Jerry let me know that a merger was possible and I, open to further expansion, contacted Roseman who presented the idea to Mildred Loomis. Consequently I went to Heathcote in 1967 to talk with Mildred about some sort of collaboration.

Mildred was much older than I had expected. Photos of her were obviously 20 years out of date. Though now in her 70s, she was still an attractive woman, vital and alive. She seemed extremely fair and open in her approach to life and willing to listen to opposing points of view. She was not dogmatic about most things, though somewhat confused in her search for meaning. The old ways were crumbling and she was trying hard to adapt to new approaches to homesteading and community living. But she was trying to do so without losing her grasp on the views that had sustained her own approach for over 25 years — an approach nurtured by Borsodi's "17 Major Problems of Living" and Henry George's economic theories (free land and land tax in lieu of economic rent.)

Back in the 30s, Mildred had been among the leftist of the leftists. Now, with the open-land movement espoused by Lou Gottlieb, Mildred's idea of organized cooperative landholding trusts was becoming immensely conservative, for the open-land viewpoint is that access to land

---

*See Chapter III for an explanation of Walden Two ideas.

requires only need, not organization or planning (See Chapter V, Hip Communes — Morning Star Ranch). It was obvious to me that Mildred, for all her efforts, was having great difficulty in truly comprehending the changing and sometimes baffling conditions around her. Most of all, perhaps, she wished to communicate her own ideas (à la Borsodi, George and others) to as many young people as possible. She was unhappy that too many of them failed to grasp the evils of the land-owning and banking monopoly in the capitalist system. She was also unhappy that the young people did not give more explicit attention to economic problems in their return to the land and community living. I realized that she saw *The Modern Utopian* as a possible vehicle to communicate her point of view.

While I was at Heathcote, Mildred was holding the annual weekend seminar devoted to homesteading problems. Pat Herron, who lived on a ranch in northern California, led a few sessions in sensory awareness — what was then a new group phenomenon just beginning to emerge on the East Coast. Pat was a very pleasant, attractive woman in her 40s and those sessions of hers were the most enjoyable meetings I attended at Heathcote.

I also met the couple who, with their five children, were at that time the year-round resident family at Heathcote. The wife ran the place, being particularly active in office work for *The Green Revolution* and *A Way Out*. The husband worked at an outside job in order to save money for their eventual goal of homesteading an isolated piece of land somewhere in the wilds of Canada. The friction between husband and wife was subtle but clear. And I surmised that their drive for isolation was perhaps an unconscious attempt to hold a crumbling marriage together. It might have been a viable alternative to the dissolution of that particular marriage, but the couple broke up a few months later — before they were able to abandon civilization together.

29

I left Heathcote much impressed with Mildred Loomis. We had established a comfortable rapport — a rapport that has lasted to the present day. However, the collaboration between *A Way Out* and *The Modern Utopian* was short-lived. My visit to Heathcote had come just before I and *The Modern Utopian* left the East and moved to the West Coast — a journey during which TMU underwent some kind of continental sea change, for in California it became increasingly radicalized and, to some people, graphically shocking. Some of Mildred's oldest friends complained and cancelled their subscriptions. Finally, as Mildred began to phase out her own activities, as she moved toward retirement, and as I temporarily lost interest in publishing, she notified me that the board of directors of the School of Living had voted to discontinue sending TMU to *A Way Out* subscribers. "I trust this is no serious blow to you," Mildred wrote. "We'd keep at it, I suppose, if there were no other place, but since we have one journal and publishing arrangement, it seems logical and right to combine them." Thus it was decided to make *A Way Out* part of *The Green Revolution;* Roger Wilks at Heathcote would be the new editor as Mildred was retiring. As a result of this decision a few pages were added to the paper and its coverage became more communal and contemporary.

PARADISE PLANTERS LOST

Hope and idealism are common qualities among people interested in community living. So, alas, is gullibility. My stop at Heathcote provided me with a saddening example of this and a subsequent issue of *The Green Revolution* provided the sequel.

One of the speakers at the seminar on homesteading was a Texan by the name of Bill Marshall, dressed in white suit, black tie, and the ritual ten-gallon hat. He was there to promote the settlement of land in San Blas, along the

Caribbean coast of Panama. He sketched the loveliest utopian picture of the climate, the terrain, and the local inhabitants of this Central American country. He came on so strong and so flamboyantly, I couldn't imagine anyone really taking him seriously. But many did. One young woman with a two-year-old child was ready to join Marshall's venture. Others indicated they would settle their affairs and go along later. This response surprised me. Even though I know I am not lacking in naïveté myself, I felt disgusted at the gullibility of these people. Nevertheless, it seemed apparent that, dissatisfied with their lot in life, they had little to lose. San Blas promised to be a new and exciting adventure — hope renewed.

A few months after this meeting, a letter from the San Blas settlers appeared in *The Green Revolution*. The letter said, in part:

After moving to San Blas, Panama, we found these conditions to exist there:

1. The climate is hot and very humid. We learned from a reliable source that the humidity is very nearly 100% almost all year. Books, shoes, and tents all showed evidence of mildew in a few days.

2. Internal parasites and skin diseases are extremely common and very difficult to avoid.

3. Gardening would be impractical on the islands, and the mainland is infested with mosquitoes and sand flies.

4. Fruits are scarce in the area and fresh vegetables almost unknown.

We decided that the tropics are not suitable for homesteading. We found that Bill Marshall does *not* have the cooperation of the leaders among the Kuna Indians. They are working with Panamanian officials for the development of their country. We think Mr. Marshall has shown poor judgment in his evaluation of San Blas and its potentials.

We were disappointed, of course, that our "tropical paradise" doesn't really exist, but our spirits are high and we are making new plans.

31

Good luck—I wonder if they learned anything about themselves from that experience. They certainly learned that San Blas is full of flies and Marshall full of shit.

Mildred Loomis' History of Heathcote

At my request, Mildred wrote an article for TMU about the evolution and development of the community of Heathcote. I think it ranks as one of her best pieces. Here it is:*

The pleasant name Heathcote signifies a home in a meadow. The Heathcotes, early settlers in northern Maryland, built in the mid-80s a large stone mill, powered by water diverted from a stone dam across the brook. It became known as Heathcote Mill on Heathcote Road in Heathcote Hollow. For more than half a century, huge stone burrs (now steps to the building) ground grain into good flour. But after years of disuse, the old building and 37 acres were purchased in 1965 by School of Living members for their eastern headquarters and community. Their purpose was to gradually renovate the old building, pay off the borrowed money, mail out their 20-year-old publication (now called *The Green Revolution*), and try to form an education-centered community of modern homesteaders.

HEATHCOTE. A SYMBOL

Members saw much of their own history, goals, and values symbolized in Heathcote. Their remaking the old mill epitomized their remaking society. At their first workbee, New Year's Day 1965, a member said, "Shovelling out 50 years of dust and debris is like digging at the error and ugliness in today's world." The thick stone walls and sturdy beams represent the sound values of the past— simplicity and honesty. The charming meadow, lively brook, and wooded hills are a source of beauty and quiet. The mineral-laden

---

* Reprinted from *The Modern Utopian*, vol. 3, no 2, Spring, 1969, with minor style changes.

small fields, a source of good food and work. The large rooms in the building provide space for forums, classes, and dormitory.

Summers have been high spots of interest for groups, for conferences, and for the annual meeting of the nationwide School of Living members. Later workbees made one 7-room, 2-story wing habitable. A small kitchen with gas stove was installed; water, electricity were also installed, and a good fireplace restored in the living room.

There have been four major problems at Heathcote:

1. Physical Comfort: In the winter of 1965–66, the old stone building was hard to heat, firewood was scant or wet, and there was little money for gas or electricity. Vision and enthusiasm dwindled with the increasing cold and isolation. Nevertheless the family who lived there survived sicknesses and personal problems, added partitions and beautiful cabinets, and tastefully refinished the walls and

bathroom. They interacted with people constructively, and they effectively interpreted and represented the School of Living. They had a wonderful garden on very average soil (via rodent control with an electric fence, plus attaching a pump and hose to the brook during a drought). Old couches and mattresses were brought in to "furnish" the meeting room and dormitories. Our Community Conference and Summer Family Week were exceptional in 1966.

Nevertheless, this family wanted to move on. They found living in a somewhat public center too distracting for family life. They longed for the wilds of Canada. Difficulty with the local school authorities in the fall of 1966 hastened their departure. The school demanded the vaccination of the three children at Heathcote (aged 7, 13, and 15). The children were in excellent health, none had a single dental cavity, nor had ever visited a doctor except for routine checkups. The family believed that they could assume the responsibility for their own good health via good living habits and sound nutrition. They had grown up in Colorado where vaccination is not required. To the Maryland dictum of "Vaccination or Nonattendance" the family said "No." When mother was arrested, tried, and jailed—for "neglect of children"—the family's request for dismissal of charges if they left the state was granted. Thus, in January 1967, Heathcote School of Living Center was suddenly without residents and leaders.

The next applicants, a young couple with a baby, recent graduates of Antioch College, found it hard to adjust from a glass-walled broadloomed apartment to the austere Heathcote setting. The husband needed more time for writing his novel. They did not last out their six-month agreement when they got a writing scholarship for summer school. Their leaving was more crucial since the School's subscription, bookkeeping, and mailing work had been transferred from Lane's End Homestead to Heathcote.

2. *Records and Business:* The performance of office work associated with a School of Living headquarters proved the second source of difficulty. Subscribers send money, records must be kept, reports made, letters answered, papers mailed, postal regulations met.

A family of seven had come to Heathcote for the summer, preliminary to a planned move to Canada later. The wife eagerly took over the office at Heathcote for the $100 per month now made possible by 25 special friends of the School. Several summer seminars went well, and for three months the office was creditably handled. Then work began to lag. It was turned over to a resourceful 20-year-old girl, who had "joined" the "community" at Heathcote. She did well, but in another six months a crisis in her personal relationships necessitated her leaving, and another shift.

3. *Human Relations:* Emotional tangles beyond the ability of the persons involved to handle them was the third problem at Heathcote. Such problems were present in all the "regimes" there, but seemed to reach the greatest intensity while the third family was in charge. People thought this was a close-knit, successful husband-wife partnership that even extended to agreement between them on sexual experimentation. Unhandled resentments and personal frustrations between them, however, were interfering with good performance in all areas, including their relationship with their children, with School of Living visitors and officers, with handling of the office work and their physical environment. The place grew cluttered, fireplace and stove unattended. They took the easy way, turned up the thermostat and relied on the gas furnace. Utilities charges shot up and the budget allowance was exceeded. In late January 1968 the family and Board Members agreed on the termination of the family's work and residence there. Legal separation of the husband and wife took place at the same time.

These experiences added weight to plans for increasing emphasis in the School of Living on group dynamics, and sensitivity and encounter training.

4. *Principles vs. Practices:* A fourth source of difficulty stemmed from uncertainty about School of Living goals, its organizational structure, and the use of the term "freedom."

In late 1967, the husband in charge began asking questions: "What is this School of Living, anyway, with its big ideas? What is being accomplished? Who are 'They' to supervise us here at the center, and tell us who or what kind of people shall come here? This is our home, and why can't we be spontaneous, and live the way we want to? Why charge visitors for meals and rooms here? 'They' talk about freedom; do they really believe in it?" And so forth.

These questions and feelings called for several sessions of interaction with the School of Living Board and friends. Efforts were made at clarification and integration of differences.

In the Spring of 1968, a single man of some experience in experimental schools and communities attended a Heathcote conference on decentralization. He expressed his concern for a community of close association and deep emotional ties. He suggested joining Heathcote as a volunteer, giving what services might be useful. The Board accepted this offer and invited him to serve as director of promotion. Four additional seminars, and a two-week seminar on Peacemakers at Heathcote, made a busy season. By summer's end our new volunteer had decided that he now wanted to be an "individualist" with very little, if any, commitment to "community."

In September 1968, three Ohio School of Living members came to live at Heathcote—myself until January 1969, and Ruth and Martin Tilton through March. I keep busy editing, writing, winterizing, "housekeeping," and initiating or helping in office work, which has again fallen behind. Ruth Tilton has taken over records and mailing with dispatch and efficiency. Martin works part-time (as do some others) with Anacker's Tree Experts in Baltimore, and initiates discussions and educational and community projects at the center.

In mid-November 1968, the group consists of nine adults and one child, varying in participation in our community. The Anackers live in their modern farm home on the other side of the brook. Bill is a trustee; attends both official and informal meetings. Since the fall of 1967, a mother and her grade-school daughter live in a trailer; the Ohio couple have a well-equipped camper. Our young repairman, gone temporarily on a carpenter's job in Washington, D.C., has nearly completed his own quarters in the corncrib. Our current individualist lives in the Spring House. I live in a comfortable trailer. Another associate member—and short-term guests—come in frequently from a distance. After last winter's adventure in family living (called "community") under one roof, there seems now to be a trend toward privacy. We share the evening meal (we rotate preparation), share food costs, housekeeping, and community projects. We have frequent discussions, a kind of T-grouping (probing and sharing of feelings), and have posted a long list of concerns to discuss and work on.

PROGRESS?

Community? The good life? Are the two synonymous? For some of us at Heathcote nothing less than work at the complex, comprehensive adventure called a "good life" is an adequate goal. Some of us express it as "self-realization." Most of us think it includes thinking, feeling, and acting on several levels. It includes the physical — growing and processing food, caring for land and animals, building and maintaining shelter. It includes the psychological — sharing and interacting on as close and intimate a level as we can. It includes the intellectual — reflection, study, reading, discussions, seminars. It includes the social — developing new practices and institutions like group holding of land (or "land trusts"), cooperative credit, mutual exchanges of goods and labor, etc. It includes the cosmic — meditation on the nature of man and the universe, exercises (for some it's Yoga) for stilling the body and mind and experiencing the Ultimate. For some of us it more specifically involves confronting and dealing with all our major problems of living. We have a long way to go.

Roughly a year later, in the fall of 1969, Mildred wrote to me as follows:

Yes, times (meaning people) have changed. The group here are part of the new people — little concerned in the old work, luxury and success patterns, and definitely concerned with simple living, direct experience, honest and open and warm relationships. They spend time together; they play a lot; they eat at their own convenience, which means the kitchen is almost always in use and in disarray; they are not careful or tidy in this pattern, so unless someone values tidiness and does a lot of sweeping and "putting things away" the place can be quite disorderly. This can bother and upset older people — though we have not had any real hassles to date.

Even so a good deal gets done around here, on a very do-it-yourself, unscheduled, unplanned basis. Two wonderful and huge gardens are producing most of the food for 15 to 30 persons daily; some people are digging a root cellar for storing carrots, potatoes, squash, cabbage, etc. The building is better organized and new office space has been developed. Love, Mildred.

To think and write of Mildred Loomis makes me feel warm and joyous. Would that all elderly ladies were as young and vital and gentle of soul as she. I'm sure she was one of those who "values tidiness and does a lot of sweeping and 'putting things away.'" But I imagined she would have the wisdom to acknowledge this as her peculiarity rather than to accuse others of being irresponsible and sloppy. She could accept the life styles of others and be open to their values though she herself might prefer a different style.

As cold weather approached and the wind swept through the old walls at Heathcote, Mildred began to look for another home, warmer and more tidy than with the anarchists in Maryland. John had died a few months earlier and she did not wish to return to Lane's End at that time. I received a note saying she'd be at Pat Herron's ranch in northern California for the winter; then it would be back to Ohio in the spring and summer to build a community at the old homestead.

COLD MOUNTAIN FARM

In July 1967, I came across the following news item in the *East Village Other*, one of the first underground newspapers:

A small group of Lower East Side people have moved to the country, both to get away from the City and to provide free, organically-grown food for the East Side Community. Operating now with a nucleus of six, Cold Mountain Farm (RFD 1, Hobart, New York) is making great progress, but needs more people willing to work.

The farm covers 400 acres of black, rich valley land, which has always been farmed organically. Local farmers, interested to see young city folks getting together to work, have been assisting by giving instruction and providing some equipment.

Living off the land, the Cold Mountain people are putting together macrobiotic meals from local roots and flowers. They live in a twelve-room house, provided with fresh spring water and free electricity.

Their plans envision a larger, self-sufficient community complete with school for the kids.

Joyce Gardiner's Account of Cold Mountain Farm

That was the first and last time I heard of Cold Mountain Farm until a friend of mine, Elaine, handed me a copy of a long paper written by Joyce Gardiner. The paper was then edited and published in *The Modern Utopian* magazine, as follows:*

The Modern Utopian, vol. 2, no. 6, Sept., 1968, with minor changes.

Given: 450 acres of land—12 usable for farming or pasture, the remainder being old, neglected apple orchards (also pear, plum, and cherry trees) and young woods—in a mountainous, upstate New York dairy-farming area. A beautiful piece of land, with three running streams in the springtime, but only one good spring for water in the summer, close to the five-bedroom house. The farm is one mile off the main road, at the end of a rugged dirt road, a mile from the closest neighbor. There is no rent, no electricity, no telephone—and to acquire any of these would be extremely costly.

The Group: Anarchists. Mostly in their 20s with children under 6. A fluctuating population, up to 30. About four couples and one or two single people consider this home. Mostly former residents of NYC, but some from other parts of the East Coast. Interrelationships have existed for as long as five years.

History: Goes back two-and-a-half years, to NYC, where a communal loft once existed, with shared dinners and other occasions. Or back three years, when at least two families shared an apartment together for a few months. Or to last spring and summer, when a group of NYC anarchists used half an acre of a friend's land to farm on weekends.

More concretely, June 1966, to a Community Conference at the School of Living in Heathcote, Md., out of which emerged a new community—Sunrise Hill—at Conway, Mass. At least one person, loosely connected with NYC anarchists, went to live there.

The rest of us continued to farm our friend's land on weekends during the summer, meeting at least once a month at different places in the country during the winter—living together for a few days, getting to know one another better, and making plans to start our own farm the following spring. Some people from Sunrise Hill also attended these meetings.

We finally located this place through a friend. About that time, Sunrise Hill was suffering its final collapse—due to internal conflicts—and four people from there eventually would join us.

ONTO THE LAND

Starting a community farm is an incredibly difficult thing. We didn't fully realize this when we began. Setting up a new farm—or rather, rehabilitating an old and neglected one—was at least a season's work. Not to mention compensating for the work which should have been done the previous autumn.

It was still cold, there was occasional snow, the house was difficult to heat, and no one was prepared to move in. The dirt road was all but impassable, we walked the mile through snow and later mud—carrying babies, supplies, bedding, etc.

Meanwhile we had to find a tractor immediately to haul manure for compost heaps. They should have been started the year before as they require three month's time to rot properly and we wanted to farm organically. We'd have to prune the neglected fruit trees within a month, since pruning too late in the season would shock them.

On the many rainy days we had to make the house liveable: build shelves, worktable, bookshelves, a toolshed, a mailbox; install a sink; acquire tools and materials. Somehow, whatever needed to be done, there was always someone who knew how to do it or who was willing to find out how. But with each person having some particular responsibility upon himself there wasn't time to work on group projects.

Well, we had a farm, didn't we? All we had to do was go there when it got nice and warm, plow the land, plant our seed, and wait for the vegetables to come. We didn't even have to pay any rent! It was so simple. No rush to get out there while it was still so cold.

Consequently, the farm was completely deserted until the end of April. Then news got out fast (we couldn't help but brag a little), and we found we had hundreds of friends who wanted to "come to the country." So we had to bite our tongues and violate all the laws of Lower East Side hospitality to avoid creating a youth hostel or country resort. We lost a lot of friends that way.

Meanwhile, in NYC, an infinite number of conflicts existed growing out of two difficult years of coexistence, trying to work out an ideology based on anarchism-community-ecology-technology in an environment which presented a constant contradiction to it.

We had discouraged the city people. No one came. The land cried out to be tended, but people were preoccupied with their own personal grievances. The farm was all but deserted. The work fell entirely on the shoulders of a few people. Without telephone and often without car, we waited daily for friends and supplies to show up; waiting for reinforcements. Finally three friends arrived from Conway, [Massachusetts] reassuringly bringing all their worldly goods. The man started out at once, hooking up running water in the house, pruning some apple trees, then driving to a nearby town without a license or proper registration, and spending three days in jail. Soon he bought us a much-needed tractor. It was precisely this tractor (to this day still only half paid for) which shuttled up and down the one-mile dirt road, hauling cow shit (from neighboring farmers, who proved surprisingly friendly) and transporting little children to the nearby town — and then, as the time to plow grew nigh, flatly refused to budge.

There was absolutely nothing anyone could do. We had to wait for our friend from Florida to return. He was our only mechanic. Days passed and finally a few people started digging their own gardens — such a pathetic task for a farm that hoped to support some 30 people and then give out free food in the city.

But all this time there were small compensations. We had an opportunity now to explore this incredible land, watch the seasons

change, see the snow melt and trees slowly push forth buds, see birds moving in and laying eggs; spy on porcupines each night loudly chomping on the house, make friends with cows and four wild horses grazing on neighboring fields, start to know one another in that unique way that comes only from living together.

TRIBAL FEELINGS

Now a few more old friends began to arrive. There was an incredible feeling of warmth, of family. We were becoming a tribe. There were long, good discussions around the fire, into the night. Slowly, things were beginning to take shape. In those days I loved to look into the "community room" and see a bunch of people sprawled out on cushions around the floor, all so brown, their bodies so well-developed, their faces relaxed, naked or wearing clothes often of their own making. You could always spot someone from the city — by the whiteness of their flesh, the tenseness of their body.

It was my dream — and certainly no one openly disagreed with me — to become a tribe, a family of "incestuous brothers and sisters." Unfortunately, living so close, we probably made love less than when we lived in separate apartments in the city. And there was so much fear and tension in the air about *potential* affairs that actual love-making all too seldom took place, and even physical contact became a rare thing. Even though we created our own environment at the farm, we still carried with us the repressions of the old environment, in our bodies and our minds.

While others were not actually opposed to these ideas, most people didn't feel quite ready for them, and certainly no one else bespoke the same vision. If we could find a form by which our visions could be shared. . . .

INCREDIBLE TRACTOR

Waiting for the tractor to be fixed (it took about a week-and-a-half of hard labor), living our usual lives, making our own bread and yogurt, etc., we spoke to a nearby farmer and learned of a barn full of manure which he paid men to haul away for him. We offered to do it for him free, in exchange for manure to use as compost. He was so overjoyed that he offered to come up and plow our land in exchange for our labor. We thought he was joking, but a couple days later we heard a loud and unfamiliar motor coming up the hill, and there was that huge, incredible tractor. "Well, where do you want it?" And that's how we got six acres of land plowed and harrowed (later, we would plow a couple more acres ourselves). A couple of days later we got our own tractor fixed in order to start hauling manure and planting at a furious pace, trying to get the crops in before it was too late. We were already at least a week behind most everyone else in the area . . . in a place with *a very short* growing season.

These people were so overwhelmingly happy to finally have the tractor, after weeks of frustrated waiting and digging by hand, that one person actually planted some 40 mounds of zucchini and 80 mounds of acorn squash and several rows of corn in one day, by hand! Then he devised a method whereby he could dig five furrows at a time by building a drag with teeth for the tractor and installing three women as weights on the drag, where they could drop onion sets into the rows. That last part didn't work so well (all the onion sets had to be spaced again, by hand), but nonetheless by the time the other folks got home about a week later, close to an acre of land had been planted.

Now that there were more of us, we were not so close. There was no real sense of community between us. There was good feeling, but no center, no clear-cut purpose. Some of the men felt an unfulfilled need to fight. The women felt an unfulfilled need to love.

About this time we undertook—or were overtaken by—what I consider one of our most challenging feats: trying to assimilate a young lawyer and his family, including two girls, ages 4 and 6. Many a group meeting centered around the problem of "the kids." Because they were breaking out of a sick environment, their parents felt they needed a maximum of patience and love and understanding. Others felt they needed simply to be treated as human beings and that their mother should not repress the anger and frustration which she obviously felt.

Most of us felt we should in fact try to let them work *through* their hang-ups and hopefully eventually come out the other side. Let them yell "penis" and "vagina" at the top of their lungs. Let them throw

Raggedy Ann into the cellar and elaborate upon her tortures while chanting "No, you *can't* come out of the cellar!" all day long. But what no one seemed to be able to endure were the howls and wails which rose from the lungs of one sister after the other, particularly on rainy days, of which there were many, when we were all locked up with them in the house all day long.

Apparently we just weren't strong enough nor healthy enough ourselves to be able to cope with these children. And their parents, who had had such great hopes of finding in us a healthy environment, soon had to build their own shelter in order to remove themselves from our environment.

By this time the house had become so generally unbearable that everyone else as well had decided to move out. Just before then, there had been 20 adults and 10 children—with only 3 or 4 adults and 1 child sleeping outside—living so close together in that house. It seemed absurd to try to keep the house clean (anarchism does not necessarily mean chaos). And the flies were so bad that if we hung five strips of flypaper fresh each day in each room, by evening they were dripping with puddles of gooey flies. It was just barely possible to exist in the midst of all these copulating multitudes. (We didn't like the idea of using poison sprays, with all the cats and babies.)

And so, in a burst of desperation to escape the noise, children, chaos, flies, tension . . . everybody dropped everything and for a few days did nothing but work on their own shelters. The house was almost deserted.

People who get into community too often forget about the importance of solitude. And we were lucky enough to have plenty of land so that everyone could have their own shelter. But personal possessions (especially kitchen stuff), which had originally been pooled with a great sense of communal enthusiasm, were righteously carted off to their owners' shelters.

HOSTILE OUTSIDERS

About this time we started coming into conflict with the outside world. Ever since it got warm, we had all been walking around more or less nude most of the time. Unfortunately, we had to discontinue this most pleasant practice when neighbors started to mention casually that they could "see everything" from their property on the hill and that "people were talking." Our local reputation was getting progressively worse. There were too many articles in the mass media about hippies, often loosely connected with legalizing marijuana. The local people, who had originally just thought of us as "strange" and had then begun to accept us as old-fashioned organic farmers, could now call us "hippies" and forbid their kids to have anything to do with ours.

The local sheriff began to take an interest in us. Whenever we went into town we were stopped by the cops. And a friendly gas-station attendant told us the highway patrol had been told to watch us. It was easy to be paranoid, to imagine their trying to take our kids away for nudity. It was terrible to compromise, but most of us began to wear clothes again. That was a great loss.

ECONOMIC ARGUMENT

I suppose our first and worst economic argument was whether or not to buy chickens. At first, it was incredible how little problem money had been. Whoever came just threw in whatever they had— $100 or $200 perhaps—and we'd live off that until someone got a tax return, a welfare check, or whatever. We never did spend more than $25 a week on food—even when there were 30 people. But the chicken crisis involved all sorts of things. Did we eat the eggs (wasn't wheat germ good enough)? Was it morally right to take eggs from chickens; wasn't it cruel to keep chickens caged—but if we didn't cage them how would we keep them out of the garden? Were we really saving money on eggs, if we had to spend money on the chickens, chicken wire, and all kinds of feed? Who was going to plant an acre of millet and an acre of corn to feed them? Who would build the chicken coop? This was the first time I remember hearing anyone say, "Well, *I* won't give any money for chickens"—using money as a weapon, a personal source of power. And it wasn't long before money again became a personal possession.

BAD TIMES

I liked the young lawyer and his wife because they often spoke at meetings on a personal level, about how they *felt* about things, while most of our people maintained a kind of cold objectivity, only discussing things external to themselves. It was this lack of "feeling" which brought the lawyer to say that *Cold* Mountain was certainly an apt name for the place. And his wife complained, not unjustly, that there was not enough making of music, not enough dancing, and she felt her joy was being stifled here.

We seemed to have reached an all-time low. We had passed the summer solstice. Our money was all but depleted. We could work at haying for local farmers, but $1 an hour wasn't a hell of a lot. Until now we seemed to have been subsisting mostly on enthusiasm. Now it was hot and even our enthusiasm was gone. There was a general feeling of emptiness. Times were very bad, but we tried to hold on until the times were more favorable.

We decided to limit ourselves to just a few staples (rice, oil, powdered milk, soy sauce, flour, salt, soybeans, brewer's yeast, molasses, grass — always purchased in huge quantities to save money) and whatever we could get from our environment — at this time of year, dandelion greens, wintergreen, and burdock root and, in a little while, fresh strawberries, rhubarb, and wild leeks. And we'd soon be getting edible weeds from the garden: milkweed, sorrel, lamb's-quarters. And then we would discover violet leaves, for salads. Still later, there would be mushrooms, raspberries, currants, and blackberries; wild mint, thyme, and oregano; green apples, pears and plums — and by then we would be getting at least zucchini, peas, and baby onions from the garden.

Then, one morning, someone took the shotgun and killed a groundhog. We'd been talking about hunting for a long time, but most of us were vegetarians and meat was a rare sight in these parts (the hunter himself hadn't eaten meat for the last two years!). But that night he cooked up a fine groundhog stew. Which he ate. And that big pot of stew sat on the stove and people thought about it and talked about it and went to bed without dinner. In the middle of the night a couple of us woke up and had a little. Next day some of us had some for lunch. Only four people remained staunch in their vegetarianism, and mostly they didn't condemn the rest. Each of us worked it out in our own way.

Still, the diet wasn't satisfying. Subsistence living was one thing, but we all felt damned hungry. We called a meeting and decided this had a great deal to do with the cooking—which, until then, had been just a matter of chance impulse, so that the task usually fell into the hands of the same people every day. Their boredom with cooking showed up in the quality of their meals. It seemed reasonable enough that if two different people were responsible for the kitchen each day there would be more interest and variety in cooking, the house would be kept neater and more organized, and it would leave the other people free to concentrate completely on the garden or whatever. At that time we had 14 adults, so it was pleasant enough to know you only had to cook and clean one day per week.

It's amazing how much this helped. We'd all begun to grow so discouraged with each other and the mess we were living in. We all felt like pigs and everyone blamed the next person. Our morale was sinking fast, the kids were screaming, and we were at each other's throats. Now suddenly the house was clean—spick and span, almost.

We felt we had been reborn. We'd stuck it out through hard times and now virtue had its reward.

At that time, four Puerto Rican friends from the city joined us. They emanated new energy and worked hard. And they had a certain revolutionary spirit which none of us quite had. One would say, "Communism and capitalism—they are both no good. But if I had something like this farm to fight for—why, I would give my life for it." At night you could hear the guitars and there were big fires, and dancing and singing. The hardest work was over. All we had to do now was weed and mulch. Now we had time to make music.

PUBLICITY

About this time, an article appeared about us in the *East Village Other*—without our knowledge or consent—claiming we needed people to help out on the farm (as if we hadn't had enough trouble discouraging people we *knew* from coming up!). And we were soon flooded with letters, and every two or three days a new visitor would arrive. It created terrible tensions to have to ask them to leave, to tell them it was all a mistake. And then a couple of people we *did* know arrived and announced their intention to move in. Some of us didn't want to live with these people, while others either wanted them to stay or felt we didn't have any right to ask them to leave. We had decided a long time ago that if this happened, each person in the community would just do as he felt best, and there would be no group decisions.

But how can you ask someone that you know to leave—particularly when they've brought all their things and say they have no place else to go? I think this must be a dilemma suffered by all communities. Certainly my way of dealing with it (absolute frank honesty) was far from effective. They just stayed. And stayed. And gradually, for this reason and others, the warmth and trust and sharing between us began to die. Whatever tribal or family feelings we had were gone.

We weren't ready to define who we were; we certainly weren't prepared to define who we weren't—it was still just a matter of intuition. We had come together for various reasons—not overtly for a common idea or ideal, but primarily because there was land and there was supposed to be a "community." Even in the original community there were people who thought of themselves (and their reason for being here) as being primarily communitarians, or primarily farmers and back-to-the-soil revolutionaries, or primarily political revolutionaries (anarchists) or "tao-archists" for whom farming and community was just one integral part of the totality, or just plain hermits who wanted to live in the woods. All of these different people managed to work together side-by-side for awhile, but the fact was that there was really no shared vision.

And then still more people arrived — people we had all been looking forward to seeing. And the house was very full. And there was a lot of confusion. And it was very difficult to cook for that many people. Again, tensions began to mount. There was so little money, and now there were three or four pregnant women here, and one or two nursing mothers. Their dietary needs were very specific and important, and the community was unable to fulfill them. They were forced to fall back on their own resources. In similar ways, one began to feel they couldn't trust the community to meet their needs, to take care of them in an emergency. There was a feeling of general malaise. The garden wasn't being weeded. The grass was growing higher and higher. Everyone felt as if everyone else was irresponsible.

In a community, things happen on such a large scale that you need the cooperation of other people in order to accomplish almost anything. But now one began to feel as if it was easier to do a thing by oneself. It was hot. Laziness had set in, very firmly. The word "failure" was being tossed around a lot. People began to just look after themselves and to talk as if the only reason they were here was the land. The City suddenly seemed to hold a great attraction, and whenever there was a car going in it would be filled to capacity. The young lawyer and his family finally left, quietly.

There was one ray of light in these somber times. A new couple arrived, to stay. Nobody knew them when they came, but everyone liked them at once. They brought new energies with them and they lifted our spirits. Slowly, all the stragglers had left — empty people who had come to fill themselves, sapping our energies, needing to be taken care of and giving nothing at all — and now there were only between four and six couples and a few single people left.

WINTER APPROACHES

So we all lived together, peaceably enough, until one night it was very, very cold, and wet and windy, and we could smell the coming of autumn. Then it was time to begin thinking about what we'd be doing in the winter—staying here or moving on—and making plans accordingly. Mostly we had to consider the hardship of a very cold winter, no gas or electricity, a one-mile dirt road which would probably be inaccessible because of heavy snow (even during the summer, only jeeps and four-wheel-drive cars and trucks could climb that road.)

There were five couples, three of the women were pregnant, and a fourth was nursing. The babies were due in October, November, and February. The first two couples wanted to deliver their own but not take the chance of doing it here. A single girl was already building a small stone house for the winter. Another man intended to live in the big house for the winter. Almost all hoped to be here early next spring. By this time, two couples and a girl had moved entirely into their own shelters.

The communal garden was a monstrous failure. After the original enthusiasm of planting, hardly anyone cared enough to weed the rows. (Of course, the huge amount of rain this year retarded the growth of the crops and caused the weeds to grow like crazy! And six acres is a hell of a lot of land to weed by hand. If we try again next year, we'll certainly have to get a cultivator.) At least two acres of garden were lost, either because they weren't weeded adequately, or because they were planted too late and the growing season was too short, or because there wasn't enough sun and there was too much rain, or because of the aphids, or the potato blight. . . .

We didn't become NEW people—we just became physically healthy people. We didn't find a way of sharing our visions (in fact, we didn't even have a conscious understanding of the *need* for such a thing), and we didn't have a shared vision to bring us and hold us together.

We had plowed and begun to plant the earth, but we had not pierced our own ego skins. Decay and stagnation had already set in. I went into the woods to meditate. The woods explained: it was high time we plowed the earth of this community. We must apply the blade to ourselves and cut back the outer skin to expose the pulsing flesh.

And then we must harrow and pulverize the outer skin and use our egos for compost. Then, in the new flesh, we must plant the seeds of the people we wish to become.

The few of us who remained at the farm were doing fairly well, enjoying the fruits of our labors in gobbling up the zucchini, baby onions, carrots and parsnips; savoring the apples, pears and plums; gathering myriad blackberries, chokecherries and gooseberries for preserves; eating delicious brown fertile eggs.

Sandy had been feeling unusually weak. He rested and fasted but only grew worse and Louise took him to the doctor and he was hospitalized with hepatitis. A few days later Sue Ellen and Dan complained of similar symptoms, Dan also going to the hospital.

The health inspector was obviously appalled by the way we lived, but was quieted down by our landlord (who has some monied influence in the area), who claimed we were just a summer "camp."

Neighbors who had been our friends now avoided us. All their secret thoughts about how unclean we were could now be vindicated.

After a couple of weeks more on the farm, I too succumbed and took a bus back to New York. In the city our monstrous failure was greeted with "I told you so" and "I'm not surprised." Being a lone individual suddenly and having to live on concrete, in filth, almost no sunlight, trees, or earth—I was completely shattered.

I was in bed with the flu when I first met Joyce. She and Elaine barged into my room, insisting on talking with me. Joyce was angry about the editing job; like most budding young authors, she didn't want one precious word deleted without her permission. Elaine disclaimed any responsibility for encouraging me to print the paper. And I, although the editing had been done by other staff members, reluctantly took the blame as publisher. In order to make amends I encouraged Joyce to write any additions or changes, which I would then publish in the next issue. She agreed and after editing and checking with her for approval, the following material appeared in the magazine:*

*The Modern Utopian, vol. 3, no. 2, spring, 1969.

The foregoing article on Cold Mountain was *extremely* condensed from a much longer article. It is impossible to give a truly fair description of community life in just a few pages. Consequently, the majority of space was devoted to the problems we suffered. Fortunately, our problems did not destroy us and many of the people who lived at Cold Mountain are still living together at a community in Vermont and elsewhere.

The community in (Southern) Vermont is a lot like Cold Mountain—particularly in how beautiful it is and how seldom its members ever see that beauty. Our heads are so full of our communities' shortcomings that we do not verbally express what our bodies show: the goodness of this way of life, sharing together, and being close to the land.

Now, while it is still fresh in my mind, is the time to express the beauty of our life. The way we all work and live together without any power or authority structure, simply following our own consciousness of what should be done each day. (Of course, some things have to be more structured than others—milking the cow, for example.) The way that children are cared for, with the men also caring for them. The way that tasks and chores are taken on by people, according to inclination rather than sex, men cooking, women chopping wood—*if* that was what they wanted to do or what had to be done. And nudity, bodies of all shapes, readily accepted as part of nature. And almost no clash of egos.

And the way the kids play together—sharing ecstatic joyful moments! Not that they don't fight or cry—but immediately on the surface and not repressed and distorted, so they love with as much confidence and fearless energy as they hate, they create as fiercely and passionately as they destroy, and they relax as magnificently and totally as they rebel.

And how seldom, with so many people living so close (about a dozen people in a 10-room house), anyone ever argues or bickers—except for real explosions of anger over real and immediate things—anger which clears the air and refreshens.

There seems to be less sexual uptightness here. You can touch anybody and speak intimately with them, without feeling the force of tremendous psychic tensions from their spouse or anyone else.

This is a wealthy community. Woody provides the money for whatever is "necessary," though it is desirable that soon the community be self-supporting. The standard of living these people set for themselves is almost identical to Cold Mountain. Except here are greater facilities for cleanliness (a toilet, warm running water, a tub) and sanitation (a refrigerator, big sinks for washing clothes — and an old-fashioned wringer) and warmth (two huge wood-burning stoves, a chain saw). Also, there is electricity, although it's only used for two big lamps — one in the kitchen and one in the reading room.

It takes a little bit of humility to realize that, at least at first, no aspect of farming is likely to be easy for most people. We still have to establish certain rhythms with the seasons and the land. Once you're in a place you know that in the spring you'll plant, in the fall you'll harvest, and during the summer and winter you'll have time for yourself and friends. But if you're just moving into a new place, then everything must be done at once, and at least in the first year there is very little hope of having anything but chaos. If only we'd have *expected* that before we began, then it wouldn't have upset us so much.

Here there are also the same kinds of problems as at Cold Mountain, like the same small group doing all the work and taking care of the lazy transient people who only suck energy from the community *and contribute almost nothing.* At least here there *is* a constant small group of people who are truly committed and they know who they are and so does everyone else. At Cold Mountain, the conflict between city and country rendered even our consistent people unstable. Here the tree stands firm at the center though the leaves come and go.

CHAPTER THREE

I WAS A THEOLOGICAL STUDENT more interested in humanistic psychology than the behavioral form when I first read B. F. Skinner's novel *Walden Two*. Nevertheless, the book turned me on; it was sort of a composite of many previous utopian visions — communal dining, egalitarian economics, professional child-rearing, labor credit system, and so on.

My initial enthusiasm was so great that I immediately got out the phone book, looked up Dr. Skinner, and called him. His cordial invitation and our subsequent meeting left me as positive as ever.

A short while later I came across an interesting classified advertisement in Ralph Ginzburg's *Fact* magazine. It said that Gerald Baker of Cresco, Iowa, was looking for people to form a Walden Two community. I contacted Baker and discovered that the rudiments of such a community had already been formed by other people in Washington, D.C.

WALDEN HOUSE

I visited the nascent community in the spring of 1966 — it was my first visit to a commune — and found it located in a poor section of the nation's capital. Here, half a dozen idealists had gathered to start a new society. One of the founders, Bill, had studied at Meadville Theological School in Chicago. But instead of going into the ministry after graduating, he returned to Washington, D.C. where he and some friends began to develop his utopian schemes. In essence, Bill wanted to combine the ideas of Walden Two with the practice of group marriage.

In 1965 he and a friend financed the purchase of an old, narrow four-story house wedged between similar 19th-century buildings. Brick walls caked with deposits of soot disclosed the building's run-down appearance. There was a tiny yard in front and a slightly larger yard in back.

The two men advertised widely and conducted meetings in hopes of finding others to join them at Walden House, as they called it. This was a difficult process. And in order to keep up payments on the house they took in boarders.

George, one of their first members, was industrious and responsible. He would have been an asset to any community as he had a practical inclination and could fix things. His main interests were in various applications of the physical sciences — electronics, mechanics, etc. He was the only person in the house who had these kinds of interests or aptitudes. When I visited Walden House, George was converting the plumbing so that their newly acquired dishwasher could be installed. He had just built an electric-powered turtle that would have been a joy to any young child — but there were no youngsters at Walden House.

Kathleen came along soon after George. She was a divorcee with a teen-age daughter, Susan. Well aware of the pitfalls and disadvantages of the isolated monogamous family structure, Kathleen enthusiastically embraced the ideas of Walden Two.

When I was there the community had one or two other members, as well as two boarders. Members and boarders paid the same amount of money per week for rent and food and had about the same benefits. Boarders, however, did not have to do household chores. On the other hand, they could be asked to leave on short notice if new members were admitted and the room was needed. And they could neither vote nor have a voice in the purchase of equipment made from the common purse. New members had to wait through a trial period of three-to-six months before they could vote. It all seemed a little too complex and messy to me.

At the time of my visit, Bill was no longer a member, although he still lived in the house, in the front room on the second floor. He no longer ate with the group nor participated in its activities. He drove a taxi by day and wrote his utopian ideals by night. In the beginning, Bill had envisioned a group-marriage community where adult members would rotate sleeping partners. As Kathleen was the only adult female member at the time, she was the crucial factor in this experiment. But she did not want to sleep with anyone except George. So Bill resigned and sold the house to the group with the understanding that he could stay on for a time. Bill's original partner had sold out to him sometime previously.

Kathleen had administrative abilities, as well as a strong personality. In addition to writing and editing the newsletter the group had begun, she also handled the money, and supervised household chores; in short, she ran the house on a practical basis. She and George were an essential team to make a project like this work: she the congenial organizer and taskmaster; he, the efficient handyman.

During the day each member of the commune had to work at an outside job in order to pay for the group's practical necessities of life. It is not surprising then that, exhausted from a full day's work, they had little energy left over for their own needed household repairs and interior decorations.

But it was not all hard work for all people at Walden House. Consider, for example, one short-term visiting member—a stout, ex-Army colonel. He was around the house all day. He spent the time reading and relaxing. At dinnertime, I recall, he would relish the meal with audible groans of delight, mouthful after ecstatic mouthful. I kept my eyes glued to the food, not daring to look at anyone for fear that I would burst out in uncontrollable laughter.

Irrespective of their concern about improving the building, the members did not consider Walden House to be anything but a temporary home. Their goal was to find a better place, preferably in the country. Eventually they did find such a place in the adjoining state of Virginia — after a useful trip to Michigan.

In the summer of that year (1966), Kathleen and George, having just been married by a justice of the peace, took a trip to Michigan to attend the first annual Walden Two convention. It was staged by a few behavioral psychologists who hoped to found a full-blown Walden Two community based on Skinnerian principles, with the aid (they fondly hoped) of a huge foundation grant and the cooperation of some pliable utopian people.

Among the other people attending the convention were Rudy and Dusty, two university students from Atlanta, Georgia. They had recently begun a newsletter called *Walden Pool* in cooperation with Gerald Baker. The contents of their paper included, among other subjects, theoretical ideas on how to create a Walden Two community, letters from enthusiastic readers, and a summary of important ideas from Skinner's book. They themselves were impatient with talk and theories and anxious to create the real thing.

The Walden Two convention brought Walden House and *Walden Pool* together. During the next few months, much discussion and exchange of visitors materialized between the two groups. A third party in this interaction was a Virginia businessman named Kurt, who had also attended the convention in Michigan. Kurt enthusiastically backed the Walden Two idea (unlike his wife, who, opposing his involvement, divorced him). He offered the collective groups money on a low-interest, long-term basis in order to buy a farm. The offer was accepted, a farm was found and purchased, and a community was begun.

TWIN OAKS TAKES ROOT

The new community, called Twin Oaks, was established at what had been a 123-acre tobacco farm near a Virginian town far from any large city. Rudy, his bride, and Dusty made the move from Atlanta. Kathleen, Susan, George, and two others arrived from Washington. They all settled in at Twin Oaks on June 16, 1967.

When I visited the community in August its population had jumped to ten. Everyone was hard at work, making rope hammocks and harvesting the crops (the previous owner had conveniently planted many vegetables and acres of corn).

Even at that time the group not only had many visitors but also a well-defined policy for handling them. Visitors were required to work a specified number of hours and to pay a fee according to the length of their stay. As I discovered, it was fun to be a visitor — picking and shelling peas, husking corn, and watching the tomatoes stew in a big outdoor vat. The members had already canned enough vegetables to last the winter, but were now worried about the lack of freezer space; they had no money to buy another freezer.

Kathleen showed me around the farm. The house was small, a one-family dwelling hardly large enough for the ten members. But it was summer, so most of the members slept outdoors. One problem they faced with equanimity was the very inadequate water supply. All baths were taken at the swimming hole across the road. The toilet was flushed only a few times a day. And nothing was washed under running water. This problem was greatly aggravated by the influx of visitors, which sometimes doubled the population, especially on weekends. Still, the situation was handled with a minimum of tension. This seemed characteristic of Twin Oaks, for an energetic and buoyant spirit permeated the place.

In addition to the tiny farmhouse and one or two storage sheds, there was also a workshop for the making of wooden sections for the hammocks. This same building accommodated the printing-press shop. The members had purchased an old multilith and were trying to produce a good newsletter. This paper was important to them: it enabled them to tell the outside world about their attempt to create an alternative society and it also brought income into the community. Dusty was in charge of running the newsletter operation, although Kathleen continued to do most of the writing.

A dairy cow and hay feed were kept in a small run-down barn. But at the time I was there the milk and butter were all being sold to the outside because the cash income was sorely needed. The members also hoped to make and sell enough hammocks to avoid the necessity of taking jobs for cash on the outside during the winter. And they were raising a few hogs so that they would have meat during the cold months ahead.

A First Interview with Kathleen:

THE COMMUNITY AT THREE MONTHS

Much of what I learned as a result of that first visit to Twin Oaks came from Kathleen, who took the time to answer my many questions. The following is part of her response:

DICK: Did you deliberately choose a farm that would be so far from any large city?

KATHLEEN: No. That choice was dictated by price. You can't buy a farm within reach of a large city for the money we had available.

DICK: Why did you decide to name the place Twin Oaks? I thought you would use a name with "Walden" in it.

KATHLEEN: The name was a compromise. We couldn't seem to come to any agreement on a name that any of us were crazy about, so we eventually settled on the neutral, descriptive name of Twin Oaks. That's the twin oak tree there, by the well. The "Walden" names were vigorously championed by some, but we couldn't get consensus. Others were opposed to using "Walden" because so many starry-eyed people would show up expecting us to be just like the book. It isn't fun to be in a position of consistently disappointing people.

DICK: Are you still accepting new members, Kathleen?

KATHLEEN: Certainly—provided they are people able to accept our crowded conditions and severe economics. We have a very serious housing shortage right now. We are going to build a large structure this fall which will contain several bedrooms, in addition to work space for our hammock industry on the first floor.

DICK: Tell me about those hammocks.

KATHLEEN: The hammocks are made of cotton rope and kept in comfortable shape by oak stretchers. They sell for $25 to $35 each, the price depending on the size. They come complete with the hardware for attaching them to trees or porches, and we are developing a hammock-stand for people who don't have any trees to hang them from. We don't make a big profit on them, because the materials cost a large part of the price. But it is a means of putting our labor to use on our own premises. It is much more pleasant and better for the community than going to work in the nearby towns.

DICK: The hammock makers seem to be having a good time, not like working in a factory, for sure.

KATHLEEN: I don't know many factory managers who would put up with that amount of joking and singing, or with the hi-fi that alternately blasts them with the Beatles and Gregorian chants. We find that most work done in compatible groups is relatively pleasant.

62

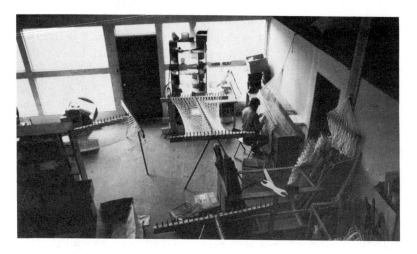

DICK: Quite often people who tell about their communities tell only the good things. It always leaves us wondering what is left unsaid. How about people getting the work done? What about interpersonal conflict?

KATHLEEN: Dick, you must realize that we are talking about a community that is less than three months old. We are still on our honeymoon. Interpersonal difficulties are minimal. So far we find a great deal more satisfaction from each other's company than we do annoyance from each other's idiosyncrasies. Of course there is the person who always spills water on the bathroom floor, and another who can never remember to clean up after herself on cooking and baking projects. But remember we have the whole outdoors and several barns to work in, so we aren't stepping on each other's feet too much in the summer months, which minimizes petty annoyances. We realize that this kind of thing can be a problem, though, and we have thought up a means of dealing with it. Along with our other managers, we appointed one called the Generalized Bastard. His job is to be officially nasty. For example, suppose that a certain member has a habit of letting his work partner do the dirty part of the work and of skipping out on the last ten minutes of cleanup on a shared job. If this happens once or twice, his work partner ignores it. If it keeps happening, his partner begins to resent it but hates to say, "Hey, how about doing a full share of this job for a change." In order to avoid a building-up of resentment, the complaining member goes to the Generalized Bastard and explains the situation. Then it is the Bastard's job to carry his complaint to the offender, which he can do in an objective way.

DICK: Isn't that a bit roundabout? Couldn't you just encourage people to be frank with each other? It seems like a cop-out on the whole idea of community to have people unable to confront each other face to face with a problem. What kind of depth can develop in a relationship if frustrations can't be expressed directly? I'd resent it if someone had to get another person, official Bastard notwithstanding, to complain to me.

KATHLEEN: Maybe you're right ideally; but we've found the Generalized Bastard helps things to run smoothly.

DICK: You mentioned that managers had been appointed. That sounds like *Walden Two*. What kind of system have you set up?

KATHLEEN: We spent five weeks without government. Everybody did what seemed to him appropriate for him to do, and we got along all right. Occasionally we would have a meeting and try to get consensus on something important, like spending a large amount of money on some particular item. We would still be carrying on our business in that manner except for one thing: some of us couldn't stand meetings. Some objected to what they termed "wasted time." Others always got upset because of disagreements that arose at the meetings. What happened is that we had fewer and fewer meetings because they were so unpleasant. And as a result we found that decisions were going unmade, except when one member would just do something on his own initiative. Like, one weekend, one person just went and bought some wire and wired the shop. He figured that if he waited for a meeting on the subject, it would be winter before the shop got any electricity, and the printing press that was there doesn't run on treadle power. Now we have elected a board of planners with broad powers. And the board in turn appoints managers to various areas of work. I can't tell you how well this system works because at this point it is too new. We have a hammock-making manager, community-health manager, vegetable-garden manager, visitor manager.

DICK: And you're the one who manages visitors?

KATHLEEN: Actually, I'm three managers. All of us are at least two. There are more jobs than people. I tell visitors where to pitch their tents and remind them to pay for their meals. I'm not required to entertain them. We can't spare the labor for that.

DICK: How do you divide up your labor?

KATHLEEN: Our labor credit system is very much in the experimental stages. Right now we divide the work weekly by means of a kind of card game, where everyone is dealt a hand and passes his unwanted cards to the right until he accumulates the right number of credits and the jobs he prefers.

DICK: Is it working out well?

KATHLEEN: It seems to be fair to everyone and there has been general goodwill toward the system, but it takes a long time. We keep imagining what it would be like if we had 50 members instead of 10.

DICK: What would you do here if someone refused to do his share of the work?

KATHLEEN: Ask him to leave. That everyone works is a fundamental assumption at Twin Oaks. There is a lot to be done and we are not in a position to afford any loafers.

DICK: So you consider yourselves an experimental community in the same sense that Skinner intended in *Walden Two?*

KATHLEEN: Yes. Of course we aren't the avant-garde of the sexual revolution. So far we are sticking to patterns which give the feeling of free choice; and free choice for a woman could mean a one-to-one relationship that is fairly stable. We are different from society at large in that we merely *practice* marriage. Society at large virtually *requires* it. In our community the practice of lifetime marriage will endure just exactly as long as it is functional and no longer. Society at large regards it as a sacrament in itself greater and more important than the happiness or unhappiness it produces.

DICK: How about marijuana? Do you people smoke?

KATHLEEN: We are asking members and guests not to use it at all on the premises.

DICK: Doesn't that strike you as rather a conservative stand for an experimental community?

KATHLEEN: Yes. Most of us favor liberal legislation on the drug question. But pot is illegal. And adding indignant neighbors to the list of our difficulties is more than we can handle — a raid by the police we don't need! Even people off on their private illusions is more than we need when we are trying to get a lot of work done.

DICK: Couldn't this sort of thing be done with discretion, so that the neighbors and the police need not be involved?

KATHLEEN: Conceivably. If we had a population with a strong personal desire to smoke pot or drop acid, we might have to take risks like that. But our membership at present has virtually no interest in drugs. And if we did have, we wouldn't have the money for it. A liberal stand would benefit only our potential guest population, and we don't see any reason to risk the community's local reputation just for guests.

DICK: What about free love?

KATHLEEN: The community doesn't take a stand on free love. We take it for granted that couples will find each other and seek the kind of relationship that they mutually consider desirable. We foresee no reason to regulate it.

DICK: You seek to regulate some behaviors and not others, according to whether you feel they need regulating. Tell me, have you found certain pressures in community living that are not found in ordinary life?

KATHLEEN: Some. We have to remember to clean up after ourselves, to put tools back in their places, to do our work at a reasonable time so that other work which follows it will not be held up. Community life is not entirely free of restrictions. On the other hand, we escape a great many pressures by being here. We dress as we please; our schedule is more flexible than it would be if we worked at a city job; there are no artificial standards we have to meet, such as qualifying for a degree or earning a promotion. I personally feel very free here.

DICK: How many hours a day are you people working?

KATHLEEN: We average about six, but a lot of things get done outside the labor credit system. I don't think anybody got labor credits for arranging the library, for instance. I wouldn't be surprised if we were all averaging closer to seven hours a day. That should go up when emergency projects are added, such as the actual construction of the building that is now being planned.

DICK: What do most of the members do for fun?

KATHLEEN: In a group this small, recreational interests always vary a great deal. One member plays a clarinet, using a phonograph record for his back-up orchestra. Another is interested in ham radio. The most organized activity we have is the Repulsive Quartet. That's a group that meets whenever the mood strikes and sings hymns in four-part harmony. I imagine it will eventually develop into a good choir — given time, practice, and the addition of some more voices. But in the meantime we are out-of-tune fairly often. When we get to sounding better, maybe we will change the name.

DICK: So most of you just follow individual hobbies?

KATHLEEN: Yes, or sit around and talk, which is quite a recreation in itself. This summer has been great for conversational games.

DICK: If conversation is a common recreation, you probably are a group with a great deal in common. Would you agree?

KATHLEEN: A number of people have commented that we are a lot alike. From inside the group it doesn't seem that way. We can see our differences much more clearly than our similarities. Probably the very fact that we are here indicates something about us. Certainly we have a set of common opinions on a few subjects. We all think society is in bad shape; we all think intentional community is a reasonable way to make at least a small improvement in it.

DICK: How does a person become a member of Twin Oaks?

KATHLEEN: First, he visits us and talks to us about it. Then he would have to move in and live here for three months. If he is acceptable after his three-month trial period, he becomes a member.

DICK: Does he have to give all his money to the community?

KATHLEEN: The simple answer to that question is "yes." Actually, there are some exceptions, but they aren't important enough to talk about except to individuals whom they might affect.

DICK: How about the personal property the member brings in? What happens to it?

KATHLEEN: It remains his. But frankly, these things have not been important so far. Everyone has shared his things very freely, and there had been no abuse that I know of. All the sharing is voluntary, however, so if an incoming member had some precious possession he felt very special about, no one would even hint that he should share it.

DICK: What is your prognosis for the survival of Twin Oaks?

KATHLEEN: Finances look bad and the draft is a serious threat, but I still think we have a fair chance of surviving. We are on the farm and will not go hungry. There is no lack of potential members. They pour confusedly out of colleges every spring. We will not get bored and we are not likely to be intimidated easily. We are building good relations with our neighbors. Above all we are prepared to change our policies as they prove unworkable and make new ones that suit our purposes.

THE GROWTH OF TWIN OAKS

Since those early days in the summer of 1967, Twin Oaks has continued to grow — not by leaps and bounds, but gradually and consistently. It has avoided both stagnation and abrupt change — thereby giving itself a better-than-average chance for survival.

BUILDING FOR THE FUTURE

There has been a great deal of construction, as well as physical reorganization, at Twin Oaks since 1967. The new building was erected as planned and made livable before the weather became intolerable. The first floor of this building became the hammock factory, with private rooms tucked along both sides of the common work space. In addition, part of this work space was made into a living room and library; the printing press was moved into a new building, a photographic darkroom was set up and a communal clothes closet was built there too.

In February 1970 the members completed the main floor of another wood-frame building. They named the new structure the Oneida Building, in honor of that famous 19th-century community. With seven bedrooms on the finished main floor, the workers were now busy building a second floor that would provide another seven. Because of all this expansion, the woodworking shop was moved into the first new structure — dubbed the Hammock Building—which would eventually be converted into shops entirely.

The tiny farmhouse, which had formerly been divided into living room, dining room, kitchen, bedrooms, etc., was redesigned to accommodate the community's kitchen, dining area, laundry, and office. And the water supply was improved, thereby remedying another of the community's initial inadequacies.

CHANGING THE LABOR CREDIT SYSTEM

Since the community's inception, the labor credit system has been the basic method for getting the work done. Under this system, each member is required to earn the same number of labor credits per week. The labor credit manager decides how much work and what jobs need to be done. He makes and posts a weekly list. Members sign up for the work they prefer. The amount of time each person works depends on the desirability of the jobs he selects. If more than one person signs up for a job, that job is considered desirable work and its credit value diminishes; if nobody signs up, then the job is considered undesirable and the credit value goes up. This job is then assigned to someone at random. Theoretically, people who perform the least desirable job work the fewest hours per week, because they accumulate the required number of credits faster.

For three years the labor credit system worked fairly well. But then the community decided to modify the system. This change was discussed in *The Leaves of Twin Oaks*, the community's newsletter, in its issue of October 1970:

What we became discontented with was the overall quality of the work done. Many a hopeful member would take a managership with the intention of seeing the department thrive under his care, only to find that the other members working in his department just didn't

69

care enough to do a good job, and good projects were continually being sabotaged by indifference. . . . Under the old system you might clean the kitchen one morning and somebody else the next; then you were on hammock weaving, which you had only five hours of, and the next day you were mending fences. Most people had a schedule like that. Presumably, most members liked the variety, because they continued to choose it. Nevertheless, its natural results were that if you left a jar of spoiled tomatoes on the counter, somebody on another shift would have to clean it up; and if you left the saw out in the barn, somebody else would have to go look for it. The most elementary behavioral theory told us that we were not set up to get a good job done. . . .

So with a sigh of regret we turned away from the hectic variableness of schedule and began to encourage specialization. The work shifts began to be arranged so that on every meal shift and every cleaning shift in a given week, at least one and preferably two, people were assigned throughout the week and were familiar with the work. The system quickly extended to garden work and even office work.

Specialization meant signing up in blocks of 14 to 21 hours, and this made the old competition and random assignment system untenable. For, if you lost a 21-hour block at the flip of a coin, you would have to be assigned 21 hours of something undesirable in its place. Large blocks just did not lend themselves to a sign-up system at all. Something new had to be devised.

What we are working with now is a simple preference list. Each member has a list of all the job categories and is asked to number them from 1 to 40 in the order of his preference. From there, the labor credit crew takes the preference lists and makes up all the individual schedules, giving each member as much as possible those jobs which he rated high, and assigning all unpopular jobs as much as possible to those who dislike them least.

Another change that has been made . . . is a new way of awarding labor credits. It is now possible to give labor credits on the basis of the individual preference rather than the group preference. That is, you get 0.9 per hour for your first preference, 1.0 for the next few on your list, and so forth. Three people may be mending fences together, and each of them earning different credits, depending on how much he likes the job.

Most of the members are content with the new system. Their schedules are usually less aversive then they were under the old random-assignment rules. A few people prefer the old system because they didn't mind any kind of work very much, and could take advantage of other people's dislikes by signing up for unpopular work at high credits, thus working fewer hours than the average member. Under the new system this is no longer possible. . . .

The improvement in the work itself is very noticeable. Managers are not so discouraged as they were. A lot of members are becoming quite interested in their work. The people on lunch are likely to recognize the leftovers, so they don't become moldy in the refrigerator; the people on cleaning remember that they didn't do any woodwork last week, so it's time to look at it this week. . . .

This is probably not the last change the labor credit system will ever see. It is interesting to note that we can make sweeping changes in it and still stay within the general framework of the system described in *Walden Two*. The principle remains the same — the more aversive the work, the less you have to do of it.

CHILDREN IN THE COMMUNITY

There have been families with children at Twin Oaks from time to time, but such an arrangement has yet to prove really successful. A child-raising manager is in charge of handling discipline problems with the children in the community. The biological parents are not allowed to discipline their own children. However, few parents are able to adhere to this prescription as their life experiences have been in the structure and values of the traditional family. No such families have stayed long at Twin Oaks.

Kathleen's daughter, Susan, already mature for a girl in her budding teens, elected to study at home soon after she and her mother moved to the community. She no longer attended public school. Instead, members of the community offered to teach her specific subjects—history, English, etc. It worked so well for Susan that gradually a whole series of classes were organized for other members as well. Anyone who wanted to teach could do so; then, if there were any takers, the classes began.

NOVELTY, CHANGE AND EXPERIMENT

New activities are constantly being devised by the members and are often reported in *The Leaves of Twin Oaks*. The May 1970 issue of the newsletter, for example, described the beginnings of a folk-dance group:

About once a week these days we carry all the hammock jigs out of the workshop and set up the record player. Cramped quarters limit the kinds of dances that can be taught. We started with American square dances and have now added Serbian and Israeli circle dances to our repertoire.

Another new activity was the sleep experiment initiated by six members who decided they'd like to find out if they could "function happily taking their sleep in three-hour shifts rather than whole nights at a time." They scheduled their days and nights to sleep three hours at a stretch, and then remain awake for five, thereby giving themselves nine hours of sleep in each twenty-four hour period. Under the labor credit system they were free to work when they chose, so this was no barrier to arranging their time.

An experimental program of mutual criticism begun in the summer of 1969 is still in existence. Under this program (modeled on the practice initiated by John Humphrey Noyes in the Oneida Community), a different member of the community volunteers to be the subject of criticism each week. He sits quietly, listening and does not reply as each member in turn tells what is liked and disliked about him. This, from my point of view, is a great improvement over the use of the Generalized Bastard, although it still seems a bit too structured. It is important to realize though, that at least the structuring at Twin Oaks is not rigid and inflexible and that it shows no signs of becoming that way.

One of the reasons for so much change despite structure at Twin Oaks has been the continual turnover of personnel. Of the original group, only Kathleen and Susan remain. Rudy's wife left; Rudy moved to Richmond much later; George departed; Dusty moved to San Francisco where he got in and out of the Haight street-drug culture, as well as in and out of a "Gurdjieff" society. Kurt, the businessman who had put up the money for the farm's purchase, lived at Twin Oaks for a while, but then left shortly thereafter because he was dissatisfied with the way the community was being run.

The October 1970 newsletter reported a reduction in membership turnover, asserting that:

The population turnover at Twin Oaks is coming to a slow halt. . . . The average stay is closer to six months now; it used to be three months. . . .

There is still a steady influx of new people but for the last eight months or so there has been no major, jarring exodus. The membership has hovered at around 25 during the year which is the maximum number that the community can physically support at present.

Innovation has frequently meant progress at Twin Oaks, but not always. The following lines indicate how one experiment failed completely. In search of work that would provide adequate support for 25 people, Twin Oaks began raising veal calves and beef cattle in 1969. But one problem after another developed: for example, the community's sole resident cattle expert left; two heifers died; and baby calves couldn't be purchased on the market. Finally, after losing about $1,500 in feed and expenses plus the depreciation on the animals caused by underfeeding, Twin Oaks went out of the cattle business. The community now contents itself with keeping only a few cows and a few replacement heifers, plus the knowledge derived from having tried something new (even if it did fail).

Another new enterprise is the community's country store, which was opened in the spring of 1970. Working in shifts, the members keep the store open 14 hours a day. True, it does not bring much income into the community, but it does provide the members with different and enjoyable work.*

Another job enjoyed by Twin Oaks members is lecturing. Churches, colleges, and schools in the general area frequently invite members to come and talk about themselves and the Twin Oaks community. The cash income derived from these lecturing activities is, like that from the store, small in amount, but this is offset by another, intangible factor.

Since March 1968, it has been necessary for members to take regular outside jobs, in order to help meet the mounting needs of the community. Although they provide a major source of income, these are the least popular jobs. One of the reasons for this lack of popularity is the commuting distance between the place of work and home. The prospect of rising in the morning at 5:30 in order to work long hours at unskilled work at some distant place is not attractive. Nevertheless, at any given time 8 of the 25 members must be working at outside jobs. So each member takes his turn. The method of selection is rotation, based on the length of time spent as a community member. New members have to work the 40-day stint soon after they join. Those who can survive this ordeal settle into the potentially more pleasant atmosphere of the community with the knowledge that they'll not have to do an outside job again for at least another 4 to 12 months.

---

*The store is now closed (summer, 1971). The operation was not a financial disaster but the income from it was not enough to justify the time and energy expended by community members in its maintenance.

A Second Interview with Kathleen:

THREE-PLUS YEARS LATER

After writing the foregoing information about Twin Oaks, I made my second trip to the community, where I talked at great length with Kathleen—now known as Kat—and others to bring the story of Twin Oaks up-to-date, the date being late December 1970. What follows is the transcript of a good portion of that discussion:

DICK: How many people have been members at Twin Oaks in the last three years?

KAT: Seventy-two. There was an average of 15 members per month in 1968; lower than that in 1969. We jumped to 25 in 1970. Now we're up to 31.

DICK: With that many members are you each able to have a private room?

KAT: We've never had a private-room policy. The only time anyone's ever had a private room is when we've been real low on membership and there was space. A lot of us would really like to have private rooms, but everytime you say "we are going to have a private room," you are saying "we are going to turn someone away who wants to join." So naturally there's pressure inside each individual. No member has a very clear point of view on this. He says to himself, "I really think we ought to have private rooms and the standard of living at this point is more important than expansion of membership." Then he turns right around and says, "But I've got this little brother, see, and he really needs to find an alternative and I'm wondering if we can take him."

DICK: How much money did it take to start this commune?

KAT: It took about $35,000 for land and one building—a little more than that counting the well, come to think of it; add another thousand for the well.

Dick: For how many people?

KAT: Fifteen people were comfortably housed, at that level. Since then we've put another five or six thousand into building. That five

75

or six thousand has come from internal donations. A member joins who has a thousand in the bank, and he says let's build a building with this. Of course a lot of the building fund comes directly out of our own income — Twin Oaks outside-worker income or hammock income or whatever. We put money into construction every month.

DICK: How much money does Twin Oaks need to keep going?

KAT: We live on $700 a year per member — that's food and clothing and medical and gasoline and stuff like that. But we put so much money into trying to get industry started, and one thing and another that oh, good heavens, we went through $50,000 last year. And we didn't have as large a membership then. I think we probably go through a couple of thousand per member per year altogether.

DICK: The problem is trying to find industry that will bring in that amount of money, rather than outside jobs?

LUKE: Something like three or four thousand a month is what we take in at the moment.

KAT: Donations from members that are joining —

TAMARA: —quite a bit comes from hammocks, believe it or not.

KAT: —and the lectures.

TAMARA: Yeah, those have been contributing quite a bit too. But the highest figures on the income page are hammocks and guest meals and right after that members' salaries from outside jobs.

DICK: Who handles the money for the community as a whole? This is very crucial I would think, trying to keep the books straight and know how to budget things.

KAT: Well, it's a managership like everything else. There's a budget manager. Books are kept by fairly conventional methods, and taxes are paid just like any business would pay them. Our taxes are more complicated than business taxes, because we are not just a business, we are a living arrangement. Money is handled communally; there's no such thing as a private income. All money from outside jobs, regardless of how much it is or who makes it, comes back into the central treasury. The outside workers who might be bringing in, oh, about a hundred a week, they take their 32 cents a day for snack money and they pack a sack lunch. We try to keep expenses down as far as possible.

DICK: Do members rotate on the same jobs?

KAT: No, we seldom get anything where people can rotate on the job. It sometimes happens one member will quit a job and another will walk in and get the same job, but we each are responsible for finding whatever job we can.

DICK: All this must amount to a great deal of bookkeeping?

KAT: A great deal of bookkeeping in comparison to what? In comparison to the bookkeeping in most corporations? No, much less. In comparison to an anarchist, free-style commune? Much more. But with it we have equality; they don't.

DICK: What's that mean?

KAT: What's that mean? That means nobody rips off more than anybody else.

DICK: You mean actually dollar-wise?

KAT: Yeah.

DICK: Does that make equality?

KAT: No, it can't, but it's a start. Nor do we assume that equality equals happiness either. We may agree that inequalities produce unhappiness, though. If we can keep sort of a rough equality going by saying that everybody gets 75 cents a week to buy candy and coke or what ever they want. . . . So you say that isn't equality? True. Some people are more attractive than others and they can get friendship more easily; some people have hot tempers; some people have placid dispositions. People are not born equal.

* * *

DICK: Now, getting back to reinforcement and equality. Some people like obviously, you and Susan, have gotten the most reinforcement out of Twin Oaks because you're both still here. So it's an unequal situation in that sense — in that in the community different people get more reinforcement from the community than others. This may have to do with their own personalities, but from a psychological point of view there is an inequality that may be a permanent necessity.

KAT: I don't know what we can do about it.

DICK: I don't know either, but it's definitely an inequality.

KAT: But I don't see that we should push inequality and shrug our shoulders and say, "Well, all right, you can't do it so forget it." Now the kind of a stance we take is: "You can't do it completely, but let's give it a try; let's minimize inequality."

DICK: Have you had any problems of equality with Christmas presents?

KAT: We just don't get them. We don't give them.

DICK: I mean someone in the community getting them from parents or some other outside source.

KAT: We let people keep the presents they get from their parents, but most people don't. If they get something good to eat, for instance, they generally put it out and everybody eats it. If they get something to wear, they might wear it once before it goes into community clothes.

* * *

DICK: It's mainly on the economic level that you're dealing, or is it?

KAT: Primarily, but that has so much influence. That's powerful. On other levels, on personal levels, we don't think of it in terms of equalization; we think of our struggles to work out personal problems simply as working out personal problems.

DICK: But has your economics really been the major problem in the last three-and-a-half years?

KAT: I would say so. It means that so many people in our community have to do outside work every day. They leave very very early in the morning and they get back late at night. They have to work for at least two months.

DICK: This has been going on since the beginning?

KAT: Yeah. Well, no. The first six months we didn't have to work outside because we lived off the money we brought with us. That's how long most communes last, until the initial money is gone.

DICK: That's changed now. Maybe the same people don't go on, but once a place is established in the country, it seems to go on.

KAT: Other people come in with their assets until they run out. . . . Well, in any case, the way we do it is to go on outside work. Outside work is really very unpleasant and undesirable for us. You can't call that anything else but an economic problem.

DICK: Is economics a major factor in interpersonal relations, in terms of a group of people staying together?

KAT: Now, it's pretty hard for me to put my finger on what's supposed to be a major interpersonal problem. I don't know. What's a major interpersonal problem? Sex? Problems of sexual arrangements at Twin Oaks just aren't that heavy. Here's our interpersonal manager. Come close to the microphone.

DICK: You have an interpersonal manager?

KAT: No, I'm being funny.

TAMARA: We can't supply all of everybody's needs — that's what all our problems are. We don't have private rooms and so there are problems of arrangements between two people who are sharing rooms.

LUKE: And we can't afford all the recreation facilities that we'd like to have so it sort of vexes people.

DICK: Members aren't able to use their leisure time the way they would like to because of the lack of facilities.

KAT: Exactly.

TAMARA: And so you get theoretical discussions, like standard of living versus growth. It's because we don't have enough money to do both.

* * *

DICK: Of the 41 people who have left, could you give an account of some of the reasons?

KAT: There are a number of reasons. One of the major ones is that they never intended to stay in the first place. We have a very young population. They say to themselves, "I think I'll live in a community for a while because that would be an interesting experience. I'm interested in personal growth. This is something I want to do." So they stay six months, eight months, a year. Then they've done it, so they go do something else. They do not come up with: "This is the way life ought to be. This is the way society ought to be set up. I'm going to dedicate my life to this" — or anything else of that sort. They're not just simple people who say "I want to find a comfortable nest for myself and settle down." They're young people doing adventures. And this is one of their adventures. And they come and they go. I don't think we can help that. Furthermore I don't even think it's bad.

DICK: It hasn't been disruptive of the group at all?

KAT: No. Well, it tears down morale when somebody leaves, 'cause you can't help saying to yourself, "If we were sufficiently wonderful he would have stayed." But I'm not certain just how wonderful you'd have to be for that! The sense of adventure — "I'm going to go hitchhike across the country; I'm gonna go to Africa; I'm going to visit all the communes; I'm going to . . . ," you know, one adventure or another — that's what takes a lot of them. Now that isn't the only reason people leave. Some people leave because they have personal problems that they came hoping Twin Oaks would solve. Let's say their mating problem or friendship problem or their deep, personal psychological problems. And they go off to some place else that doesn't help either. I should mention that there must be eight different people who have gone and come back. That seems to be a trend. Another reason people have left is because they stay for a while and realize there are distinct ideological differences between the core group — the power structure, Twin Oaks Establishment, so to speak — and themselves. They say: "This is not what I meant. I don't think things should go this way. I think they should go some other way." And then they say: "I'm going off to form my own commune," and of course they don't.

DICK: Could you give me an example or two of that ideological difference?

KAT: Sure, any number. One is: "I don't think equality is so important after all. I think that if you're going to run a commune successfully it is necessary that competent people be in charge of industries and be in charge of the progress of the community. Those competent people have power in their hands to do something; they shouldn't have to be forever stumbling over neurotics and children and teenagers and longhairs and incompetent, inefficient . . . ," you know, you get the general gist? I call it an ideological difference but you can sense that there's something more to it.

DICK: Yeah, but I'm not quite sure what you're saying. I am sure that the people who, as I understand it, make the major policy decisions is the board of planners. So in other words, these people you're referring to aren't on the board of planners?

KAT: They certainly aren't.

DICK: So it would seem to me that what they are saying is that they want to be on the board of planners and what you're saying is that they don't get there that quickly.

KAT: Well, maybe they don't get there at all. Maybe there's something about their point of view so that the group says we don't want those people in. Incidentally, cleanliness is another big issue. There have been people who have left because it's simply too dirty.

DICK: Really? Twin Oaks doesn't look too dirty.

KAT: You're comparing it with other communes. No, Twin Oaks is not a dirty commune at all. It's cleaned every day. The floor is scrubbed every day, and so forth. Then there are the people who want us to move ahead faster. They want us to be closer to the American middle-class standard. They like the communal ideal. In *Walden Two* everything was, you know, so affluent. They think Twin Oaks can get to be like that. They say "I believe if I put my effort into it we could soon get ahead"; then they discover perhaps that their financial ideas disagree with ours, or perhaps we're going to continue to take young people that don't have any particular skill and who will leave tools out in the rain; so they say to themselves, "With people like this, we'll never get ahead," or something of that sort. Then they get discouraged about ever becoming really well-off, comfortable — someplace like Camp Hill up in Copack, New York. Have you ever been there? Now there's a well-to-do commune: everything's in beautiful order, like the Shakers used to be or the Hutterites are.

Where everything runs smoothly. I think we'll get to that stage, but it'll probably take about five or six times longer than those certain people are willing to wait.

DICK: What's happened to some of the people who have left Twin Oaks?

KAT: I think that the average person who leaves simply goes back into the Establishment—back to doing whatever he was doing before he got here. A couple or three have left to get into other ideological work. There are other ideologies that pull people in other directions, like Rudy and Scott. People who come here are quite often heavily ideological. They want to be certain their life counts for something. If they decide the community isn't worth it, or it isn't what they want their lives to count for, then they will go into some other self-sacrificing ideological thing.

DICK: Why do people stay? What's so reinforcing about Twin Oaks?

KAT: I stay because it's my life's work. It's reinforcing in every way. In the first place, all my basic, all my ordinary, needs are taken care of and my rather unordinary needs are taken care of too. That is, you know, the food is excellent, except sometimes it is lousy. But it's a whole lot better than I would cook for myself, or that I ever had before.

DICK: You're not so crazy about cooking three times a day?

KAT: I'm certainly not. And my laundry is done and the house is . . . not neat, but neater than I would keep it. That sort of need is taken care of for me. I'm entirely relieved of housework. I'm supported with dignity, with honor; by that I mean—without any sense of guilt on my part—by doing things I don't mind doing, like waiting on the store and typing; and I don't have to work too many hours a day. So those are the physical basics that would really appall me to have to leave and go somewhere and work for a living again. To have to work 37½ hours a week in an office and travel back and forth to an apartment and clean up the apartment and do my own laundry and find a meal somewhere—oh, I would hate that! So communal living offers its physical advantages. But that's sort of minor. The quality of friendships, the quality of people that I associate with, is so much higher at Twin Oaks—more so than anywhere I've ever been. One can find interesting people in college, but how do college people sustain that kind of environment when they leave college? They've got to go out and leave that highly stimulating atmosphere. At Twin Oaks it never stops.

DICK: You're in college all the time.

KAT: Well, in a way. I'm not sure we'd want to use that for a slogan. But it's much more than that. What one wants, what I want, is something worthwhile to do—to put my energies somewhere that I feel is worthwhile, worth doing. As I see the world and as I see the social situation, working in a commune and making it a success is worth it for itself and for the people who are there now. In addition, if we can make another commune, then it's worth it for the people in it as well. In addition, if we can contribute to a movement, then it makes a real difference to the social structure as a whole, to the nation as a whole.

DICK: Can I ask you a question, Luke? While we're on this, are there reasons you'd like to contribute to this as to why you came back after leaving for six months? What is it that made this more important to you than, say, getting another job—or, say, going into another commune?

LUKE: Well, pretty much the same things that Kat said. I've found that Kat usually speaks my mind. It's pretty much the same things.

DICK: Just thought I'd check.

KAT: And then you'd ask us what we do with our leisure time? Is that well taken care of? Well, in my case it is—very well. This is part of the same answer, going back to what we were saying, as to what's reinforcing about the community: in terms of general aims, in terms of physical comforts, and in terms of fun and games. What I like to do in my leisure time is to play around with theory and have intellectual arguments with people and things like that. Which is a constant activity at Twin Oaks. We have a tradition of putting up theoretical papers on the bulletin board, on subjects that relate directly to the community. You'll find one up there now called "Positive Reinforcement is a Farce," and another one called "Punishment is no Joke." They are arguing things that you probably wouldn't even understand because you haven't been here during the planners' meeting that they refer to and so forth. And we answer each other with theoretical papers on the bulletin board.

DICK: You answer by other papers?

KAT: Sometimes. But we sit around and argue about them at the dinner table mostly. Only a few of us like to write papers.

*   *   *

DICK: Are you really sharing clothes communally now?

KAT: It's just too much of a nuisance to do otherwise. I think the whole clothing situation is a nuisance. There's this big closet where we keep all the clothes. You want something to wear? If it fits, wear it. You can have your own clothes if you want to, but most people can't be bothered. There's no rule about community clothes, never has been. Never been legislated. It's evolved by itself. I think the reason is that in this country the superfluity of clothes is outrageous. Everyone's got more clothes than he can possibly use.

DICK: I remember once you told me that the interpersonal and sexual aspects of a person's life were left up to each individual.

KAT: Most of us feel that the sex-love thing is sacred. We just have a special feeling about it and we want to be left alone in it. I wouldn't say it was contrary to our philosophy or doctrine to introduce experiments in sex and love, but I will tell you this: we would not publicize it if we did. We would not go to *The Modern Utopian* and say "Write us an article on it." In fact, we would sit here and tell you blatantly that we never did anything of the kind. It's just simply that publicity would be dangerous and harmful in those areas. Those are private areas.

DICK: One of the biggest problems I've seen in communes is the inability of couples to stay together.

KAT: Well, we don't call it a problem. We certainly know what you're talking about and can contribute to the statistics. There has been one marriage to survive Twin Oaks so far.

DICK: There has been one to survive and still live here?

KAT: They moved back to Carmel, California.

DICK: They left?

KAT: They came into the community and left and are still married.

DICK: But they had to leave in order to stay married?

KAT: I'm not sure that would be the case with them. This was an older couple in their 40s. Wait a minute, L___ and M___ also made it.

84

DICK: So what's the reason for married couples breaking up in communes?

KAT: It's very simple. Marriage is a very very weak institution. It's supported on the outside by all sorts of pressures which are removed as soon as you get into the community. We remove the pressures and make alternatives available and people do what comes naturally. They will choose to stay married only if that's reinforcing. If it isn't reinforcing, what for?

DICK: Is there some sort of dependency thing in the nature of monogamous marriage which gets taken away in a community setting?

KAT: We don't know that people are less dependent in community, but there are more people to be depended upon. Your alternatives are greater. It's not us two against all the world; it's you, an individual in this community, and me, an individual in this community. If we dig each other, great. Generally one or the other will find another friend, quite often both do, and if the marriage survives multiple relations, great. Sometimes it does. There have been three couples who have gotten married because of the community too — three couples met in the community, left the community, and got married.

DICK: I'd like to try to deal with this a little more in depth. I'm not sure how. It's a very complex thing, this business of interpersonal relationships; especially couples and their breaking up and coming together, and the reasons for it. Do you think that maybe a lot of people who get interested in the community as couples do so because of a certain dissatisfaction with each other in the first place?

KAT: I suspect so. I don't know for sure. I can just think of an example or two that fits into that category. I can think of examples immediately that don't, too.

DICK: So maybe it doesn't?

KAT: I doubt very seriously there would be a generalization. If you took a slice of married couples anywhere you would find that most of them are not happy with each other. Marriage is a bummer. Of course, I wouldn't go so far as to say that the pair has no function, because there are people at Twin Oaks who pair up and stay paired for a long time. I have not been including them in the term "married." I am using it in its ordinary sense. I don't think the reasons for marriage on the outside have a whole lot to do with interpersonal relations. They do at first, but they have to do with things like, OK, the need for sex, and a place and time to do it, reasonably and legally without parent hassles, police hassles, and so forth. That was more true in my time than now. Second of all there's a problem of support. Somebody has to make a living, and marriage has been traditionally a way for a woman to make a living. That tradition is also fading, but then so is marriage. Also, it's a place and a way to raise children. In a community these things are totally meaningless: everybody makes his own living, and sex is readily available and not disapproved of.

DICK: How about the emotional relationships that keep people together?

KAT: There are pairs. There are couplings that take place and stay together.

TAMARA: It's a security thing, on both sides. The security a person would need a marriage for—to insure that there was somebody who cared. In the community there are people who have committed themselves to each other and who realize that the only way they can really stay together happily is if they do care about each other and they do reinforce each other. Otherwise, they won't receive the reinforcement to the extent it requires.

DICK: Have you ever experienced in Twin Oaks the situation where a pair got together with another pair and it's worked out satisfactorily—emotionally satisfactorily?

KAT: I don't know what you mean by "worked out satisfactorily." Generally we have seen these things and can say "yes, they have worked out satisfactorily." And three months later they split up. I think they're very very hard to do, very hard.

DICK: So the usual thing is a temporary pairing.

KAT: I'm talking about temporary quadrupling.

DICK: Right, right. But I was saying the usual thing is—

KAT: —and one mate is out, usually with the change.

DICK: The tendency is to go back to couples.

KAT: Yes, but not the same couple. I have sometimes cynically suspected that group pairings take place because one of the pair is more attracted to a member of the other pair than he is to his own mate. That's the original impetus for it and of course the real goal of it. When this goal is firmly accomplished the peripheries on the side drop off. But, as I say, that's cynicism.

DICK: Yeah, that's my cynicism too, I'm afraid. I wish it weren't so. There ought to be a better way for things to develop than simply that way. But somehow or other it usually turns out that way. So my cynicism gets reinforced. Let's talk about your board of planners — the people here who make the major policy decisions. Just how does a person get to be a planner at Twin Oaks?

KAT: Well, for one thing, planners are chosen for their general agreement with the kinds of policies we've already set and for their ability to think out problems logically and unemotionally. By unemotionally I don't mean they don't feel anything; I mean they are able to separate their opinions from their feelings.

DICK: I'm not sure that's possible.

KAT: To a reasonable degree it is — at least to try. There are some people who are obviously not very self-aware, who are obviously self-deceived. These people will never be on the board of planners. Most of what a planner does in our group — and there's some criticism of this but it is the biggest part of his job — is judicial. An issue comes up: may this member have or may this member not have such and such special privilege, which is not technically equal but it might be a good thing anyway. The planners have to decide — in case after case after case. It's like being a judge.

DICK: It's making decisions the group itself is not willing to make?

KAT: Well, this is the way the group makes a decision.

DICK: They make a decision by referring it to the planners.

KAT: Yeah, otherwise how can the group make a decision? Somebody gets a present, somebody wants to go to school and take a certain class. Well, we figure schooling is recreation and the community can't afford it. But the person says, "My mother will pay for it." We say, "We haven't all got mothers to pay for our private recreations." Are we all allowed to write home to our mothers and say, "Gee, I'd like a canoe; gee, I'd like a trip to Europe; gee, I'd like this, I'd like that?" Can we all write home to our mothers and say, "Will you finance it?" It seems unequal. Part of the community will be saying,

"That's not fair." On the other hand, the individual says, "Look, this is a thing that I've always wanted. It's only a six-week course. It doesn't cost a whole lot. I don't think it's a bad precedent. I personally would enjoy it very much and I don't really think anybody cares." Then the other people say, "For heaven's sake let her have it, who cares?" This is the kind of problem that comes up to the board of planners and they sit there for four hours and scratch their heads. Planners are quite often chosen for their ability to think through that kind of thing—without letting their personal prejudices get in their way, or personal friendships. 'Course, there's more to being a planner than that. The question of using some judgment in how to spend money, or whether to spend money is another.

DICK: The planners make major decisions for the community as a whole and those judicial kinds of decisions regarding individuals. Now as I understand it planners are appointed on a rotating basis and there are three planners all together. The original planners were you, Kat, Rudy and Scott.

KAT: Scott left ages ago.

DICK: Then you appointed someone else?

KAT: Well, back then we were electing, but under our current system we would simply have appointed someone to take Scott's place. That kind of thing still goes on. The mortality rate on planners is terrible. Eighteen months is his supposed term. He goes out of office in 18 months and is replaced by the same process, by appointment. This is appointment with a majority overrule possible. There's a veto box placed after every planner appointment; if the group doesn't want a particular planner, all they have to do is say so. All it takes is a simple majority. In other words, we don't vote for our planners, but we vote against them.

DICK: Before a planner is appointed, he is suggested to the group? Is that it?

KAT: Yeah, we have chosen so and so to be the next planner. The veto box is over by the phone. It will be there for a week. Now after he's a planner it will take two-thirds to get rid of him. Two-thirds of the group can do anything—to that extent we are a democracy.

DICK: Good, it's very good to get this cleared up because I think that's a very crucial thing about *Walden Two:* the question of democ-

racy versus oligarchy. How about the planning board's meetings? Do you have them regularly or once a month?

KAT: Once a week. Oftener if necessary.

DICK: Is anyone able to observe or be around?

KAT: Oh yes, planners' meetings are open. The only time they're closed is when they're appointing managers. Those are closed sessions because quite often you have to say things about a manager or about a person's qualifications that you wouldn't care to say in public. We have, as you may remember, an anti-gossip rule. We do not discuss each other's personalities, faults, failings, or whatever, behind their backs. Planners can and have to do this when it comes to appointing someone to a responsible position. If somebody can't handle money, you're not going to say that in public. You don't yell out, "This person will probably rip off the money." You say it quietly.

DICK: There is "criticism," though. Is that a mechanism for saying this to the person himself?

KAT: We practice criticism, but I don't think we practice it as well as Oneida did. I sometimes think the institution is dying, but we still do it.

DICK: Why do you think it's dying?

KAT: Because I've seen some sessions where there was obviously something to be said, something that needed saying, and it didn't get said. People were too polite, withheld their comments. People think: Well, it's true, I could say that but I would be saying it in front of everybody in the group and there are people here who don't know. It's the same reason for the anti-gossip rule. If we all knew each other intimately and well and someone was particularly unaware about his own faults, then it would be time to say it. It could be said publicly without damage. But, considering what the turnover is here, there are people who have only been here a couple of months and don't know that so and so has the habit of doing such and such. Better they shouldn't know. A lot of members don't feel like exposing their friend in front of people who might never have known. There was a time when you could expect to hear the truth; now, you hear comments that are very gentle, very very, all the way up to too gentle. In my particular case I once called a criticism especially because I wanted to know something in particular and I wasn't told. I needed to know and I wasn't told.

DICK: How did you find out?

KAT: Well, I don't want to go into it. They let me know.

DICK: Well, is there any way to make something like that work?

KAT: I don't know. There's a lot of theoretical discussions. Some people feel very strongly that it's not an appropriate institution for Twin Oaks and does too much damage. They won't go and they won't contribute their comments and their spirit. This is the thing about a voluntary commune. You do not say, "OK, we will now have group criticism and all people will attend." You can't do that and wouldn't want to.

DICK: The board of planners doesn't make that kind of decision?

KAT: Board of planners doesn't have that kind of control. We don't give *anybody* that kind of control. We are very free people and we attend meetings if and when we damn well choose.

DICK: Someone in another community said that too much structure was violence, that structure could be a violent thing, like if everyone has to eat between 5 and 6 P.M. This is violence to the individual because eating is a personal thing and so forth. How would you respond to that?

KAT: I would respect what he said but it wouldn't have occurred to me to use the word "violence." I think of it in terms of freedom and of everybody having to give up some freedom in order to have others, or in order for other people to have others. At Twin Oaks the person who wants to eat any hour of the day or night, may; all he had to do is fix it for himself. A person who wants a full-scale meal served at 10 o'clock at night — well, his freedom to eat that full-scale meal conflicts with my freedom not to fix it. We have just enough structure that anybody who wants a hot, well-prepared meal gets there at 6:30 to eat it. If you don't want that then you eat at some other hour. Big deal. It's unreasonable to suppose that we're going to serve tremendous meals all hours of the day or night. Nor do I think your anarchist friend would expect us to.

DICK: If you had steam cabinets you would be able to set it up in the morning and whenever anyone wanted to eat, they could eat.

KAT: Yeah, but not your anarchist friend. I mean, he would probably shudder at that. Technology — good heavens! It probably does violence to his sensibilities.

DICK: There are a lot of people who are that way. They don't want to use technology anymore. Which from my point of view is ridiculous, because it's here to stay until we all disappear anyway. We have to use the best parts of it and discard the worse.

KAT: Twin Oaks is not against technology at all, neither theoretically nor practically.

* * *

DICK: Picking up leadership, again: regardless of structure or no structure, isn't it really leadership based upon individual personalities — those that are aggressive and leader types, which tends to influence the direction of a community?

KAT: That's still true. I don't think it's going to be true for always but it's still true now. The time will come when rational decisions will rule the community regardless of what kind of personalities are behind them.

DICK: You hope.

KAT: I . . . hope.

* * *

DICK: I've always had a problem with the jargon of behaviorists! These words "manager" and "planner." Personally, I like the way you do things. I just don't like the way you *call* things. I read about Twin Oaks, you know, and I said, "Oh, Jesus Christ!" But then I see Twin Oaks, and I know Twin Oaks, and I say, "Hey, things are pretty good."

KAT: Yeah, you find that the kitchen manager is someone so young and so pretty, who bites her nails, and then you say, "Oh, for Christ's sake, what's the problem?"

DICK: Isn't there any way to get around this "language"?

KAT: I refuse to worry about it until we are begging for members. As long as they're pounding on our doors — I don't care what people think of our nomenclature.

DICK: But it's important what kind of image you project. That's part of what you exist for, right? To turn other people on to doing it. You have to care in that sense. You don't care in terms of recruiting but —

KAT: OK, OK, OK. I care. But I don't know what else to call them. Overseers? It wouldn't matter. You could choose any word and it would be just as objectionable. People come by Twin Oaks and say, "If this is all behavioral engineering means, I'm not afraid of it." Some members feel that the *Walden Two* image hurts us; they would like to rewrite the book. They'd like to write a book explaining the same ideas in terms that would be more palatable to today's young people. It's a good idea if somebody did it. Is there going to be a meeting of the "board of fascists" this afternoon? Oh, wow! We could extinguish the reaction to those words in about three weeks. See, that's what happens here. People come here and they join. They have your attitude and they shudder and say "Oh well, it looks like a neat place." Within a week the word "manager" has lost all its emotional connotations. A manager is just the member next to you. And you'll probably be one, or two or three, if you stay another three weeks.

LUKE: Why don't we just call the managers "LACKEYS OF THE FAS-CIST PIGS!"

DICK: Yes, that's the real difference between a fascist system, which has planners and managers, and a community like this, which has planners and managers. Everyone knows each other in this community; in the fascist system there's just some guy up there.

KAT: It isn't just that, Dick. It's a question of what you get for being a planner or manager: whether the position is simply a responsibility with a little slop-over of prestige, perhaps, plus personal satisfaction; or whether you're actually getting a salary or power over people.

LUKE: Any manager who came up with something strongly opposed by the rest of the people wouldn't have any support. All "manager" says is that the person who is best qualified in a field should direct it.

* * *

DICK: Most communes dislike publicity because it means they are going to be innundated with visitors as a result. That's not a problem for you, is it?

KAT: No, but I feel very sorry for the anarchist communes, because they don't have any way of handling visitors. The reason we continually expose ourselves to publicity is because we can manage. And the reason we can manage is because—OK, we've got a visitor manager.

DICK: That's why you manage!

KAT: The visitor manager says, "So many and no more," and tells the correspondence manager "So many and no more." The correspondence manager writes back and says, "I'm sorry but we're filled up. Would you like to make a date for March?" We are currently making dates for March. This is December. January is filled. February, I believe, is filled. We have decided among us a little at a time, through experience, how many visitors we can reasonably live with. It turns out not to be the limit of how many beds there are or how many places there are to sleep. It's much more than that. It's how many strangers can we have on the premises at a time without feeling that this is not our commune anymore.

DICK: That's a very important question. Have you developed any kind of ratio?

KAT: I don't think it's a ratio. Our current thing is we can have six or eight long-term people who stay a week or more. If they stay a month or more, we can have ten, because by then they're just like members. In January we're going to have ten long-term visitors. That's all we can handle. We're not taking any short-timers in January at all. We don't like to have more than three or four short-time people on the property at a time. So, we simply limit them. We've got the structures to limit them with; and this is what the hippie commune doesn't have. They don't know what to do about it, so they're swamped. Boy, am I sympathetic. You're not at home anymore when you've got three newspaper reporters and six people down from New York in their high heels and their upsweep hairdos, plus 20,000 hippies from the nearest city who are drifting by to see if there's any dope.

DICK: Yeah, the manager thing. Isn't that very difficult to work out?

KAT: It's difficult to find enough competent people. It's not difficult to choose among them because there are plenty of managerships to go around and there are no goodies that go with managing except just the pleasure of managing. If you have somebody who wants to be kitchen manager, and Tamara's doing all right at it, but this person is superlatively good, you would say, "Well, start working with Tamara." And pretty soon Tamara would say, "Look, this person knows so much more than I do, I think I'll do something else." And so she would just kinda drop off.

TAMARA: Queen for a Day!

DICK: Do you have any skill requirements for new members? In other words, can they come without any money, without any skills, without anything?

KAT: That has been true to date, but now that we have the lid on the membership we'll take the person on the waiting list whom we want most. And that might be determined by skills in certain situations. We had three people on the waiting list a short time ago with one opening. And the person we took was one who knew how to repair automobiles. As it happened we also like him quite well. Still, you notice it was a skilled person we took when we had a choice. Before, when our doors were open, we took the first person who came along. When our doors are closed, we choose. As time goes on we'll be more and more choosy. We're just getting into that now. It's a very hairy problem when you have to choose against people and they say, "We know what you're doing, you're discriminating against that person because of the way he's dressed," or whatever—it makes you feel crummy.

DICK: The planners are the ones who decide who comes in?

KAT: The membership manager makes a recommendation, the board of planners makes the decision, but the group is polled in instances where they know. If they don't know the person then the membership manager and the board of planners sort of . . . the membership manager gets acquainted and makes the best recommendation she can.

DICK: How about if a person has a job he likes and yet he might like to live at Twin Oaks? How do you attract that kind of person?

KAT: We get the income.

DICK: Yeah, but he has to make the income within a reasonable distance of Twin Oaks? I was thinking of a person who had an occupation that he liked but really wasn't interested in doing all these managerial-type functions. He wanted to spend most of his time on his own specialization, say, like something that might bring a lot of income into the community. I'm not sure how that would work in terms of the equalitarian spirit of the community.

KAT: As long as he doesn't get more than his share, it's OK.

DICK: In other words, could a person come and be a member of the community and spend his six hours a day, or whatever, strictly developing programs which would bring income into the community? He wouldn't have to wash dishes. He wouldn't have to—

KAT:—it would depend on how much of the labor credit quota he does, providing he does as many hours as everyone else.

TAMARA: If it were possible for him to teach other people what he has done so that they could do it as well, then maybe his quota wouldn't be filled.

KAT: Hardly anybody has to wash dishes right now; I don't touch dishes. Anybody who has work that she likes and it takes enough of her time to fill her quota doesn't have to do anything she doesn't want to do. It's just that some of us are lucky enough to like work that's available and some of us aren't. A doctor, for example, would obviously have work available because there's a shortage of doctors in small towns, but a behavioral engineer isn't likely to unless he had something going by mail. Ray doesn't have to wash dishes.

DICK: Who's Ray?

KAT: Our professor at the University of Virginia. He works in the community on weekends only, since he doesn't quite get all of his quota in at the university.

LUKE: He only works four or five hours a day at the university.

DICK: Your setup is on an hourly basis?

KAT: Yes, he comes back here every night and doesn't have to leave until 10 in the morning.

DICK: Does he have to pack a lunch like the other outside workers?

KAT: Yes.

DICK: He isn't able to get a hot meal in the cafeteria or something like that?

KAT: No.

DICK: He must really love the commune.

KAT: No more than the rest of us.

LUKE: People do get an extra allowance if they work at outside jobs because they need it.

KAT: The same is true if you work in the store. You get a certain amount of goodies just because you're surrounded with all this temptation all the time. You're allowed 15 cents a shift for goodies.

LUKE: At wholesale rates.

KAT: In other words, what's common sense.

*　*　*

DICK: At present, the emphasis is upon expanding at Twin Oaks rather than setting up at any other locations?

KAT: No, I wouldn't say that. I wouldn't say that at all. What Twin Oaks can do in terms of setting up other communes is fairly limited. If we had the membership on the premises that we want and the facilities that we are after, if we had reached what seems to us a reasonable limit—then we would say, "Okay, let's split down the middle, like was done in the book." We'd take three competent people and call them a board of planners and six or eight competent people and put them in charge of the major managerships and then we'd make the down payment on a farm 50 miles from here, or in another state or whatever, preferably reasonably close so that we could trade with one another. But we are nowhere near ready for that, because if we had that kind of money we would expand on Twin Oaks premises. There's a whole lot ahead of us on our own premises. For one thing, getting children on the grounds. We haven't even started raising children yet. We are interested in expansion of the movement. We are very much interested in giving any kind of advice or help of any kind to anybody who's trying to start a commune. We can't do much in the line of finances, but we're going to have a conference next summer [1971], on Twin Oaks property, specifically for people who like our general kind of commune and who would like to set up one something like this one. We are hoping that there will be people at the conference, families with children, for example; we're not in a position to take children here at the moment, but a commune could start with people who already had children. We would hope to give the people as much advice and help as we could. They might have enough assets on their own to go ahead and start up one.

*   *   *

DICK: What if you all of a sudden had a black couple who wanted to join?

KAT: We would take them without any question.

DICK: Do you think there would be any adverse problems in the area?

KAT: People would talk about us a lot. But I don't believe they would come out here with shotguns. No, I think that everybody in the neighborhood knows that we are interracially minded, that we are among the liberal set. They shake their heads over that kind of thing, but I don't believe we would have any persecution.

DICK: How about working in the store?

KAT: We would not hesitate to put blacks as employees in the store. In the first place, nine-tenths of our customers are black; in the second place, the nearest competing store is run by blacks. It wouldn't be particularly extraordinary. If they work in the store, everybody will know they are from Twin Oaks, but everybody's going to know anyhow.

DICK: Right, everything gets known very fast in a small community.

KAT: Relatively. Now a mixed couple, black and white—we might be wise to ask them if they would not hold hands in town. Other than that our stand on race is unequivocal.

* * *

DICK: Now how does behavioral psychology really have anything to do with how you set things up here? I mean really? From a nittygritty level?

KAT: What behavioral psychology has to do with it is that we set up our institutions in such a way that the kind of behavior we want is reinforced by those institutions. For example, there is nothing to reinforce competitive behavior. You wash dishes faster than the guy next to you, it gets the dishes done faster. That's all.

DICK: Well, that's a very good benefit.

KAT: Yeah, insofar as it's a natural benefit, it's fine.

DICK: What I'm saying is I don't think you have to know anything about behavioral psychology to have Twin Oaks as a community.

KAT: No. Don't tell Skinner that.

DICK: Don't tell Skinner that? He's impressed with Twin Oaks now, isn't he?

KAT: Well, maybe because we're still here. We're going to get him down here one of these days and talk to him. Twin Oaks could have been conceived entirely without the idea of behavioral engineering and be pretty much what it is now. It's an economic theory. It couldn't have been conceived very well without the communal theory.

DICK: The book, *Walden Two*, is a cementing force, or at least was initially.

KAT: All of our institutions come from *Walden Two*, with the exception of criticism, which comes from Oneida.

DICK: Of course a lot of those institutions come from other utopian writers, like Bellamy.

KAT: Yes, that's true. But it was Skinner's genius that cemented them.

98

LUKE: I wonder, was it genius or just that he was knowledgeable about what was happening?

DICK: He is a knowledgeable man. Still, I don't think you can take genius away from him. Genius is putting something together that hasn't been put together the same way before. Like, Picasso took a bicycle handlebar and seat and made an oxhead out of it.

KAT: I saw it. And I am not impressed.

DICK: You're not impressed? Oh, I'm impressed.

KAT: I think that you're saying that precisely because Picasso did it and for no other reason.

DICK: Maybe. I look at it and I say: well, I could have done that myself. But the point is I didn't; and that's a major difference between genius and mediocrity.

KAT: A lot of people may have done it, but nobody paid any attention to them.

DICK: Well, there are a lot of geniuses in the world who'll never get recognized. We can always point to at least one.

AN ALTERNATIVE

Behind all of these details, however, is one central and solidifying belief of Twin Oaks members: this Walden

Two community offers an alternative — an alternative to working for the military-industrial complex, an alternative to aggressive, violent and destructive opposition to the system.

The concept behind Twin Oaks offers a radical approach to revolution — that of creating the post-revolutionary society now, during one's own lifetime. The community has, in fact, published a little booklet entitled "The Revolution is Over: We Won!"

By dropping out of the system and creating communities that will hopefully cooperate economically and socially, activists are increasing the possibilities that a whole new type of society can eventually emerge, from the grass roots upward. The members of Twin Oaks, like most community folk, see revolution as a radical restructuring of both the society and the individual so that people become "committed to nonaggression . . . concerned for one another . . . where one man's gain is not another man's loss . . . where disagreeable work is minimized and leisure is valued; an economic system of equality and a society which is constantly trying to improve in its ability to create happy, productive, creative people."*

*The Revolution is Over: We Won! published by Twin Oaks Community, 1969.

CHAPTER FOUR

MODERN RELIGIOUS COMMUNES

THE OREGON FAMILY

IF YOU VISIT communes long enough you will eventually trek up a long, narrow, dusty road that winds through the woods and opens onto a clearing filled with beautiful naked maidens. At least that was my in-person introduction to The Oregon Family.

Friends had told me about this group, which was now in its third year of existence. Its founders were devout fundamentalist Christians, mostly in their mid-20s, very industrious and committed.

I had listed The Family's post office address in the

Commune Directory (published annually by Alternatives Foundation). So when I began to revise the list of communes, I wrote to The Family in order to find out if they cared to continue the listing. The secretary, El Twig, replied:

Dear Brothers and Sisters —

The Lord bless you and fill you with His Light. We wish our name and address to be immediately *deleted* from your magazine.

This is our home, not a tourist vacation spa. We are trying to gain, spread, promulgate the love of Jesus the Christ and find it necessary to control the number of brothers and sisters who share here with us. We also seek more subtle methods of soul-mating than computerizing. We appreciate your inclusion of our address, and now would appreciate your exclusion of same. Kindly R.S.V.P. that this has been done.

> Love and Peace
> El Twig, secretary

When I arrived on a Thursday morning to R.S.V.P., I found a sign at the entrance that read, "No vehicles beyond this point. Visitors on Saturday only." Hoping to respect their wishes, I decided not to go in but to drive farther north instead, visit other communes, and stop back there on my return. I returned on Friday afternoon, still too early, although several other vehicles were already parked there.

There in the forest, somewhere in Oregon, The Family had erected an immense circle structure, architecturally a rural gem for communal living. Constructed of logs and timber, the building had an interior that consisted of a single room, space uninterrupted. The kitchen, occupying the end of this room next to the entrance, was amply equipped with stoves, cupboards and counter space. A long, wide table extended from the kitchen area into the middle of the room. Toward the other end of the room were two semi-circular tiers of connecting bunks. Adequate space between tiers enabled a person on a lower bunk to sit up comfortably without hitting his head or straining his neck.

When I entered the main building, I noticed a few people resting on the top bunk tier. And someone sitting near a corner was lightly strumming a guitar. Most of the women were in the kitchen baking bread and preparing other foods. A few sat outside nursing their babies. It was a warm day and all of the women were either totally naked or naked from the waist up. All, that is, except for several visitors and one resident couple who were talking to some of their guests.

The few men present were visitors. I talked with several persons in the area of the main structure. They were all visitors. Finally one of the younger naked ladies mentioned that many of the residents had gone away for the week. The men who remained were working in the huge garden at the foot of the hill or constructing new housing in different areas on the hillside.

Some families had decided to build their own separate dwellings among the trees along the winding road beyond the main communal area. The landscape was beautiful, the buildings rustic and sturdy. Among them stood a large food-storage house near the main clearing, a spacious and green garden—well irrigated and promising a good harvest.

I had heard that The Family had experimented with group marriage for a time, probably with everyone housed in the main communal structure. But the marriage "hadn't worked out"—that was all the information I could obtain. Now, those who wished to could live in the main building and others could take separate shelter. Since warm weather had arrived, the hillside was speckled with campsites, tents and tepees belonging to the many visitors as well as the residents.

At a large, wooden picnic-type table near the main building, I found the resident couple talking with three women and a man. This couple, as well as the rest of the men and women members of the commune, could only be described as hippies. Their dress (what there was of it), their manner, their hair all reflected this new life style; yet they seemed as fanatically committed to Jesus as were any of their more conservative, straight-type brethren, four of whom were sitting around the table discussing numerology and the Bible and Sin and Salvation and the Glories of the Lord.

"Bless you." "Be born again in Jesus." "Love God." These seemed to be the prevalent slogans as I brashly took a seat at one corner and listened in. I had nothing to say.

All four visitors were almost middle-aged and seemed to me to have just come from some Bible-Baptist prayer meeting. One of the outsiders, a seedy-looking man with short black hair and huge grim smile, seemed to be the numerology freak, as the others listened to him with indulgent Christian kindness. One woman dressed in her finest suit, probably straight out of a Montgomery Ward catalog, was talking with relish about how she believed in sin. And she elaborated lavishly when her hippie friends humbly disagreed with her assertion that "without evil how would you know good." And somehow, without actually agreeing, they all came round to the conclusion that Jesus was the answer. It was a mind-blowing scene. Four uptight, tight-lipped, straitlaced, well-groomed conventionally dressed, knit-browed Oregon Okies talking with two dusty clothed, freaky-hatted, longhaired, land-loving, out-of-sight Christian hippies.

The visitors—unconverted by any of this, as were their hosts—left with nervous smiles. They had spoken with "objectivity" and had assumed an unbiased demeanor. But never had they dared to discuss their feelings and beliefs about their personal life styles. I felt certain that the old gal who believed in sin would soon be telling the others how sinful were those who wore no clothes.

I was tired of being a reporter and of harassing people with questions about their home—which is, after all, what a commune is. It is not a tourist spa. Anyway, I didn't feel too comfortable with Bible-thumping Christians, however hip, though no one had collared me with a "have you been

saved, brother" routine. The sun was going down so I decided to split.

Bob Carey and the Family:

GETTING IT TOGETHER IN THE WOODS

The following account of The Oregon Family comes
from a long interview with Bob Carey, one of the founders
of the commune. The interview was conducted by Edmund Helminski who has omitted his questions here in
order to give continuity to the interviewee's responses.
Here are Bob Carey's words:

"One of the things that is noticeable here is that when we first
came out here, we had the idea that by coming here, by dropping out,
by making this move, we'd all drop all our hang-ups; but everyone
brought all their little things with them, their little things. So the
first thing was to bust the bubble of how we imagined it would all be
and then go back to working things out for real. There is nothing
here to blame your hang-ups on. You can't say it's society, because
it's *your* society here. I used to sculpt. That was my thing before I
dropped out. The whole transformation from doing individual things
for myself, from making little pieces of sculpture, that whole thing
was transformed into making myself into a piece of art and finding
art in the daily things around me. Like the cabin we built, it's not the
best piece of sculpture I've ever seen, aesthetically speaking, but it's
a beautiful, funky piece of sculpture.

"This county here has a large accumulation of surplus food and
they give it out to anyone who wants it. So we go in and get it. Oregon
happens to be one of the down-and-out states as far as the economy
goes. The only thing it has is logging and tourists. There's hardly any
other employment, so the government ships in surplus food to this
area since it's one of the poorest in the nation. Right now anyone
who does farming is self-employed and anyone whose net annual income is less than one thousand dollars for a family is entitled to
surplus food. A lot of these farmers don't make any more than that

because most of their business is carried on in trade. They don't have to handle much money. Everything like machinery and most of their supplies is knocked off and so they hardly ever have more than a thousand dollars cash. Now I don't want to have anything to do with the system, because the more we stay away, the better off we are; but I went down there with this guy just to see where it was at and they were really nice, they were open, they welcomed us, and they gave us the food. We get cheese and butter and it really saves us a lot of money.

"It's really unbelievable what those chicks have learned to do over a fire that's nothing more than a hole in the ground. I think we're really lucky and I've been in a lot of communes before this, three of them before we got together. If the chicks aren't making it, if the chicks don't have any energy and don't want to do anything, like be chicks, you know, wash dishes, cook, then you're in for trouble because there's nothing worse than not getting your food, having all the dishes stacked up. We used to go through so many changes in the other communes. A lot of the young people don't want to center their energy, they're afraid to, they're afraid they're going to get hung up, so they stay so scattered that they're useless, they're like parasites. You've eventually got to say, 'Dig man, you want to eat, you got to work like the rest of us, because that's what's happening here.' And then they say, 'That's just a cop-out, man, we'll just lay around here and God will feed us.' So I say, 'OK, you go find some other God, because this God ain't going to feed you unless you work.' There's got to be a certain inner strength, not the-world-owes-me-a-living theory of man. Some of these people have had such rough times with their families that they think that anything that has anything to do with the system is really ugly and anything like work is a bummer. The Zen monk that was up here was really good about that. He really laid a trip on everybody. He was about forty-three and his trip was that work was where it was at. He got a lot of them off of their asses. I work about four hard hours a day and I feel healthy too, I feel clean. Five days a week, four hours, and it has to be done anyway because we need cabins. We need shelter, we need the water developed, we need our garden. It gives you an inner strength to be your own feeder.

"Down in Santa Cruz we had lots and lots of people always coming in and out, but things got so out of hand, you know, stuff all over the place, and nobody was doing anything. Everybody was just smoking and watching television and then we got up here and it was a whole different trip, man. People don't smoke and they're meditating, and occasionally we have a good session. It happens maybe once a month, when everybody will really get high at meditation. In the morning and right after lunch we have an hour for meditation, and Sunday's the day when we usually go off and fast.

"There's one thing about drugs, and we all realize that it wasn't an end in itself, but it sure brought us a long way—and fast. I don't know where we're going, but we've left drugs, and I believe what we're doing is right, or not even 'right,' it's just good. A lot of love is being generated, a lot of energy is in our place. Very magnetic, because even isolated up here we get visitors every week. We have people come in here from Maine, and we don't even know how they found us.

"The right diet and a little physical exercise really puts people into shape after they come up from the city. All the girls are healthy. They're beautiful. Some of the girls are a lot stronger than some of the male members of the family. I don't know what it is, but sometimes there are a lot of ego games involved, sometimes with the males.

"I've got a pretty strong will, but I don't try to impose it on anybody. I just try to flow with the group consciousness. But a lot of times, especially when I bought the property, and said, you know, 'Let's all move to Oregon,' there was an immediate ego clash with some of the males, who would say 'Well, Bob's taking us on his trip,' you know, 'I don't want to go on *his* trip.' They'd start separating themselves. But it's not my trip, man, it's everybody's trip. This is just a piece of property that we can use. But that changed too after everybody saw what was happening.

"Jim, the Zen monk, has a degree. He's got a doctorate in psychology. Ron has a BA, Twig has a master's, and Sonny has a BA, and they're figuring on getting their certificates, you know, to teach the kids. During the year we'll have eight children altogether. The people with graduate degrees won't have any trouble at all and those with bachelor's can get temporary certificates. Actually, I don't even

108

want to get into that part of it, because I'm sort of into the maintenance part of it all, and the economics. Everybody's got their role,
where everybody's got something they've done previously that's
going to play an important part in the community. I want to set up a
complete workshop for ceramics. All my education was in art —
casting, metal work, welding, forging, and pottery. The workshop
would be something for everybody to be able to trip on. If you don't
get on an ego trip with art, going into shows and all that, it's really a
good catharsis, therapy. Right now everybody's making vests and
leather pants. Rat Face makes drums. We use a lot of that Indian
print material for dresses and shirts and things. Another thing is that
everybody's interested in occult things, so some people are into the
tarot and some are heavy on astrology, some read the *I Ching* all the
time.

"Everybody's sort of waiting. The people from the communes in
this area sort of get together south of here occasionally, and every-

body's going through very heavy changes about what's happening. Everybody's questioning it, so to speak, like it's awfully heavy, but we don't know what's happening. But every time we get together, it comes up. Kesey, too, says his group is experiencing something. It makes you feel good. You know you're not alone.

"Most of the people have been into a life something like this for at least a couple of years. I think Ron is the most recent. He was a computer programmer in L.A. only a year ago, until he turned on, until he saw cops beating people, old ladies, straight people even, just for demonstrating against the war.

"Whenever somebody comes here from the city, the energy, the vibration is changed. They bring in a lot of the scattered energy. A lot of strange games come in too, but it's really fun. I'll have to go down to San Francisco this week to pick up the tepees. It'll be my first time out in a few months. It should be interesting. At least I'll have something to compare it to. If you're in the city all the time, you have nothing to compare it to. Your whole center is right there, while our whole center is right here. What goes on in the city means nothing to us, but when you go in you have some kind of measuring rod. Now, of the people in the city, there are those at the temples and ashrams who manage to turn out some very positive vibrations, but I don't want to get into positive and negative because that's not what's happening either.

"Last Sunday we had ourselves a family gathering. Everybody came up from the city. There were about forty people here. It was really powerful, because the people who were up here were so much more serene and flowing than the others, who have so much nervous energy.

"There's a fear towards the unknown. To make the change, to go through it sometimes seems like hell when you're doing it. It's very intense and maybe you experience a fear trip, but then when you pop out on the other side, it was nothing. You wonder why you were fearing the change when it was nothing at all. Because once you're out here, you don't want to go back. I don't know what's going to happen here, but I know there's no going back.

"Most of the local people have been very open and beautiful. They're really very hip in their own way. One of the reasons is that we don't try to freak anybody. A lot of hip, turned-on people try to freak people. We just try to go on their trip and love them for what they are, and then it's just beautiful, because they really give themselves to you. There's no reason to freak anybody. People will blow their own minds when they're supposed to, that's the Buddhist way.

"This piece of property here has everything we need on it. We've got lumber to market, if we should ever want to. We have one hundred and eighty acres that have never been logged. We can just cut poles down if we want to. They sell them for seven bucks a piece. Then we have a friend who is psychic and pretty dependable. He's already told us where the gold is on this land, maybe eight thousand dollars worth. But we don't want to get into that yet. There's a slow change-over going on because some of us are still making money privately and we intend to be a nonprofit religious organization. But people can give us things and deduct it from their taxes, and there are a lot of people who want to do that. We have a deal with the rice company, where they give us various grains, like a donation. Right now, in Florida, my parents have really turned on to our trip and they're going around collecting blankets and ponchos and things like that for us. They're getting companies to donate materials so that we can build more. It's coming about slowly, but it will work itself to the point where we will be able, without having to go out and get jobs, to live and work on our land. This year, though, we plan to do some work for local farmers and bring in just a little bit of money that way. We also have a good friend who owns a leather shop in San Francisco, and he'll sell some of the things we make here. But I don't want to get into that kind of thing yet. I want to see if we can do without it. I want people to make their own clothes, and for people to make clothes for others in the community. I want that exchange to happen before we ever get into a commercial thing. We don't need that right now.

"A leader has to be someone who has enough energy to be able to center the energy of the other people, to get it all right in there. It takes an awful lot of energy to do that. It dragged me down for a while, because you've got to keep reminding people, because a lot of people are so unsure. They've dropped out of so much that they don't quite know what they're into yet. They can't focus their energy. You keep saying to yourself that you don't want to do anything wrong

111

with your energy. Once everybody became really unsure. They would say, 'Are you sure that we want to cut down these trees? Aren't we desecrating the land? Shouldn't we just worry about eating berries and roots and things like that? Do we need those things we're doing? Do we need to clear the land? Do we need to develop the water?' Now I have the feeling — and I felt it then — and I said, 'All right, if you can live off of the land and you don't need shelter or water, then we won't do it.' Then we all sat around for about fifteen minutes and thought about it and then everybody said, 'OK, let's get to work.' None of us are that strong, that we can just walk out like that. I walked out once to fast for four days by myself, and I realized that I wasn't that strong yet to separate myself; well, it's not a matter of separating myself — to put myself in a place where I am strong enough to be in control of what's happening, in other words, spiritually and physically. You can take a bag of food with you and stay for four days, but to go out and do it with nothing, then it's a matter of faith. That means that you have to have an absolute faith in yourself. I can see why very few of even the Indians were able to go alone, because fasting by yourself is much different than fasting with a group.

"When I first joined up with Kesey, someone asked me why I thought I should be with them and why I thought I should be able to travel on the bus with them. I said that I didn't know, but that it seemed like what I was supposed to do, and immediately that was a good enough answer. If I had laid some bullshit on them, they probably would have told me to get out. I can't say no to anyone who wants to live with us or to learn or to share or whatever. Your whole trip is to be open and to love and when people come up, it's hard to turn them away. Once there was a guy along the road who stopped us and said that he wanted to follow along. We were all going down to the river. When we got to the river he was almost crying, man, he got out and said, 'You people are really beautiful,' and then he said, 'I don't know what's happening, but I want to learn, can I come with you?' And I said, 'Sure man, if you want to, we're all brothers.' So he followed us and everybody was walking barefoot. We were used to that kind of thing. He wasn't. He took off his boots, and I imagined he hadn't walked barefoot in his life. I told him that he should wear his boots, but he wouldn't listen to me. He started following us and we walked for about three miles, but he only got halfway, his feet were hurting him so much. He had this ego thing about him. He wasn't ready yet. Water seeks its own level. If he had listened to us, he could have come. We never saw him again. See, everybody was carrying things and he wanted to carry things, and that only made it worse on his feet. He really went on an ego trip. It was a bummer. He just wasn't ready for our trip. None of the hang-ups are out here, you bring them, they're all yours."

THE LAMA FOUNDATION

It was practically impossible for us to find the Lama Foundation. We drove up and down, back and forth, along a wet, snowy mountain road in northern New Mexico. The road was rutted and downright goddamned dangerous. In exasperation we decided to give up and return to the main highway. Rounding a curve, I almost hit a truck coming toward us. Its occupants were friendly. We explained that we had been looking for Lama. "Well, follow us," the driver replied, "we're on our way there."

It was unbelievable. We had been on the same road before, but we couldn't see how anyone could live that far out in the woods. We drove and drove, fearing all the time we'd lose another muffler. Finally, we came to a parking area and the driver of the pickup pulled us over and said, "You better park here and ride the rest of the way with us. It gets even worse from here on in." I gladly parked; Consuelo bruised her leg as we jumped into the back of the truck.

"This is as far as we can go." The truck couldn't get through the ruts of mud, so the driver pulled off the road. "We can walk the rest of the way. It isn't far." He was a young clean-cut, collegiate-looking guy with an equally all-American hip girl companion. They made their way up the road on foot. We followed. They stopped at an old school bus, now their home, and we continued on toward the central area.

I had seen pictures of Lama, but I now saw that they had not done justice to the beauty of the place. It was situated on top of a mountain, commanding a view that extended for miles. Even though we arrived at dusk, the view was almost incredibly fantastic. It was like standing on top of the world.

Midway between the main building and one of the smaller domes, one of the leaders greeted us. Consuelo and I stood there in the cool night air, explaining who we were and why (?) we were there. We were given information about the Lama Foundation, most of which was contained in a descriptive brochure.

One fellow hurried by, stopping briefly to chat. He was another of the basic support group and sort of the overall administrator. He was busy trying to get an old Peace Corps kerosene slide-projector to work for the evening's entertainment.

Our reception was rather formal and businesslike, in

contrast to the more casual response at other communes we visited. Lama had the vibes of a rather hip Esalen-style retreat; its inhabitants seemed hip because of fashion rather than life style. When we looked inside the main building, people were gathered around a warm fireplace and appeared comfortable and snugly middle-class.

Each family or individual who takes up residence at Lama has to provide their or his own separate housing on the land. But no one is allowed to build winter housing until he has been there one whole working season.

This residency requirement seemed to explain the apparent middle-class quality of the place. Not only would a person need the wherewithall to construct his own living quarters but also he must have previously accumulated enough money to meet his living expenses. This would come to $660 for a six-month period ($360 for room and board, $300 for tuition—limited scholarships available).

The full working season at Lama extends from early April through October. The busiest period of operation is during the summer months—June, July, and August—when guest teachers are added to the study program. Many students from all over the country attend this program, called "The School for Basic Studies." The daily schedule, we were told, includes "meditation, chanting and body movement exercises such as Tai Chi Chuan, Yoga, etc., depending on the availability of suitable instruction."

From its modest beginnings as a non-profit foundation in the spring of 1967, Lama has grown impressively. Physically it is an imposing community, with constructed roads, greenhouse, garden, summer cabins, year-round living quarters, and the gigantic domed main building. The architecture of this central structure is a massive combination of old adobe and new wooden dome work. Without doubt, Lama is well on its way to even more growth.

STEVE DURKY AND THE DEVELOPMENT OF LAMA

Learning about Lama came not so much from admiring the fine dome work as from talking with the people responsible for and living in this isolated community. The following discourse about Lama is taken from this interview with Steve Durky, one of the founders, when the community was only about 15 months old. To quote Steve Durky:

"How did it all begin? Five years ago someone sent me a letter, and in the letter it was said that the only place that one should live is where the heart is and where there is love, a radiance of love. Prior to that I had only heard that from people in India. So it was obvious that one should find out who that person was, and we came to this area on a camping trip and met this man. He said that nothing was possible at the present due to that fact that the psychic vehicle was oscillating and spinning from the effect of drugs at too rapid a rate; in other words, that the only possibility for spiritual growth comes when your flame is burning steady. So he said, you know, 'Go on about your business.' At the same time someone said that it was possible, if we found some land, to get it. Whereupon we spent many summers driving back and forth across America looking for land. Two summers looking for land. And we sort of narrowed it down to here. At the same time — you see, this is a very strange place, because what it actually is is a place for graduates, graduates of *high* school. That's what this is about. When you really want to be high — because none of us really know how to do that yet. That's what this is all about. We have to find a mountain. So then, after many times of seeing him, the flame was beginning to burn steadier. You know, we drove transcontinentally back and forth and this is where we would always stop. And he'd like always tell you where your flame was at. So the last time, which was about two-and-a-half years ago, as I came through, he said, 'If you want to come back, go to New York and finish what you have to do.' So we went to New York, and all of us at that time did something together in New York. It started on Mother's Day and ended on Father's Day. My father died the night we left. We left and that was the end. There was a decision that was reached that year by a number of us. Before that, we had always tried to fit ourselves into shells; in other words, it was the end of the shell period. And it was the beginning of trying to create something out of nothing, of furnishing our rooms.

"That was the beginning. We came out here — there were three of us at first — and we'd drive around every day looking for land. We were living on an Indian reservation south of here, and we made a map and kept looking. Finally that man said, 'Why don't you look at a place called———?' Well, New Year's Day was the first day we came up here, New Year's Day 1967. We had $4,000 in our pockets and we came to look at this land; but it wasn't this land, it was over on the other side of the mountains, same acreage but twice as much money. The person who had so kindly offered to help us was only into it for a certain amount, about half of what this other land was going to cost. In other words, that land was 44; this was 21 — the number of the tarot and also very meaningful. But we had come with $4,000 in our pocket and were going to buy it, but this man said, 'Don't do it.' Now, that night an angel came to see this man, and the angel told him to see another guy, and when this man went to see this other guy, this other guy had only two weeks earlier decided to sell the land we've

117

got now for exactly the sum that this very kind person had offered to begin this world. So, boom! We clicked in and this was the place.

"It became apparent to us that we had reached a crossroad, and we had come by many different ways, by car, by foot, by boat, by train; we were all at the same point. The point was that we could see our way up, but it was obvious that if we were to go up by this path, we had to leave a lot of things behind us, like drugs and that whole world. In other words, to grow you have to sacrifice. I don't know if everybody here agrees with that, but that's how I see spiritual growth. It's not really a sacrifice but you have to let go of something, because the body, the being on whatever plain, can only hold so much. So we let go, but a lot of us who were originally involved didn't want to let go. They wanted to maintain it. So those of us who wanted to did let go, plus new people; that's why I say it's like graduation, I mean that this is a new thing, a new grouping, a conglomeration of people who came out of a lot of different scenes, out of the very straight world, out of Indian scenes, out of bhakti, raja, hatha, etc. In some way, all of these disparate things have to be woven into one seamless garment, and that's what this is an attempt to do. And each person, like this person over here, his head, his being, is rooted in the Tao and Chinese philosophy, and this person here comes out of the ethos of the eternal living God as manifest in human form, and another person comes out of the world of the university, which is no longer alive. The university, you know, began when a number of teachers came together and people flocked to them because they were alive, which, to a great extent, the university world isn't anymore. And what I've just said is about the mental side of how this all happened. But the thing to realize is that it's always this weaving of different threads.

"The other thing that's important to say is that we're not so much against the government as *for* changing it. In other words, there are groups that say, 'Boom! government.' My forefathers signed the Declaration of Independence and the Constitution, and if you read those things, and really understand what they say, you'll realize that something's gotten lost, and when something's lost, it either has to be found, or you can just forget it.

"So what we did in relation to the government is that we became a nonprofit, tax-exempt foundation, founded for educational and scientific purposes, because, as we see ourselves, we are a center for basic studies. And by basic studies I mean how to make an adobe brick, or learning how to plumb and how to carpenter, learning what's basic, learning what it is that people really need and what are their desires, and what is the relationship between needs and desires. And also, what is basic, is the relationship to the earth, to the sky, and to each other.

"We're learning how to provide for ourselves as much as we need and no more, living with the grace of God. Very much of it has to do with our limitation and understanding that limitation. The fact that certain societies are cut up in a way, a certain way, where the spiritual is divorced from the practical, this is what we wanted to change for ourselves. The world that makes sense is a world where each man and each woman lives out time and the cycles of the seasons, where no man is a priest and every man is a priest, and where the duty to maintain the cosmos is dependent on everybody instead of just a select few. In other words, we're anti-priesthood. There are no priests here because everybody is a priest. There are none other than the elect.

"The real basis of the whole thing is that growth can only come about through the direct experience of that ultimate that is all around us, and that when you have a direct experience of that ultimate, you know who you are. You begin by understanding that you're only beginning. That's the first understanding. Then you also have to understand that growth comes out of a sincere desire to know the truth about yourself, and as much as I am able to help you, I will help you, and as much as you are able to help me, you will help me, and that all our growth has to occur on three planes simultaneously — the physical plane, the mental plane, and the spiritual plane.

"We applied for a federal tax exemption and got it and then we got a small foundation grant which handled about fifty percent of the construction costs last year. We hope to put together a brochure next year to raise more money, or less money, I don't know. We have a five-year plan, and by the end of five years we hope to be financially independent. It's based on three different approaches: a school; the establishing of workshops, since a lot of us are artisans or artists; and publishing, because we're obliged to publish under our federal

119

tax exemption. This year we'll be publishing two books: the *Dome Cookbook*, which is about zonal polyhedral construction, and *The Eight Sacred Directions*. Each year we hope to have a technical book, which is a help to people starting communities, and a spiritual book, one oriented towards growth. We believe that the essence of spirituality is practicality. It's not up there, it's right here, right here, *right here*, and everytime you go up there you're forgetting what it's about. As Jesus says: the Kingdom of God is within you. Or as the Buddha says: when you get high, bring it back with you. The other thing about publishing is that as explorers we should bring back, you know, a map. And another thing is that the community is only one aspect of all this—the residential aspect.

"Another thing is that we consider very slow growth an important thing. I've been into communal scenes for seven years now, and the

two things that really do communities in are rapid expansion and believing that you're further along than you are. For instance, you're my brother, right? And she's my sister. On the other hand, I still need my individuality and my privacy, let's say, and you need yours. Many groups say, well, if you're my brother and so forth and we're all one, let's live in a heap. But you look at these people around here, and at people all over the world, you see that they've evolved something, not by going against nature, but by going with it. If something is to be, it will be. It's not to be had by simply saying that I'm ready for that, because we know from experience, from having tried it, how far we are from it. It's like understanding all the time where you are and not trying to say that we're enlightened.

"Our ideal is no more than thirty people. Let me make one thing clear. We have two levels going here. One is to establish a firm focal point on the physical plane, and to do that we're going to grow by about one family a year until we have eight families that live here all year. Those will be the building blocks. We want to do it slowly so that we can integrate things well. Then there's the summer thing. It's kind of like life: in the summer everything expands and in the winter things shrink back. One of the screens we have against too rapid expansion is the rule that you cannot build any winter housing until you've spent one whole working season here—April to October, when all your energies are spent on the communal thing. It's just very natural.

"Now, all of us here have a very strong belief that this is the time of the coming-together. Now you can call this East and West. The way of the West is exploitation, rape, and also a brilliant mind thing, you know, solving the material thing first; and the East is much more the way of flowing with it, you know, if you don't have crops one year you don't let it get you down, you meditate in hunger. In the West if you don't have food you do something about it. Now is a time when all this is coming together, and you see this in many ways, like the war in Vietnam, where the only way that East and West can get together is through killing, which is an act of love in itself. It's the same as when you kill a deer and start taking its guts out—you establish a very close relationship with that thing. It's easy to see unless you're hung up on death. If you think that this is it, then it gets pretty scary, but

121

if you see that it's all part of a whole, if you can see beyond the end, then you can get someplace. So this is all coming back together and one of the things we'd like to do is to bring some of the people from the East here, because they have some brothers here and, in some way, we'd like to help them get together. We don't know exactly how we're going to do this, but it's very clear that it has to be done. We will probably do it by becoming a center of attraction, the way people are drawn to India because it's a center of attraction, not because people put up big banners saying: 'Spiritual Life in Ten Easy Lessons—Come to Benares for the Summer.' If we are at all able to be what we're talking about, then it will happen.

"We make certain requirements of people. The reason for this can be simply explained. We have all found that there have been things in our life that we've wanted to do but found ourselves incapable of doing. We've lacked the necessary discipline to do them. We all admit that we're undisciplined in relation to the spiritual life, and we believe that through the centuries there have been very clear precepts for spiritual growth laid down that worked—at least they seem to have worked judging from people we have seen and met and learned about. We would all admit that. Now 99% of us, especially those who have dropped out of the drug or hip world, are still very undisciplined people, out of tune with ourselves and one another. By applying from the outside a form of discipline, so that everybody gets used to it. . . . Why do we get up every morning at six-thirty? Why do we chant? It's not just to get up early. It's not just to chant. It's to begin accustoming ourselves to a new rhythm. A good word is tuning. The instrument is still being tuned, both in terms of the individual and the larger organism. You're talking about a community, you're talking about an organism which, to some extent, is greater than its components. It is not merely that there are 20 people here who have accidentally come together, but that there is something that's evolving. I keep reiterating this, but it's just a *beginning*. Our feeling is that you cannot just jump all the way from the bottom all the way to the top.

"Something that's above and beyond all of this is just the wonder of it all. It just feels good."

Telling it on the Mountain:

AN EVENING DISCUSSION AT LAMA

In 1968 when the following discussion at Lama was taped, members of the Lama Foundation met almost every evening to discuss problems, business and practical matters, and on this particular evening like others, their interpersonal and spiritual relationships. The participants in this particular account were Cody, Nancy, Rachel — female; and Ray, Mike, Jim, Tory, Job, Jonathan — male.

CODY: Do we have a subject for this evening?

RAY: Well, we had a number of things we were going to talk about. Let's see, work? I think work is a perfect subject.

NANCY: Could I say something first? I wanted to ask Mike about something he said today.

MIKE: What's that?

NANCY: Well, you sort of mumbled something about you were glad to see me finally doing something.

MIKE: I think that was in reference to the sawhorse, and I didn't think I made it personal.

CODY: I'd just like to inject something, because it seems to be typical.

MIKE: What?

CODY: It's that whole thing about the women and the men.

RAY: It's that the men are very arrogant and overbearing and —

CODY: — for one thing, the women work more steadily and harder and longer hours than the men.

MIKE: OK. Maybe what I said was in very poor taste.

RAY: I knew we had a punk on the crew. (*Laughter.*)

CODY: OK. So let's talk about work.

JIM: I have two questions. One is that I've been working at a generally lower and lower level because of fatigue, not through hard work necessarily, just a lack of energy. It seems to correlate very highly with lack of sleep. The other thing is that it seems that I've had very little time to be with Rachel, because it seems that we're always too tired when we're together. I saw Henry in town today and

I explained the problem, and he said that both of these things were undoubtedly true, and those are the breaks, and just do my work. (*Laughter.*) And I indicated that that was the worst advice I had ever heard from him. (*Laughter.*) But he indicated that that was just a personal response to me and not a general law of the situation — necessarily.

RAY: I would like to say something about that. I've noticed in the past week that you were slowing down, and I was talking about it with Job and Cody. What we were discussing was — since we know from our highest moments that energy absolutely permeates the universe and that energy is not dependent on anything other than our receptivity to it — that a lack of energy really isn't so much a lack of one thing or another, it's just that we're not receptive to the energy that's available. Now I do think that lack of sleep might make one less receptive (*laughter*), but in view of what you were saying today about seeing yourself as a facilitator or an expediter in some sense, it suggests that when you're fulfilling that role you have plenty of energy, because you're doing what you want to do. What your question really relates to is how you can pick up on the energy again. Being able to put in a good eight hours a day is directly related to finding your own role within our structure. So one of the things that may be useful is for everyone to state in some way just who they think they are. Like you feel that you are a facilitator, and you feel that very deeply. Now that may be a stereotyped image of yourself that will prevent you from growing, because you feel comfortable in that role. But accepting that for now, what or who do people feel they are?

CODY: Let's go clockwise. Start with Tory.

TORY: Who me? Why don't we go the other way.

CODY: Well, we've got this superstitious fellow here who insists that everything go clockwise.

RAY: I've noticed that a lot of people around here have been telling children to run clockwise and building to be done clockwise. Not only me.

CODY: So who mentioned your name?

RAY: You said we have this superstitious fellow here.

CODY: Well, he could even be on another plane.

RAY: Go ahead.

TORY: I don't know what to say.

RAY: You mean you don't know who you are.

JIM: There are two very different kinds of questions: who you are and what role you fulfill. In a sense, what I was saying to Ray was that I seem to operate most easily and effectively in a group when I'm not instigating, but facilitating or helping or kind of seeing the incongruities in a work-flow or anything else. I suggested to Ray that he's more of an instigator.

RAY: Yes, but I think everybody has a concept of who they are.

JOB: But isn't the concept you're asking for in terms of this supposed organism that we all participate in, that's growing here?

RAY: But not only this one. Like whoever's been in groups before finds that one normally —

JIM: — what kind of roles do you gravitate toward or like or prefer or feel most at ease in? Not who you are, which is a lot tougher question. I don't think that I am a facilitator or the facilitator.

RAY: OK. Sure, whatever, so that we can talk about it. What do you think you are, Job?

JOB: A hand. A large part of what I am is a hand.

JONATHAN: What I think you are to a large extent is somebody who notices details and someone who is very keen on what has to be taken care of. A noticer. . . .

RAY: You feel happy when you're doing this?

JOB: Yeah, but it's an old pattern of mine.

RAY: What do you aspire to that's new?

JOB: You mean beyond that?

RAY: How would you change the pattern?

JOB: By expanding it, by enlarging it until I notice everything.

RAY: And you feel you do that here, you have a chance to do that here?

JOB: Sure. As far as I'm concerned there's only that one goal, and everything I would say along these lines would be in terms of that. The goal being infinite consciousness. Noticing is just one aspect of consciousness.

JONATHAN: What are the things you don't notice?

JOB: Well, if I don't notice them, it's very difficult to — (laughter)

JONATHAN: No, no, I wasn't talking about details. I was talking

126

about areas. What are the areas in which that capacity doesn't function so well?

JOB: I don't know.

JIM: That's a very good question.

JOB: Noticing is just another way of talking about awareness.

RAY: What he's really asking you is: where do you fail at the job? And since you're aware that you're evolving, you must evolve out of your failures.

JOB: My failures are best described by other people than myself.

JIM: Where are you growing?

RAY: Jim's so positive. (*laughter.*)

JOB: Probably the greatest area — well, 99 percent of what I do has nothing to do with my thing. All of my life I've spent most of my time doing things for myself. Now I spend practically none of my time doing things for myself.

CODY: What is it? What is it that we are? Brothers? What is it?

RAY: That's a whole other world.

CODY: Well, I want to mark that down.

RAY: O.K. Mark it down. . . .

JIM: How do you see yourself, Ray, since today when I called you an instigator, you sort of reacted against it?

RAY: Well, I feel that in many instances I do instigate, but even more than that I feel that I coordinate.

JONATHAN: I see you also as a flash sometimes. That is very helpful for maybe a brief moment, but everybody can see something at that moment, and then we go back to the darkness, but that moment or in that moment there's a visibility that's very helpful.

JOB: He's the intuitor.

RACHEL: I think intuition runs pretty high in the group.

JONATHAN: Women are pretty intuitive.

JOB: That's just a stereotype.

CODY: Job can't hear anything about women.

JOB: Well, a woman's intuition is a myth perpetrated by men, because men believe that they're intellectual, and they believe that intuition is inferior, so they give that to women. It's a whole Western trip.

RACHEL: But men always talk about women as though they were a different category of being.

MIKE: I've been thinking about that all day, and I've been wondering just how much the women are falling prey to the trip the men are on.

JOB: My feeling is that a lot of that is reinforced by the women themselves. They're very quick to stand up for women or make it a woman's issue.

RACHEL: Right.

JOB: There is a polarity that's enforced. Cody's a great one for insisting that there are women and there are men. Then she turns around and says that it's the men who are enforcing the polarity.

RAY: I think it's true. I think that there are two races that cohabit.

CODY: But the only people I find it polarized in are Job and Ray. With the rest of the people they're friends or something else, but with you there's this very strong thing that goes on.

JOB: It separates women from men?

CODY: No. It separates you and the women as friends.

JONATHAN: How do the other women feel?

RACHEL: I think it's true. I respond to Job as a woman, but it stands in the way of friendship.

NANCY: I think that Ray, for instance, often comes across as this very authoritarian figure, but I've been feeling it less and less.

RAY: But that's because you're doing your thing better and better. I feel that my presence on the job is a spur to almost everybody else's work, but when people start taking responsibility for their own work I can fall more and more into the background, and then I don't have to be that kind of person, who I don't enjoy being. But I do see, in terms of seeing, on a large scale what has to be done.

CODY: But you're no longer alone in that job.

RAY: Well sure. As much as everybody takes responsibility, it becomes our job, not my job. . . .

RACHEL: I have an interesting question I'd like to throw out, and it's about how Jim and I can live what feels to be a good life for part of the year in San Francisco and then we come out here in the country and are faced with all kinds of things.

RAY: Can you clarify that question a little more?

128

JONATHAN: I think that—and it goes for all of us to some extent, and that's the reason we're here and the only reason to be here, as I see it—left to ourselves, we can reinforce our games, our ideals, which are also our illusions about ourselves, and often our ideals are quite different from the reality. Here you really have to see that even though we're all aspiring towards something, we have a long way to go, and since we can see the steps, and we take the steps, and we see how hard it is, we no longer can sit at the bottom and dream we're at the top; you know, we begin to climb. Something like that. Since both of you are extremely competent in your normal mode, you don't have any shock necessarily to make you wonder about it. Do you know what I mean?

RACHEL: I know exactly what you mean. The time when I know I'm beginning to grow is when I want to leave here. It's maybe a defensive reaction of my ego, afraid of having its illusions exposed.

JONATHAN: What dismays me about the two of you now is that you're only going to be here for six weeks. You somehow came with that protection or insulation, which allows you to participate in it at a certain level, but still gives you a way out of it. You can just get in your car and that's it. Somehow you haven't burned the bridge that still has to be burned for you to really go where you want to go.

RACHEL: I guess one thing will have to happen first before we burn that bridge and that's that we'll have to feel deeply in our hearts that this is the reality we want to choose.

RAY: I was trying to say this the other morning. This place here and these people here—well, this is a place where your life has to count on what you do, and if it doesn't absolutely, no matter where it is—I mean I could live here and if my life didn't count on it, I could still live here because I could be cool enough and sometimes that's what scares me. Maybe I'm so cool or so hip to a certain thing, that this could not touch me either.

JOB: You can make it in any scene.

RAY: Yeah. That kind of hippie trip. Many of us, because of our abilities which are pretty good, could make it almost anywhere. Our worst enemy is our facility. This thing about your life counting on what you do. If something isn't done your whole life is staked upon it. And of course the Hindus say that it's absurd to ever do that, because

129

it's the greatest illusion, it's all a dance, it doesn't matter. We all carry within us our own obstacle. In other words, it may be very true, as we've said, that you have to always live on the edge of the abyss.

THE ONE WORLD FAMILY:

THE MESSIAH'S WORLD CRUSADE

I first became aware of The One World Family of the Messiah's World Crusade some three years ago (1968) through the Berkeley *Barb*. The news report in the *Barb* told how Allen Noonan, founder and leader of the Crusade, had been busted for possession of marijuana and dragged off to jail. The report continued, "Noonan, who is 52 . . . is hoping that flying saucers will intervene in his behalf by blocking traffic on both sides of the San Francisco bridges. Help may be offered at 1387 Haight Street. Flying saucers should be directed to either bridge."

Oh well, I thought, another kooky commune leader. Haight-Ashbury communes had a very short and chaotic lifespan at the time, so I dismissed this group as typical of the genre.

Time passed and I still heard whispers of the continued existence of a group called The Here and Now Commune or Messiah's World Crusade. In the summer of 1969 I read an article in another underground paper that described the group in more detail. It stated that the commune consisted of a core group of about 20 people, together with temporary visitors who came, experienced living there awhile, and then left. This experience involved working to create Allen's vision of a world environment containing "creative schools of experience, providing food, clothing, shelter, care, recreation, and transportation for all of the people on the planet as one family." The people of the commune held all things in common, with each person giving according to ability and receiving according to need. They operated a pure-food macrobiotic restaurant in San Francisco and published a newspaper called *The Universal Communicator.*

I was sympathetic toward the humanistic ideals of The One World Family, but as a "liberal" I just couldn't stomach all that strange talk about flying saucers and an inspired Messiah.

In 1970, the Messiah's World Crusade took over the famous Forum restaurant on Telegraph Avenue in Berkeley and turned it into a natural-foods restaurant named The Mustard Seed. Thursday through Sunday, from 7 to 11 P.M., The One World Family Band and Chorus performed at the restaurant.

One day I received a letter from Dian, the group's

secretary, inviting me to do an article on their commune. The literature she enclosed with the letter talked of Allen as a psychic,

adept at channelling-in high potent energies from the Higher Extra-terrestrial Beings who are guiding our planet into the New Age. . . . He is a Messiah, a Messenger—Not a Savior, for there is nothing to save. Each man must save himself from becoming a slave to matter, by raising his consciousness through service to humanity.

I could not help being reminded of Robert A. Heinlein's great novel, *Stranger in a Strange Land,* and I wondered why at this point in history so many minds were turning to a communal vision as a solution to societal stress and alienation. Sociological answers seemed inadequate.

As my own attitude toward Messiahs had broadened, I had come to feel that perhaps only a "divinely" inspired leader could possibly bring so utopian a vision into being. The literature from Dian continued,

Right now decide to no longer go along with the worn out status-quo system. Begin to form together with your friends into communes, holding all things in common, helping, loving, and lifting one another into the New Age ideas. Use our U.S. constitution and Bill of Rights in their true essence. Only by building a complete alternative healthy environment now will we ever avoid a violent revolution.

"Right on!" I exclaimed, and rushed to the phone to call Dian to make an appointment to visit the commune and talk with Allen.

"Allen has been taken to Vacaville for three month's observation," Dian said. "They want to figure out what makes him tick." She invited us to interview her instead.

Consuelo and I arrived at an impressive, two-story house that was situated on a hillside and surrounded by trees and luxuriant greenery. We tried the front door but there was no answer. Hearing voices around the back, we made our way there and came upon Dian, sitting in the sun, totally naked and unafraid, her belly large with child. She was sure to have that baby (or several, I imagined) any day.

Dian went inside to dress. We sat talking to her amid constant interruptions from the telephone and the people of the commune. She was a friendly and conscientious hostess. In spite of all the interruptions, she kept coming back to us to continue explaining about the commune and responding to our questions.

Dian was in charge of things at this house in Larkspur; she was also the community's secretary and bookkeeper (she who controls the purse-strings controls the commune).

Allen, as we already knew, was at the California State Correctional Institute at Vacaville, where he was being examined by a team of psychiatrists. The history of how he got there begins with his early days in southern California. There, beginning in 1947, he preached his gospel and set up communal living groups. Whatever his success or lack of it, he eventually headed north and wound up in San Francisco in 1966 to begin his glorious mission in the Haight. He was greeted with enthusiasm and became the focus of a commune, which materialized around him in a big mansion on Oak Street.

Allen became well-known in the area, and the word leaked back to southern California where a Bircher-oriented businessman (who had attended one of Allen's meetings) informed the San Francisco authorities that Allen was dangerous and a source of corruption regarding the morals of youth. An undercover agent was sent to entrap Allen. He succeeded. Allen was charged with the sale and possession of marijuana, with bail set at $10,000. (Marijuana is known to be used by most hip citizens in the San Francisco Bay Area. But the police rarely invade the privacy of people's homes to find it. If they did they would have to build hundreds of jails to house the offenders. The people who are charged with selling or possessing marijuana are usually those who the authorities decide are misbehaving on moral or political grounds, not legal ones.)

Allen's followers responded by sponsoring benefits at The Straight Theater in order to raise money for bail. Although these benefits did not raise the required funds, they did bring the commune together and, as Dian observed, "we had a lot of fun." Bail bond was finally obtained for Allen, but the police then charged another commune member with possession of marijuana. Apparently connected to this was the judge's decision to increase Allen's bail to $25,000. So Allen had to return to jail, where he remained for five-and-a-half months more. A hip lawyer came into the case on Allen's behalf, but it was still impossible to raise bail. As money paid for bail-bonds is forfeited, the commune was not enthusiastic about spending $25,000. Finally, someone put up a building as collateral and Allen was released.

In November 1969, Allen was put back in jail for the third time; the property put up as collateral for bail had been foreclosed upon. At his trial almost 2 years after being charged, Allen was found guilty despite a great deal of testimony on his behalf. The judge acknowledged the special nature of the case and offered Allen two options: first, to go to jail for two years; second, to go to Vacaville for a 60- to 90-day period and then be returned for further consideration. Allen chose the latter.

Allen's incarceration provided him with the time to continue the writing he had been engaged on for the past 22 years. Because he is such a high person, Dian explained, people wanted to be around him all the time, especially when he was at the commune. Under those circumstances, he had little time to write. Now, in prison, he was writing much more, preparing the text of his gospel to spread the word of the New Age across the planet Earth.

"Allen [at that time a commercial artist] was painting a sign in 1947," Dian explained, "when a bolt of white light hit him and his astral self traveled to another planet where Higher Extraterrestrial Beings, known as angels in the Bible, asked him if he would like to be the Messiah of mankind. He thought awhile about how Socrates was

Allen, the cosmic Messenger

forced to poison himself and how Jesus was crucified. After ridding himself of these negative fantasies, he said 'sure.' Through automatic writing, letting the Higher Beings guide him, he began to write The Plan that would create Absolute Freedom, Security, and Abundance to all People as One Family."

I was anxious to discover how they actually ran the commune, so I abruptly changed the subject.

"What about the current practical operations of the commune?" I asked. "You advertise openly. Don't you get a lot of people here who just want to be taken care of, who don't really want to do any work?"

"Yes, we do once in awhile," Dian replied. "But we find that most people want to serve and if they aren't doing anything it's because they don't know what to do. That's what we're here for—to show them. Sometimes all people need is a little push. Everyone who lives in our communes has to work eight-hour shifts at one of our restaurants. We've had a few people who thought they were being sent off like slave laborers. Well, they just weren't ready to join with us, so they left.

"Some people haven't learned the joy of service yet. We're working toward a time when everyone serves everyone else. From each according to his ability to each according to his need.

"Most people come into the commune with far too many material possessions. Many do not need more clothing, for instance. But when they do, they simply go to the bookkeeper and get the money to purchase what they need. Yes, everyone tends to think he needs something over and above what we really know he needs. We talk it over and come to an understanding.

"Ideally we share all things in common, including sex. But, of course, people are in different places and we feel it's okay for there to be couples who rely more heavily on one another, or who want to share the same room together. We make sure that each person in this transition stage has a physical place he can call his own. A place where he can go to be alone. We know ideally that privacy can be had without the necessity for private space, but at this stage we know also that people have to work through the conditioning of the old order. We allow for that. We deal with the jealousies and hang-ups of the Old Order as best we can by continually keeping aware of our vision of the New World Order, where all will share equally all the resources of the world as One Family.

"This house is becoming the children's house. We have 17 adults and 8 children here. Two adults per week take turns with the children. Just being around helping them when they need help. We believe children are happier when they spend most of their time with other children.

"Our other house in Berkeley operates as The Basic Schools of Experience. Our band and chorus practice over there and we're putting together a light show and multimedia environment. We encourage outlets for people's creative and artistic talents."

Dian stopped, and then asked, "Would you like to see this house?"

She showed us around. When we first entered the meditation room, a young man with a crew cut and athletic shorts was sitting on the floor bending and flexing his legs. He looked like a college basketball player just off the court. There were lots of colorful rugs spread out on the floor, with chairs and a couch against the walls; no table or plants. On one wall hung a painting, on another some flyers with photos of Allen. It was called the meditation room for still another good reason: the children obeyed the rule of no shouting or loud noise in this room.

The house had two children's rooms to accommodate both older and younger children. Several smaller rooms — all tastefully and simply decorated — provided living quarters for single adults and couples. One room was occupied by a painter who was doing signs for the restaurants. None of the rooms were occupied on a permanent basis as each person rotated from place to place according to individual and communal needs. We found the somewhat cramped kitchen crowded with members, for it was approaching the dinner hour. And in a room adjoining the kitchen, bread and pastries were being prepared for one or both of the restaurants.

Outside near the sun porch, one of the members had recently built a sauna bath from wood and other scavenged materials. It cost less than $100 he claimed. It was a fine-looking structure resembling a huge square puff of cotton candy at a fair. The pink fiber-glass insulation was still to be covered by plastic. Near the sauna was a small homemade pool; and in a large open space off to one side, four old doors had been covered with aluminum foil and braced on their sides at right angles to one another to create a solar bath. Jim, the architect of all these healthful creations, asked us to stand inside it. "Hot, huh! Stay in there for a few minutes and you can get scorched." Consuelo and I exclaimed our delight, and he offered to furnish plans for *The Modern Utopian* so that every commune could have its own inexpensive health spa. We said "Great!" He seemed to want more approval so we repeated our exclamation. He followed us around the yard. We finally slunk away, returned to Dian, and agreed to visit the Berkeley house on Sunday.

Sunday in Berkeley:

REJOICING IN THE WORDS OF THE MESSIAH

Sunday, every Sunday morning, the Messiah's World Crusade meets as a whole family—One Family—at the communal house in Berkeley. The restaurants are closed and the Larkspur and Berkeley members come together for song and for rejoicing in the Word of the Cosmic Messiah, Allen.

138

The house was a new structure, a few years old at most. The furniture and decor included wall-to-wall carpeting, ceiling-to-floor windows, and sliding doors in the front. Consuelo and I entered the living room and sat on the floor next to a couch, which I leaned upon. There were perhaps a dozen other people there. One fellow was stretched out on the floor drawing a mandala of sorts on a huge pad of paper. Mostly, the people just sat quietly and waited. After about 30 minutes a lightly built, well-tanned man entered and sat on the floor. He wore a small cap on his head, casual clothes, and a slightly ascetic look. He was older than the others in the room, probably in his late 30s. He completed his image with two bright solid-colored socks, one yellow and the other Chinese red. The woman who accompanied him was also well-tanned, possibly his age or slightly older. She had long gray hair and a brilliant smile that showed a large set of sparkling white teeth.

There were now 30 or 40 people in the room. They made up the most varied crew of people that could be imagined under one roof—longhairs, shorthairs, guys who looked like they just got out of prison, guys who appeared to be inmates of business corporations, girls who appeared bright and active, girls with a spaced-out look, and a few children for whom many of the girls enjoyed playing mother.

Someone shouted for musical instruments. While these were being obtained, a young girl distributed the Crusader's songbook. We began to sing a combination of gospel and rock tunes, mostly written by the commune members themselves. *Victorious Gospel* was one.

> We're going to love you—right into
> heaven—it's here on earth—
> We're going to give it birth—
> Come on and kiss the earth.
> Victorious Gospel—We're going to take
> it to the world—

If you want to take part in the
start of a miracle —
You can be of and — in the Messiah's
World Crusade.

Shouts erupted from various members of the audience.
"Right On!"
"Far Out!"
"Let's Get It On, Brother!"
Then Michael — he of the yellow sock and Chinese-red
sock — got down to the first order of business, which was
to introduce Sid. Sid was the man responsible for helping
the commune obtain and set up its current natural-food
restaurants. Although not a member of the commune, he
was a sympathetic businessman with 22 years of experience in restaurant sales and service. However, many of
the members felt that Allen's latest message, a five-page
typewritten article, should be read first, before Sid ad-
dressed them. Allen's message was of such import to them
that they did not want to wait. Dian had given me a copy of
it when she arrived. I followed along as one of the commune members read aloud:

Out With The Old, In With The New

To proclaim anything less than absolute freedom, security and abundance for every person on this planet as one family is sheer nonsense. Absolute freedom, security and abundance now for everyone must be the VISION OF THE PEOPLE'S REVOLUTION. . . . There are no shortages of anything except the will and understanding to make things right. Righteousness begins with self-sacrifice and self-discipline. What will you give up so that the Kingdom of God or the true communism combined with the true democracy can come in at this time?

Really when we try to give up things, we see that only the things that were not good for us in the first place are falling away and a new government is emerging in our midst. This is not a government made by men, but a government made by the Universe which is now being written in our hearts. . . .

It is unnatural to buy and sell merchandise for profit. No one is condemned because they have done this, but at last the time has come when it is no longer necessary. The One World Family is demonstrating in our communes the way all foods and services can be freely at everyone's fingertips, so there are no hangups to creating a world of absolute freedom, security and abundance for all who share and care. Those people who care enough about their eternal evolving to put first things first are now coming together to build a completely New Age.

After the article was read, Sid told the group that the Berkeley restaurant was not financially viable at present and he urged them to set up a system of more efficient operation. He suggested that the restaurant was not only a possible source of income but also a possible means for recruiting new members into The One World Family. He told them that another restaurant could be opened by them in Berkeley in a prime location if they could handle it.

The commune saxophonist gave a long and enthusiastic discourse about how they had already improved services at the Berkeley restaurant and were now ready to expand facilities in order to communicate the Word of The One

World Family. He interspersed and concluded his talk with a few "Right on's" and "Let's get it on's," in which he was joined by several other people. It was now noon and time for the shifts to begin work at the two restaurants. Michael noted, "Well, if we're a little late getting started today it means this has been an important meeting."

Plans were then made for the discussion of various projects. People who were interested in more information about the Crusade or who wished to join were to meet in an adjoining room following the meeting-session. Some members planned to meet in the music room later that afternoon to record tapes for playing at the restaurants and elsewhere. People interested in working on construction of a multimedia environment also planned to meet. Still other plans had to do with a recently purchased bus which was to convey band and chorus to schools and churches or any other organizations that might invite them. Michael then asked all people who were supposed to be working on a shift to leave.

A guitarist and a slender girl with bright eyes and a round face led the session for potential new members. While waiting for everyone to get settled, a baby-faced young girl sang a few songs of her own composition in a soft mournful voice. Everyone was called upon to introduce himself and state his interest in The One World Family.

One very straight-looking guy smiled pleasantly and said he only wanted more information. He told us he worked in Planned Parenthood. The guitarist leader appeared not to have ever heard of that organization. When he finally understood, he explained that the birth-control method used in the commune was the natural way; members followed "vibration levels." Now it was me who did not understand; I guess I was not alone, though, for the Planned Parenthood employee left. The baby-faced folk songstress said she lived in a similar commune in Minneapolis and had been called by God to come to this one to live awhile and find out if the two groups could collaborate.

A long-blond-haired guy with a pinched look about him said he was ready to join and do the work of the Crusade. I had thought he was already a member; his enthusiasm was such that he had joined in on every exclamation of "Right On" and "Let's Get It Together" during the morning session.

A guy in old khaki pants, shirt, and jacket — he looked like an Army reject — stated quietly that he wished to join. A young Jewish girl curled up on a chair in the corner said she didn't like the religious nature of the commune although she believed in the ideals. When pressed to explain, she got angry and said she never could find a place to join as there was always something about it she could not go along with. When the five Crusade members tried to convince her of the true nature of their religion, adding doses of liberal comments like "You can accept all or any part of this that you wish," she came back even more angrily with "I don't want to join a commune now; I'm too fucked up to join anything right now."

Then Michael came in and began to talk about a number of topics: first, about how important the shift schedule was to the Crusade — everyone had to take his turn at the restaurants; then about Allen as the Cosmic Messiah, bringing the true message to the world. Next, Michael asked those present who wished to serve in the Crusade to see him in order to get on the shift.

A girl with frightened eyes said she was joining and planned to live at Larkspur near her boyfriend, Brian, who was already a member. Michael continued discussing how the shift-schedule worked. He noted that it always worked out fine when certain people wanted to be near other people on the shift-schedule. There were two shifts for each restaurant and one for each house — it was all worked out.

"But isn't that extremely difficult," I inquired. "Aren't

143

there many who prefer to be with one person or another, at one time or another?"

"Yes," Michael smiled, "but they learn that it isn't necessary. I get it all worked out," he pointed to a schedule book he had on the floor.

"I want to be with Brian," the scared-eyed one emphasized.

"Okay, my dear," Michael replied indulgently. "Let me make a note of that." The schedule book fell open and miscellaneous scraps of paper flew out. Michael hastily gathered them back into the notebook and began to talk of the importance of the Crusade in creating a New Age where absolute freedom, security and abundance would be available to all the peoples of the world as One Family.

Consuelo and I introduced ourselves next. I remarked that there seemed to be no mechanism for personal growth operating within the commune. Also, I did not see them dealing with conflict and personal frustration adequately. For instance, I observed, during the morning meeting one fellow had made a negative comment and either it was ignored or subjected to such pressures as "Wow, man, you're bringing us down; we only have one meeting together as a family per week and now you're trying to bring us down."

One member explained that personal growth was achieved through service to others, by the work and activities of the Crusade. Another noted that the despondent member had been dealt with adequately in the meeting.

Now Michael took up the Bible and began to read and interpret the book of Daniel as the prophecy of the Coming of Allen, the Cosmic Messiah, and the Messiah's World Crusade: "And at that time shall Michael stand up, the great prince which standeth for the children of thy people: and there shall be a time of trouble, such as never was since there was a nation . . . and at that time thy people shall be delivered, every one that shall be found written in the book. . . ."

Michael read and interpreted for about an hour—on and on and on he read. The Jewish girl got up and left. I went to piss. When I came back Michael was explaining a passage and its relationship to the present. At some point, our ex-group leader, the guitarist, said, "Okay, but I think we'd better get on with—" he gestured toward the other two potential new members, neither of whom had yet had a chance to introduce themselves.

"Right!" said Michael, and resumed reading aloud, picking up where he had just left off in the passage from Daniel.

I laughed heartily as an obvious cover-up of the hostility I was beginning to feel toward Michael. He reminded me of a New England preacher I had to work with one time while in theological school. That man, too, had been caught up in the flame of his own ego, reading the true word, impervious to others around him.

The pinched-look one continued to intersperse his enthusiasm—"Wow! Far out! Read that again! You know, I really believe it!" Michael responded to the compliment by fanning his ego.

Soon, however, even the intersperser was saying, "Yes, Michael, I believe it but I'm hungry now. Let's go eat." It was mid-afternoon. I urged Consuelo to go, but she insisted on staying until the other two strangers had been introduced.

But Michael talked and read on. I began to look vacantly into space.

"Astrology is an important science to study in this day and age—isn't that right, Dick?"

"I don't know. I haven't studied it very much," I replied.

Michael and others then talked about the relationship of astrology to the Messiah's World Crusade.

"Wow, Michael, I really love your socks," I said abruptly yet sincerely.

Michael stopped talking and beamed for a full five

minutes. The most beautiful smile I've ever seen shined on his face and washed away all my hostility.

One of the two remaining guests said he just got out of the Army and wanted to get into a group that was organized and together and could help him get his head straightened out. He too was ready to join the Crusade. Michael noted that a week of eating healthful foods and being in the Messiah's environment would produce great changes — changes that would contrast sharply with the previous dull atmosphere of the military. He added that this youth could be a great crusader in bringing other military men into the commune. "Different people are needed in different places. You could communicate with them, while they'd just take an old Bible-thumper like me and throw me in a corner of the military chapel." Michael was in a good humor.

"Let's eat," replied the happy convert, "I'm hungry."

My stomach was growling also. I turned to Consuelo. One more guest. I walked out to the car and got some copies of the magazine to give to the commune. Michael was still talking when I returned. Michael's lady sidekick had come in and was taking the names of those who were ready to join. Consuelo was ready to leave. The final guest never did get to explain why he was there or who he was, but apparently he intended to join the commune and begin on the shift-schedule.

We decided to make a day of it by eating at the Berkeley restaurant. When we arrived, the place was crowded and there appeared to be only one waiter on the floor. We sat there, waiting, and passed the time by watching several commune members going to the kitchen and bringing out elaborately prepared dishes of food and then leisurely eating them. After about half an hour, the waiter — a tall, large-nosed athletic type, balding with long hair in the back — took down our order. I noted that there were now two waiters, but that several tables had been occupied and vacated without service. We too almost got up to leave after waiting still another half hour, but finally our food arrived. We shared a delicious meal of rice, vegetables, and so-called "macroburgers."

The crowd thinned out. Then Michael, his sidekick, and several other commune members arrived to eat and serve. Several members took up jobs, waiting on tables. Michael came up to us and began his spiel about the Crusade. We told him that they hadn't had enough help on the tables earlier.

"We operate on a plane of higher consciousness," Michael replied. "We came in because we felt the vibrations that we were needed."

"But earlier—"

Michael interrupted by returning to his rap about the Crusade.

A LETTER FROM THE MESSIAH'S SECRETARY

At my request, Dian kindly provided me with more information about the current activities of the Messiah's World Crusade (In addition to furnishing the photos that accompany this account). She wrote me the following letter in late February 1971:

. . . The MUSTARD SEED Natural Foods restaurant was closed in June 1970 when the gentleman who was collecting our rent went bankrupt and the IRS requested we stop paying him and pay them. As soon as we did that, he closed up . . . the restaurant, confiscated our musical instruments and forced us to move out.

Since that time we've been maintaining our family at about 40 members, caring for our 11 children, baking organic wholewheat bread and distributing it to local health food stores and the Co-Op super market, catering natural foods to churches and happenings, presenting feasts at our Berkeley commune at the beginning of each zodiac sign. We've also been working hard on the *Messiah's World Crusade* newspaper which explains our mission and how the MASTER

PLAN channeled from the Higher Beings and written down in trance by Allen, is the plan to synthesize the struggling yin and yang forces on this planet.

Now we are presently operating our two communal homes and offering room and board in the New Age style of living for a nominal fee to help pay the rent. . . . This also is a good way for interested people to come slowly into the communal activity.

At the beginning of March we will again open up at the corner of Haste and Telegraph. This time we have the entire building at half the rent we paid previously. . . . plus our band equipment — Good Karma. This is the People's New Age Center. . . .

We will be featuring benefits starting March 15 with all kinds of musical and live entertainment. . . .

Our band and chorus are ready to do a recording of their original songs, inspired by the channelings of the Galactic Command through Allen.

Allen (out of jail on appeal bond) is compiling his channelings compositely called *THE EVERLASTING GOSPEL* and they soon will be published in several different books. Revelations Revealed, Nature's Potions, The People's Emergency World Government.

If you wish to help, let me hear from you,
Dian

THE CITY OF LIGHT

In 1968 we noted in *The Modern Utopian* "News Digest" that The City of Light, a religious community in San Francisco, had moved to New Mexico. This commune, whose beliefs included credence in flying saucers, New Age religion, etc., reported:

¾ of our exodus is over. The last and final move will be when we move to the land to begin building The City of Light. We are going full steam ahead now that we are in New Mexico on all projects involved in building a city, including *The Luminator* newspaper.

Their tabloid was published irregularly. Most of the paper contained the usual New Age religious rhetoric about prophecy and abstract metaphysics. They did devote a bit of space to talk about their community:

We're steadily building a library from which people — especially the children, the raising and education of which is to be the City's prime concern — may learn. . . . We don't want to be trapped in the same old, limited sectarian "bag" that most utopian communities seem to have placed themselves, namely, accepting only one (usually quite restricted) way of living. We favor teaching people to *think* for themselves so that they can each find their own proper 'path.' Until people finally get it through their heads that there are at least as many 'paths' as there are people, this planet is never going to get past its blind-faith-in-a-savior hang-ups and its religion-is-bunk hang-ups that are stifling so much needed progress.

During the following year, the paper's format deteriorated to a poorly mimeographed newsletter. Then, we didn't hear from them at all.

The address for The City of Light was a Post Office box number. When we got into town I checked the phone directory, but there was no listing. We decided to inquire at the local health-food stores and bookshops. No luck. A health-food store said that the people had not been in for several months. A bookstore manager looked blank in response to my inquiry. I asked two young teenyboppers if they had heard of The City of Light — still no luck. As we were about to give up, I stopped a long-haired guy and he said he knew of two of them, an ex-truck driver and his wife. It seems that the ex-truck driver had some sort of revelation while high on bennies or something and he and his wife came to Santa Fe to start a church. The group had split up and left town several months before.

Later, after returning home, I received a New Age church newsletter in the mail. On page 8 was a story about The City of Light: "The City is still in New Mexico, and there it is to be as long as God so wills it. The Reverend Elaine Chambers is the Oracle of The City and the editor of the newspaper." The City was selling a copy of its all-prophecy issue of *The Luminator* for $1.00 and the article added, "As it has been a harsh winter, The City of Light is in need of help. So, if you can afford a donation, please do so when you can."

Elaine's husband, Lile, was also active in The City's work, and the article encouraged people to visit them in the summer. A photo of Elaine was included on the page. With short, short hair, a plump face and wide grin, she looked like a religious truck driver's wife.

A few weeks later I received a copy of the latest issue of *The Illuminator*, along with a poorly mimeographed letter explaining the delay in publication. The City of Light had moved to a small village 30 miles outside of Santa Fe and was now reorganizing. The letter requested that people postpone their visits until construction of The City was begun. Hopefully, construction would commence soon. Donations for the building fund were needed; "The City of Light is a City of God and it is your city;" the appeal ended.

THE ANANDA COOPERATIVE COMMUNITY

On my way to the Ananda Cooperative Community in Nevada City, California, I reread an article by Jim Mitchell (Helix, UPS) that I had reprinted in *The Modern Utopian* magazine: He wrote of the ". . . new and young people who have come here to settle the Sierra foothills and give them a loving consciousness. Bare or sandaled feet, long hair, beards and blue jeans, Pakistani or Indian prints—a Hari Krishna chant rises above drums and cymbals, a marriage of expectation and inward peace."

The community described hardly lacked facilities: a 70-acre Meditation Retreat with geodesic domes consisting of "a common house (for meals and meetings), office, and large temple arranged near a wooden water tank and small garden." And a mere three miles from the retreat lay the commune's 270-acre Farm Community, with A-frame cabins occupied year-round. The article concluded, "At Ananda, each person is free to build a new and beautiful reality, for such a reality need only be the sum of the spirit and body of each member—you become a new society and the strength and beauty of that society depends directly on your own spirit."

I arrived first at the Farm and was told to hurry to the Retreat for the regular Saturday afternoon outdoor concert. I wanted to look over the Farm first, but I was informed that this was where most members lived and worked and that the Retreat was for visitors. Besides, the members were all at the Retreat now and I'd better hurry if I wanted to get to the concert on time. As I drove away from the old farmhouse where Ananda members made candles and incense and published books on Yoga, I also noted a few other farm buildings — sheds, chicken house, and barn — as well as several tepees, small houses, and shelters scattered over the landscape.

Numerous signs pointed the way to the Retreat; there was no chance of getting lost or misdirected. The visitors' parking lot was clearly marked. Another sign read "Visitors Please Register At Office," and a helpful arrow pointed towards a small, bright-red geodesic dome with sliding aluminum doors and windows.

I was given the official guided tour of Ananda. First a look at the huge communal kitchen, which was being built with the help of students from Pacific High, a free school in the Palo Alto area of California. (Pacific High students had built many unique and beautiful domes at their school and many outsiders were now hiring them to help construct domes elsewhere.) The new kitchen-dome was

151

soon to be connected to the present kitchen and dining facility "common house"—another dome-like structure also used as a meeting and social facility. The temple was a large geodesic dome surrounded entirely by an exercise deck. We took off our shoes and walked inside. It was lovely and peaceful. The temple floor was covered with multi-colored mats and the walls were decorated with rugs and colorful murals depicting Yogiananda, Ananda's spiritual guru.

Back at the office, my guide presented me with a brochure that explained the history, purpose, and program of Ananda. Since Ananda is only a three-hour drive from San Francisco, many people make the journey for a weekend of meditation and spiritual regeneration. The location—some 3,000 feet above sea level, in an area of pleasantly rolling terrain that is heavily wooded with large oak and pine trees and manzanita bushes—provides a breath-taking view. Facilities for visitors at that time included a central bathhouse with hot and cold running water, several small residences, and (according to the brochure), "roomy cabin-type tents with large windows set apart from one another in secluded nooks among the trees. Campsites are also available for people with tents of their own."

There are daily meditation and exercise periods at the Retreat, though no one is explicitly required to attend them. Most of the members live at the Farm, where a separate but similar schedule is maintained. On weekends, however, a full schedule of activities at the Retreat is planned:

Friday:

    5 P.M.   Recharging exercises and Yoga postures

    6 P.M.   Meditation

    7 P.M.   Dinner

    8 P.M.   Evening Service

Saturday:

    6:15 A.M.   Strolling Kirtan (chanting)

    6:30 A.M.   Yoga postures and recharging exercises

7:30 A.M.	Meditation
8:30 A.M.	Breakfast
10:00 A.M.	Classes in "Creative Arts Through Yoga," etc.
12:30 P.M.	Lunch
2:00 P.M.	Concert
5:00 P.M.	Recharging exercises and Yoga Posture
6:00 P.M.	Meditation
6:30 P.M.	Dinner
8:00 P.M.	Evening Service
Sunday:	
Morning	Same as Saturday, with a service at 11 A.M. instead of classes
Afternoon	Tour of the Farm

These planned weekends run from mid-spring to late autumn (as long as the weather permits). Only a few people remain at the Retreat year-round — "Facilities for the life of a hermit," as they call it. The Farm, however, accommodates a larger number of married couples and families throughout the year. Visitors to the commune are charged nominal rates according to facilities used and the length of stay.

Ananda permits no hallucinogenic drugs of any kind on the property. Smoking is permissible, but only in the privacy of one's own tent. No dogs are allowed, a restriction because barking distracts people during meditation. Although not specifically excluded, young children are not particularly welcome to remain at the Retreat. Babysitting arrangements are provided at the Farm.

While I was sitting in the office, three young people with backpacks arrived. The director and guide had left the office in the care of John, a young artist and resident member. The most aggressive of the three began to inquire about the Retreat. "We want to stay a few days or longer, if we like it here. Can we set up camp anywhere we can find a convenient space?"

"Well, I'm not the one in charge here," John said. "The man who is will be back in a few minutes. I think only designated campsites can be used, though, and there is a daily or weekly fee for their use."

"Well," said the backpacker, "we don't intend to get in the way. How about if we just camp outside the campsite area in the woods somewhere?"

"This is an organized meditation retreat," John replied with a slight grin. "If you want to stay here you have to be part of the Retreat, not live on the edges. There are plenty of woods elsewhere, if all you want to do is camp out." Then he added, "Visitors are expected to participate in our programs and eat at least one meal daily with us."

I felt compelled to add, "If everyone who wanted, came here and just camped out around the edges of the Retreat, before you know it the whole hillside would be loaded down with people. I wonder whose toilet and bathing facilities they'd want to use? And where they'd leave all their trash?"

"Yes, I know," John replied, "we had that kind of open policy here at one time. It was a disaster. Now we've become organized. It's necessary. Unfortunately, most people aren't aware and sensitive enough to treat other people and their environment with the same care and attention they themselves would like."

"Well, you see, I'm writing a book on communes," the aggressive one replied, as if to explain why he should be an exception.

"God!" I exclaimed. "Everyone is writing a book on communes these days." (I get two letters a week from people writing books, articles, and masters' theses on the subject.)

"I'm not writing any ordinary book about communes," he retorted. "I'm writing a book on how to start a commune."

"Oh, show him your book," I said to John.

John moved meditatively toward the literature table and

picked up the book, *Cooperative Communities—How to Start Them and Why*, by Kriyananda. He turned abruptly and smiled broadly. "Have you seen this book?" he asked. The budding young author didn't seem to be very interested.

John was one of the most beautiful guys I had ever seen. His physical appearance was strikingly healthy; his manner was graceful and pleasant, yet direct and authentic. He was the one who had done the beautiful murals in the temple, and he was now setting up a display of some printed drawings of the past Yoga masters in history. These included Jesus seated in a cross-legged position, several Indian masters, and Yogiananda.

John was a year-round resident at the Retreat. He told me of spending his days without seeing or talking to another person. His solitude, together with a painstaking devotion to drawing portraits of great religious leaders, had obviously contributed to his own development as a spiritual being. Perhaps someone would come along to draw him and thereby gain a little of his beauty as well. I asked, "How come there is no picture of Kriyananda here?" (Kriyananda, a disciple of Yogiananda, was the founder of Ananda.)

"He is a great teacher; he is not a guru, an enlightened one," John replied. "But he is well on the road," John hastened to add, "much more advanced than most of us."

KRIYANANDA AND SELF-REALIZATION

Kriyananda was an active member and minister of the Self-Realization Fellowship (the work founded by Yogiananda). In 1962, after serving as vice-president of the Fellowship, Kriyananda began working independently, traveling throughout the world giving lectures and classes and writing books on Yoga. In 1967 he was given the option to buy the land on which he founded Ananda. He had been looking for such a site for many years. As he has remarked, "It was in 1941, when I was only fifteen, that I first gave serious thought to a communal way of life."

Kriyananda's evolution in thought regarding communal living is one which sounds very familiar to me. In the preface to his book on cooperative communities he notes the several stages through which he developed:

1. Envision an isolated society, without considering how such a society could come into existence.

2. Believe that the small community is the answer to the impersonal big city and big government.

3. Realize perfection cannot be achieved just by changing the system. First, there has to be a change in the person himself.

4. Attempt to combine personal growth with cooperative community.*

Kriyananda's emphasis is on "self-unfoldment — not as a selfish imposition on the universe (the 'Great God, EGO' of Ayn Rand) — but simply as a private and deeply personal search for Self-realization.

The result cannot but benefit man in his political, economic and social institutions as well. For all things bring harmony to men who have found inner harmony. And nothing brings it to men in whom inner discord prevails.**

Kriyananda's book about cooperative communities provides some insight into the limitations of his concept of self-realization. And these are paralleled by the limitations imposed structurally at Ananda. In addition to providing his readers with extremely good advice on how to start a community, Kriyananda tries to steer a middle course between two antithetical concepts: communal ownership and togetherness on the one hand and private ownership and isolation on the other. Because he recog-

*Cooperative Communities, Ananda Publications, Nevada City, Calif., pp. i–iii.
**Ibid., p. 6.

nizes man's weaknesses, he settles on a cooperative arrangement rather than a communal one. "People who receive everything without paying for it," he writes, "must be induced somehow to work for what they get."* Without private profit or obedience to the group (as administered by a strong leader), people will tend to take advantage. So Kriyananda fears that a strong dictatorial leadership is required in order for people to share all things in common.

Kriyananda's view, "The soundest course, it seems to me, would be to follow the pattern to which people are in any case accustomed. Let them work. . . ." He also warns that people should not be expected to "embrace a way of life too radically different from that to which they are now accustomed." He concludes, therefore, that the "safest course for any new community would be to allow each person the freedom to meet others on his own terms."

Doesn't that simply mean doing your own thing? Kriyananda, in effect, is copping out on real communal society in favor of a more cooperative form of capitalism.

But who can knock that? He's right, it is the safest course — it "works," it's practical, it requires little change from the way of life and things to which people are accustomed.

But I had thought Kriyananda was trying to build a community that promotes self-realization. Instead, the kind of community he envisions requires very little change on the part of the individual. Rather, it permits the individual to retain all of his culturally learned behavioral patterns and biases, which include being possessive, shortsighted, self-serving and profit-conscious. At best, one would be co-operating economically with others — that is, one would do something for an anticipated return — rather than learning to be free of attachments to money and material things. Thus one would not learn to give without expectation of

* *Cooperative Communities*, p. 28.

return; or, putting it the other way, one would not learn to give simply because giving is an expression of one's authentic self. The danger of Kriyananda's plans is that he has determined "how to start a cooperative community" based on people as they are, without the slightest hint that the plan could ever evolve toward a more "utopian" state if the community members were to gain greater self-realization.

"If people were all highly spiritual," he writes, "there would be no need to regiment them to be sure that they work. . . ."* But he discusses no group processes, other than meditation, body postures, and yoga as a way to gain that spirituality. Thus, while he pays lip service to individual change, the social structure he suggests merely perpetuates behavior derived from the same old cultural mold.

The administration of the community under Kriyananda's plan follows a sort of democratic planner-manager system (described in more oligarchic form in B. F. Skinner's *Walden Two*). This turns out to be another example of structuring an "ideal" future situation based on the premise that the present nature of man is not alterable through social planning—that is, that the capitalistic, self-seeking aspects of man's behavior cannot or need not be changed. In sum, it appears to me that Kriyananda actually *reduces* the chances for self-realization in his desire to create a secure, stable community.

Still another contradiction is that on one level Kriyananda is aware enough to recognize that a community which does not survive has not necessarily failed, because "The way of life is ever to grow, then die. . . . If an institution endures through the ages, in fact, it is probably because at some point in its history it chose, instead of dying, to become petrified."** Yet he criticizes 19th-

*Cooperative Communities, p. 29.
**Cooperative Communities, p. 15.

century communities because they "failed" in conventional terms — because they had "too idealistic a view of human nature," because they did not screen applicants adequately, and so forth.

Self-realization requires a constant battle in opposition to the drawbacks of increasing age (stability) and in favor of youthfulness (dynamic change). The institution or community that is intentionally created must be as flexible and open to radical change as the individual is, if self-realization is to be fully realized therein. The degree to which the community and/or individual is closed and rigid, is the degree to which the possibility for self-realization is diminished. In working out a safe community structure, Kriyananda is in danger of sacrificing his primary goal, self-realization. I'm certain that he would emphasize the power of yoga and meditation to advance the individual spiritually; The Ananda Retreat may be a great place for a hermit. But to be a fully self-realized, spiritual being *and* to live with others requires much less communal security than a cooperative venture such as Ananda strives to provide.

It was a very hot day. All of the male residents at the Ananda Retreat wore only long loose skirts and sandals. The drive up had been hot and dry and I had visions of being able to take off all my clothes at the Retreat. I peeled off my shirt and asked why there was a prohibition against nudity. One member said, "Well, I don't know; it's just part of the Hindu tradition, I guess. Kriyananda thinks it's an important tradition to uphold so we go along with it. Of course, sometimes we go nude at the Farm when we're working in the fields or swimming, you know." He winked as he said this.

Another member said, "Well, I go nude if I want to when I'm out in the woods, but not here at the Retreat. There are a lot of visitors and guests coming in and out all the time. They might be offended."

"Isn't that being a little phony and unauthentic," I inquired. "After all, if you're trying to become more spiritual and in contact with your real self and express yourself authentically, isn't that contradictory to being worried about what a visitor might think? He doesn't have to stay here if he doesn't like the way you live."

"I don't know," the other guy answered. "After all, this is a place which is open to those who wish a temporary retreat as well as permanent members. We need the income from these people in order to continue to operate. We have $1,700 a month in mortgage payments alone."

"Then you are compromising in order to appeal to more people to come here."

"I don't think so. After all, we want to be open to the larger society and help others find self-realization. Besides, I don't feel uncomfortable wearing this garment, even on a hot day."

THE HIMALAYAN ACADEMY

Not too far from California's Nevada City, where we discovered Kriyananda's Ananda Cooperative Community, is Nevada's Virginia City, where there is another commune of yogis on the spiritual quest. Both groups have much in common.

The Himalayan Academy's guru, Master Subramuniya, is also an American convert to yoga. Subramuniya, who grew up in the Lake Tahoe area, traveled to Ceylon where he trained as a yogi. In 1958 he returned to the United States to establish his own spiritual community, with a vision of integrating both Hindu and Christian principles and practices. And in 1962 he acquired property near Virginia City.

In contrast to the increasingly noisy, tension-ridden technological environment in which most of us live, the

Academy has deliberately created a setting that is restful, quiet, and beautiful — conducive to the practice of meditation and contemplation.

Like Ananda, the H.A. prefers to maintain a good public image. It tries not to either upset or provoke any negative reactions from local people and visitors. Thus, members of the community do not visit Reno and Carson City in flowing robes, long hair and shaven pates. In fact, when they go into town, some dress as smartly as any well-groomed Nevada businessman or wear the accepted local apparel complete with cowboy boots and hat. Another similarity to Ananda is that H.A. residents tend to have the gentle manners and clear eyes of people who adhere to a calm, meditative, purposeful life style.

The H.A. looks beyond its confines economically too. The Academy has its own printing press in Virginia City. In addition to printing materials that provide Yoga instruction for people all over the world, the Ponderosa Press, as it is called, does commercial printing for leading casinos in northern Nevada.

In other ways the Academy differs from Ananda. There are no geodesic temples in the Sierra woodlands. Instead, Subramuniya's followers have converted a huge deserted brewery in a historic ghost town into a religious center. In addition to doing over the brewery, they have constructed wickiup-like structures — small conical dwellings arranged in a village cluster. Made of crude materials such as burlap, these dwellings are colorfully decorated in Indian motifs.

In contrast to Ananda, which encourages family living and has no priests, monks, or religious organizational hierarchy, the Himilayan Academy requires taking vows of celibacy and poverty; all H.A. residents are considered to be in training for the priesthood. Monks outnumber nuns ten to one. And unlike the Ananda members, the Academy's residents are required to make a strong commitment to the order, to obey without reservations the

161

teachings of their guru, and to pursue completely a monastic style of life.

Although both Ananda and the H.A. espouse communal goals, residents of the Academy live much more communally. Newcomers are expected to donate all their worldly possessions to the order and to share all things in common. They try to live together in a close community because they believe this to be an essential part of the self-realization process. Learning to live in close communal harmony with others embodies the Christian precepts of love for one's neighbor and of the brotherhood of man.

In recent years the community has grown so much that Academy members well along in their training as Christian-Yoga priests have been starting separate centers or "churches" in Virginia City and the surrounding area.

CHAPTER FIVE

HIP COMMUNES, and hip people in general, have a great affinity for one another. The manner of speech, dress, and long-hair, immediately communicate between strangers when they meet, a sense of brotherhood and belonging, which continues until proven otherwise through experience (as in the case of a rip-off artist or a narc (narcotics agent) dressed in hippie clothing). Thus, all hip communes, however their differences in philosophy and practice, share a special warmth and comradery with one another.

Hip communes have gone through a great many changes during the past five years. Anyone who has followed their development can only conclude that these changes have been for the better. There is a sense of reality and joy in these communes today which is not described by the stories which follow because even a few months can make a lot of difference in the evolution of a commune. Bill Wheeler's description of the recent developments at Sheep Ridge Ranch provides an excellent example of favorable development, despite continued harrassment from outside authorities.

THE LOWER FARM

We had heard rumors of the existence of several hippie-style communes in Placitas, New Mexico. So we decided to hunt them down in April 1970. Not having much luck in locating one of these communities, we stopped in at the local post office to inquire. But we were late and the post office had already closed. Noting an elderly man sitting in front of a house just a few yards away, we sauntered over to see if he'd be open to our inquiries. He was responsive and invited us in for coffee and cookies. Mr. C. W. McFall turned out to be a retired high-school teacher who had taught in the South most of his life. Having lived in Placitas for two years, he was quite familiar with the people in the local communes. He offered to serve as our guide. We

piled into his old Volvo and headed for the Lower Farm—
home of Ulysses S. Grant who, in addition to being the
self-identified reincarnation of the other and earlier Ulysses S. Grant, was a commune leader and a candidate for
governor of New Mexico.

After leaving the main highway, we drove along a winding dirt road into a valley. Numerous adobe houses and
several tepees dotted the hillside. The sun had nearly
set when we arrived at the little village complex.

GETTING TO KNOW U.S.

One or two people were wandering around, but the
place seemed deserted. Eventually Ulysses showed up
and invited us into a back room of the main house. The
room had recently been vacated by a member who was
asked to leave, he told us. Said member had apparently
been uncooperative and the cause of trouble in the community.

"We're not a commune," Ulysses said without hesita-
tion. "Communes don't work—we're a village. We have a
mayor and courts and laws just like any other village."

We learned more. The village had been legally incorporated as a nonprofit organization, complete with and run
by a board of directors. No one who lived there was allowed to hold an outside job. The members had almost no
money. Some residents used food stamps. There was no
rent to pay because the land and buildings were owned
by the corporation and because maintenance expenses
were minimal. The property had a long history of use by
squatters. And, as Ulysses said, anyone who wished to
come and build on the land was welcome to do so. People
are not subject to the rules of the village unless they actually live in it, meaning in the main complex of seven
adobe buildings. The property was bounded on three sides
by a national forest, and on the fourth side by an uptight

165

neighbor who continually complained that the commune's horses got into his hay.

A tall lanky fellow came into the room wrapped only in a blanket. He took a seat in the corner and laughed madly at our sporadic conversation. It was now dark, so Ulysses lit a kerosene lantern. He pulled out two books he had written. One was a 16-page watercolor presentation of his candidacy and platform for Governor; the other was a larger book, illustrated with simple watercolor sketches, that explained the by-laws and purposes of the village.

I turned to Ulysses and asked, "Does the village get harassed by any local rednecks? How do you handle that?"

"Oh, once in a while a townee gets drunk or bored and comes down here to make trouble. I just beat 'im up," Ulysses responded gruffly.

I asked how the candidacy for governor was coming along. U.S. complained that he had been kept off the ballot because he did not have the $1,300 the state required for a filing fee. A poor man cannot run for high political office in this land of the free and home of the brave, where we are taught as infants that anyone can become President if he tries hard enough. Ulysses was discouraged. He didn't feel he had much of a chance with his name not even on the ballot.

As U.S. talked about rules and beating up townees, and politics, I sensed that his attitude had developed over a long period of time—that it was not a bullying or authoritarian attitude, but one recognizing that ignorance, so characteristic of a large percentage of people, required hard-headed, adamant confrontation. He was almost benign in his toughness. But then, he was not a kid but an older man past the age to be trusted.

"I've got a neighbor here," U.S. remarked, "that wants to see me in jail. He steals my horse and then, when I go to get it, he has me arrested for trespassing." (I recalled the story about the Dukhobors in Canada, about the time when their cow was shot when it was caught in a neighbor's pasture. The bereaved community—men, women and children—gathered around the dead cow and wailed and wailed so loud and long it stirred up the entire countryside.)

As we talked, I was looking casually through U.S. Grant's picture books. When my eyes fell on the bylaws of the organization, I said, "Hey, can I copy out these bylaws? Some of my readers might like to know how your village is organized."

U. S. Grant

"Sure," he replied, "but not now. It's time I called it a night. We go to bed when it gets dark around here."

Getting out of the village in darkness was not as simple as getting in by daylight. Before we got back to the main highway, our nerves were shattered from our being forced to explore every alternate road leading to deserted cabins and dead ends. We finally found someone who gave us directions on how to get out of that labyrinth. Next morning, when we returned to the village, we discovered that we had explored half the hillside in the direction of the national forest.

LIFE AND PEOPLE AT THE LOWER FARM

When we parked near the complex, we noticed two young longhairs busy repairing an old pickup. I asked one of them if he lived here. "Only temporarily," he replied. "I'm looking for a place way out in the wilderness. Too many people coming through here."

"It's pretty hard to get away from people these days," I said. "Course you can always put up a sign saying 'Visitors Not Welcome.'"

"Yeah, but who wants to do that! I'd rather find a place for my family and friends that's so far out that no one will want to visit."

"All I can say is, 'Good Luck,'" I concluded, thinking about Sam Wright, an ex-professor of mine who had moved to the wilds of Alaska, accessible only by helicopter, or by several miles of hazardous trekking on snowshoes. Even so, Sam had visitors.

A shiny white car with "Sheriff's Department" lettered on its side pulled to a stop on another roadway just above the main house. Two men got out. U.S. Grant's horse was loose on the neighbor's property again.

"We just checked our fence a day or two ago," Ulysses was saying, "all along the south range. There wasn't a hole in it. I don't know how he got onto your land. Maybe he got through the national forest. Or maybe you led him over yourself."

"Hump!" You had better keep him off my property," the tall lean man in a Texan hat said firmly.

"Listen, now," Ulysses replied, pounding his garden hoe up and down into the ground, "I don't know how that horse gets over there. But you just want to make trouble."

"I'm not trying to make trouble."

"Oh, so that's why you bring the sheriff along, eh? I know more than you think I know. I've been talking with your boy and he's told me what you say at the dinner table. You want to get my ass in jail, that's what he told me you said."

"Frank said that?"

"No, I don't know Frank. It was your youngest son, Joseph. I had a good talk with him. You're out to get me, admit it."

"Well, I'm not going to feed your horses anymore."

"I go to get my horse and what do you do? Arrest me for trespassing!"

The argument went on and on. They finally decided to take a look at the fence to see if there was any place where the horse could have gotten through. I had the urge to join them but got into a conversation with four other residents of the village instead.

One chicano guy with long hair and a Chinese-style mustache did most of the rapping, casually twirling a copy of *The Watchtower* in his hands as he spoke. The three others — a beautiful black cat named Tucker, the guy with the mad laugh from the previous evening, and an ex-middle-class coed with torn dungarees — interjected comments when they could.

"People go running back and forth and up and down like wild rabbits or crazy deer," the chicano said. "What for? Just stop and open up, be receptive to the good earth, tune in to natural vibrations, no one has to work for anything. God provides all if you don't get uptight about it.

169

That Old Man knew what he was doing when He made all of this"—gesturing with a sweep of the hand and a broad grin—"A lot of us used to live in the Haight-Ashbury. You had to shoot speed just to survive in a scene like that. It was nowhere. God meant men to be close to the land not on concrete. Cities—wow! Freeways, cars going zoom zoom here, there— Lights blinking—rush rush. Man, that ain't natural. That's insanity. The city is doomed. Those who get it together on the land will be the survivors. 'Course if you're really together, man, you can survive anywhere, even in the fuckin' city. There were a few cats like that in the Haight. Maybe a few still there. So high, so spiritual, you could tell just seeing a guy like that walking down the street. All the shit around him. Above it all. But if you're not that far along spiritually—and most of us ain't, man—the city is doomed anyway and you just catch all those bad vibes by living there. So you get a place where you feel good, like this, and everything is beautiful and you don't need speed or any of that bad dope and you don't need to worry about money or anything."

We all agreed. That conversation made me high.

The Lower Farm had a delightfully relaxed feeling about it. The buildings and their interiors were all an earthy adobe color. U.S. had been hoeing in the newly planted communal garden before we arrived and one or two others were doing a little work there off and on during the morning hours. Mostly, the people were just wandering around, relaxed and chatting with one another. U.S.'s wife was nursing her baby on the front porch of the main house. There was no electricity. The living environment was probably very much like that of my great-granddad, except that here there was no necessity to toil for bread or work in order to either survive or simply feel worthwhile. Consuelo and I sat on the porch and gave U.S.'s books a more thorough going-over.

RULES FOR A VILLAGE

It was from one of the books that I copied out the by-laws of the village, which, it turned out, went by the official name of Manerva Nueva, Incorporated. These are the village's bylaws, all 10 of them.

1. Membership is open to anyone on the Planet Earth. Access is denied no one.

2. There is one class of membership: first class or full member.

3. All property is and shall be held in common by all members.

4. Any member attending a meeting is entitled to equal voting rights with all members in attendance.

5. Annual meetings begin at sunrise July 4 of each year and continue until agreement on all issues under discussion is reached.

6. Any member may declare any question an important one which then can be acted upon only after meditation and consultation of the I CHING, an oracle.

7. All funds received by the corporation shall be held for use of all by Treasurers appointed by the Board of Directors.

8. Meetings may be called by any member or director upon notification of other members within a reasonable time prior to the holding of said meeting.

9. All major decisions must be made in agreement with the I CHING. Any issue may be declared a major issue by any member.

10. Individual members living in communities operated by Manerva Nueva may not hold private funds or property (personal belongings and effects excepted).

RUNNING FOR GOVERNOR

Ulysses S. Grant wanted to print 100,000 copies of his 16-page, full-color platform for governor. He didn't have the $5,000 to do so, but neither was he willing to print it any other way. I offered to do a 4-page black-and-white summary for him but he flatly refused. No compromises: the color — the pictures as presented — was essential to the total message. Ulysses preferred that I not copy his words verbatim but he was willing for me to write them from memory. Here's part of the written portion of his message as I recall it.

1. No one would ever be forced to do anything but there would be certain things that could not be done, like industrial air and water pollution.

2. Horse trails would be developed along with roadways and people would be encouraged to use the horse for transportation.

3. The bureaucracy would be cut in half since the use of paper in government would be reduced 50% in order to conserve our most valuable natural resource — trees.

4. Police would wear white uniforms and be used to help old ladies cross the street and help motorists change flat tires; police help instead of police force.

5. A return to the one-room schoolhouse in education.

6. Legalize marijuana.

While we were sitting there on the porch, reading, Ulysses came riding up on a great white stallion. As he dismounted I could see the yellow stripe on the side of his army-blue pants.

"I don't know how he gets out. We couldn't find any holes in the fence." He plopped down in an old overstuffed chair on the porch, pushing his crumpled blue army cap back on his head.

I asked him a few innocuous questions about communal living, but the most I can recall about his answers was "Communes don't work, 'cause people don't work. There's too many people with a lot of high-minded ideas about utopia. But there ain't no utopia. Just some cats alooking to ball a lot of chicks and people looking for someone to take care of them."

"What about your candidacy for governor, Ulysses?"

"Now that's something worth talking about!" he replied. He reached into his pocket and pulled out a soiled newspaper. "There are eight candidates for Governor. Look at 'em — I'm the only one who's smiling."

He was right. The people in the seven other photos on the page looked like men who had either just swallowed a bird or had a fight with their wives. But U.S. Grant was smiling — and he was the only one of the eight who never had a chance. Shoulder-length hair, beard, and smile to match — that's no way to appeal to the voters, especially if you come riding up on a great white stallion. The kids might be happy to see a beautiful white horse but they don't have a vote. "Mature" adults on the other hand can better identify with short-haired, middle-aged men.

As part of his platform, U.S. Grant proposed to eliminate half the state's revenue "so we won't have the money

173

to spend on things that aren't absolutely necessary." Also he called for a "reversal of the current direction society is taking. The real issues are life, stability, and taking care of the planet."

Will the next governor please stand?

But Ulysses was very discouraged about the race. Now that his name was not to be on the ballot he felt he couldn't win. Before, though, he had seriously believed he had a chance. "There are thousands of hip, poor, and dissatisfied people in this state who would vote for me."

"It doesn't seem constitutional that a man can be barred from being placed on the ballot just because he doesn't have the filing fee," I remarked.

"Yes. I've seen a lawyer and we may decide to go to court on this. I could have gotten petitions circulated and got several thousand signatures on them in order to get my name placed on the ballot, but I wasn't going to impose on people to do all that work and then have to vote again too."

MR JONES, MR GRANT, AND GOD

Two young men came up the road. One had short curly blond hair and was dressed in a suit and tie. The other, in work clothes, looked semi-hip.

"This is Bob Jones. He's looking for some people who would like to make some money cutting trees this summer," said the semi-hip one. "We thought some of you people might need the money."

U.S. sat straight up in his chair and said firmly, "Sorry. We have a rule here—no one works at outside jobs for pay. We've got enough to do right here. It's planting time now. If people go outside to earn money, who'll do all the work that needs to be done here?"

Young Mr Jones interrupted. "I understand what you mean but I used to live in the Haight-Ashbury and I know you people can use money. Couldn't you use the money to buy food and the things you need?"

U. S. Grant

"No. — You used to live in the Haight?"

"Four or five years ago. I didn't want to dress up in a suit and tie today," he gestured self-consciously toward his attire. "My boss has a funny thing about it so I go ahead. I got a wife and three kids now and I have to make a living. But I'm sympathetic to what you're doing. We could provide a trailer for two or three people to live in up there in the woods. The weather's dry so a person could sleep outdoors or in a tent. The job's just for the summer. And we'll pay $5 for every tree that's cut."

"Well, anyone who wants to *move out* of the village and

go to work for the summer, that's *his* business. You might find someone who'll be interested. Just walk around and ask them. I've got my hands full keeping things going here," Ulysses replied.

A little later I noticed that they were talking to five or six of the villagers outside one of the other adobe buildings. I don't know whether they got the help they were looking for — I was just giving those rundown adobe houses a quick once-over and didn't stop to listen in on their conversation.

Before we left, however, I tried to get one point straight with U.S.

"Several guys who live here have told me that this place belongs to God. Anyone can come and no one is in charge. Yet you said you'd rather we didn't send anyone here and it seems that whenever anyone wants anything they come to you. You seem to be running things."

"Well," he said, "it's just that I'm around all the time. A lot of people run for the hills when they see outsiders come in, especially like when the sheriff comes. Everybody scatters. You know, some guy might be dodging the draft or someone else is escaping a bust. I'm clean. I don't have to run from anybody right now. I might have to next week though. I don't fancy spending time in jail. That neighbor's out to get me, if not next week then later. I'm not going to jail. So, maybe I'll have to head for the hills too. In the meantime, if I'm not around to keep things going this place will fall to pieces. Look out there in the garden. How many people do you see working? One. It's planting time and one person is working in the garden. So I've got to stay here and see to it, see to the garden being planted."

THE SALESMAN FOR ZOOMWORKS

Later that day we visited a place that had once been a commune. It now consisted of a huge double-dome, a single dome nearby, two trailers on the hillside, and a tepee and an adobe hut across the road.

McFall knocked on the door of the double-dome, opened it, walked in, and said: "Jim, I've brought a couple of people you might like to meet."

As we stepped inside we caught a glimpse of U.S. riding up on his great white stallion. McFall introduced us and then left to visit the couple who lived in the adobe hut.

Jim, in his 30s, well-groomed hair, casually dressed, had recently bought the property. He was a salesman for Zoomworks, a company producing creative playground-equipment and other geodesic-dome-type apparatus. He and his wife and baby lived in this double-dome, which was as elegantly decorated inside as any hip home in suburbia. The other half of the building was a workshop. Electricity was provided by a generator. "I'm a capitalist pig," Jim noted. "I rent out the other places on the property except for the dome on the hill which Bill and Ann own."

U.S. came in and mentioned that one of Jim's dogs had killed a chicken at the Lower Farm. "I had to kick the son of a bitch to get him to leave," U.S. added.

"Oh, so that's how come he had a big gash on his thigh and was limping around here for several days," Jim retorted mildly.

"I didn't kick him that hard, Jim. I didn't draw any blood."

"Guess he won't be so hungry for chicken anymore," Jim smiled.

"Guess not."

Another young man, Larry, entered and talked with Jim about the progress he was making in getting one of the trailers into liveable condition.

U.S. explained how Larry could build a simple but adequate sewage system out of some corrugated metal and boards instead of installing an expensive septic tank.

"Were either of you here when this place was a commune?" I asked U.S. and Jim.

"I was," U.S. replied, "but never really belonged. They used to have some wild times in this place. Orgies, dope, the whole trip. When I was young, I used to think how great it would be to have several wives and all of us live together in one big room. But all those ideas are just bullshit. Just ideas I had 'cause I was young and horny. All that talk about loving everybody totally and equally and sharing everything. What these people really wanted was to be free of responsibility and smoke dope and ball every guy or chick around."

"Love and sex are two entirely different things," Jim added. "One isn't related to the other."

"Not necessarily related," I interjected.

I knew what they were talking about. I had been around a lot of people who didn't understand their motives for wanting to join a commune.

Consuelo and I left the Placitas area the next day. The drive north gave us time to consider what we had seen, heard and felt.

Going back to that conversation with Jim and U.S. in the double-dome, I speculated now about why some people join, or want to join, communes. And I thought of some of the people I had known myself: the mothers who wanted someone else to take care of their children; the fathers who were tired of holding down dull jobs to support a wife and children; all those people intent upon flight from responsibility. Not fleeing meant too much pressure just to survive—no time for fun, games, relaxed and fulfilling sexuality. Communes, on the other hand, represented freedom, utopia—no work, all play, no one to

178

hassle or be hassled, relaxation from stress and strain, no more senseless work at home or office.

But those who went searching for their fantasies discovered that reality all too soon slaps one in the face — hard. After a brief summer of orgies and fun in the sun, the long winter sets in and darkness brings dissatisfaction and disillusionment.

Anyone not adrift in a dream world recognizes that people don't really want complete freedom from work and responsibility. A vacation, a period of compensation for their previous life's oppression — yes. But not *just* endless fun and games. Fulfilling work is the greatest leisure. And as someone once remarked (was it Freud? Fromm?), the two essential ingredients for mental health are represented by a balanced mixture of love and work. Even more essential, we need to stop thinking in terms of opposites — work versus play, love versus sex. Our behavior is still based on a very false but very widespread tradition of psychosocial conditioning; we insist that work must be experienced as painful but not joyful, that love is spiritual, but not erotic. And once having learned irrational behavior and been conditioned to think it rational, we perpetuate it by using elaborate justifications, all of which are based on Western logic, with its faulty premises and dualistic conventions.

We need our brains and hearts washed free of all this destructive conditioning. We need to get in touch with the essential oneness of all activity, so that love-play-sex-work are neither separate nor separable. What a ball we could have if we could learn this, and truly make it part of ourselves. We wouldn't just be sitting around trying to get high by rapping about getting in touch. We'd be doing it.

U.S. Grant's pessimism, I surmised, was like that of so many others. He started with the concept of what he thought people *ought* to be, rather than the realization and acceptance of what they were. They ought to be responsible, to cooperate in keeping the property in good condition and in planting and harvesting the garden. They ought to have the foresight to prepare for the winter as well as enjoy the summer. But "ought" came to naught (as it would almost anywhere), so Grant concluded that "communes don't work."

There is nothing wrong with having ideals. Consider the "ideal" commune, where everyone does his own thing and helps everyone as well; where rules or regulations are unnecessary, because everyone is aware enough of his surroundings and of other people, so that when something needs to be done he does it without being asked. That's beautiful, but such a commune exists only in people's minds, which constitute the true realm of possible but improbable fancy. Here on earth, though, starting a commune with nothing else but ideals will almost certainly guarantee failure. More is required—from ourselves. To get discouraged because others do not live up to one's expectations—dispiritedly proclaim that "communes don't work"—is really to say: "I am unwilling or unable to find out how my behavior and thinking is imperfect, and therefore this incapacity contributes to my experience that people cannot live together in groups larger than the nuclear family."

DISASTER AT THE LOWER FARM

Early in December 1970, some three weeks before Consuelo and I had planned to return to the Lower Farm for a second visit, the following headline appeared on the front page of the Albuquerque *Tribune:*

> HIPPIE HAVEN DOUBLE SLAYING;
> BELIEVE BORROWED RIFLE USED.
> U.S. GRANT IS SOUGHT IN HIPPIE COMMUNES

The newspaper provided a lengthy account. According to the *Tribune*, this is what happened:

U. S. Grant's wife Helen

PLACITAS — A rifle believed to have been the weapon used in last night's fatal shooting of two hippie commune residents near here was recovered today as officers intensified their search for commune leader Ulysses S. Grant.

Grant is wanted for questioning in connection with the deaths of Robert Copeland, 27, and Joseph Ornas, 47, whose bullet-ridden bodies were found near his commune home last night. . . .

Bill Dolley, a Placitas farmer, told authorities that the bearded commune leader had borrowed the rifle at about 4 P.M. yesterday, adding that Grant had borrowed it on many occasions in the past.

Police also are looking for Grant's wife Helen, who disappeared after the Tuesday night shooting incident. . . .

Mrs. Grant was last seen walking through Bernalillo, carrying their one-year-old son.

Police also were trying to figure out what led to the shootings. They believe it was a dispute between Grant, Copeland and Terry D. Hardin.

Hardin and Copeland shared a house next door to Grant.

Grant filed a complaint at the Sandoval County Courthouse in Bernalillo, claiming that Copeland and Hardin had stolen furniture and doors from his home.

Records show that Hardin had filed assault charges against Grant, claiming that Grant had struck his wife.

Hardin claimed Grant hit his pregnant wife with a door.

The usually calm commune was wracked by gunfire Tuesday night, Hardin told police, when he and Copeland were ambushed by Grant at the commune's waterhole about 50 yards from Grant's home.

Hardin said he and Copeland ran about 125 yards down a dirt road when Copeland was struck by a bullet.

Copeland shouted: "I'm hit," Hardin related.

Hardin was not hit by gunfire and told police he didn't see Ornas shot.

Sheriff Emiliano Montoya said when he arrived at the commune to investigate the report of the shooting he found Ornas' body about 75 yards from the waterhole.

Sheriff Montoya said Copeland's body was not found until about an hour later. It was about 50 yards from Ornas' body.

Preliminary autopsy reports show that both men were shot twice— once in the back and once in the face.

On December 26 Consuelo and I arrived in Placitas to find the road into the Lower Farm completely shut off— chains and locks on the entrance gate and No Trespassing signs. We then hurried over to see our friend and guide, C. W. McFall, in hopes that he would be able to tell us what had happened. The tape recorder took note of our conversation, as follows:

McFALL: You want to ask questions?

CONSUELO: I'm interested in your immediate response to the news-paper stories about Ulysses.

McFALL: Well, I think it's just damn poor journalism, damn poor journalism. Because, you know, Ulysses has been in my house, six, eight, ten times. You know, you were there. I have accused Ulysses of being the craziest man I ever knew who didn't require incarceration. But I think his attitude was all a pose. I'm certain he knew damn well that he couldn't ever be elected governor. He knew damn well it's all right to criticize the Establishment and to buck it, but you don't knock your brains out trying to knock down a stone wall with your head. I think he was reasonably intelligent—in fact, maybe he was quite smart.

The newspaper report says this one fellow is the only person who can offer any information. And he says Ulysses killed those two people and shot at him but he got away. Then he says Ulysses returned the rifle to a gringo up here, another fellow. I don't know if the other fellow's straight or hippie. I happen to have heard—it's only hearsay, but it's something for the detectives to look up—that this other fellow (who owned the rifle) and Ulysses were on the outs. When Ulysses left for a few months, part of the reason he left, so hearsay tells me, was because they had this quarrel. And he returned the rifle? After he shot those two fellows? Hogwash. That doesn't hold water. Now what happened? I'd give my option on my back seat in hell to know. I am very much afraid that Helen and the baby and Ulysses, all three, have also been killed. Because you mean our law enforcement officers are so stupid they can't find a murderer—anyone that's as easy to identify as Ulysses? And his wife and baby? And every time there's two people associated they become a square of the number, four times as easy to find. And with a baby, that becomes nine times.

DICK: They were on foot, right?

McFALL: They tell me he took a station wagon and tore off, but I don't know that, not at all. People around here have actually gone up in that neighborhood where there are many—I don't know if they're caves or just mine shafts, or dry wells. . . . People around here have actually gone up there and hunted, wondering if Ulysses's body is not in there.

DICK: Who would kill Ulysses?

McFALL: I don't know. Another thing that's been reported, but only hearsay—and this I don't go along with—some people say Ulysses was playing a part up here for a particular purpose. Representing somebody else. It's also been suggested that he was on the federal payroll.

DICK: What would that be for?

McFALL: I don't know. But I'm satisfied there's lots more behind what happened, and I feel kind of interested in Ulysses and Helen and the baby.

DICK: When did you see Ulysses last? Do you think he had developed any unusual quirks in the last six months or anything?

McFALL: I saw him a month or so before this thing blew up. He and Helen and the baby; first time Helen had ever been over here. I had bawled him out (but it's the same as I quarrel with you, you know, for fun) for coming over and not bringing Helen—'course she couldn't, he just rode that horse. I don't know how they got over here. But I was tickled to see Helen, and she was nice enough. It couldn't have been more than a month before this a . . . well, my next-door neighbor, Mrs B____ told me, when I got up in the morning, "You know about Ulysses S. Grant?" And Joe, her husband, went over before the peace officers had removed the bodies. He saw the bodies.

DICK: So what do the local people think? Do they think he did it? Is there any other information?

McFALL: I don't know, I don't know, Dick. Most of the quote hippies endquote I've talked to seem to infer that Ulysses is guilty. But I don't know what the general reaction is, among the bourgeois. I don't have much to do with 'em. I would never know what their opinions are.

CONSUELO: He did have a station wagon available to him, though?

McFALL: Apparently. I don't know. I never knew about it.

DICK: He disclaimed the use of automobiles. . . .

McFALL: Well, so much of his strange views were poses. He wasn't a damn fool. I know he borrowed a pickup one time. He sort of let down his hair when he came over here and drank coffee with me. He told me one time how he picked up three of those fringe hippies who were living in the commune with him, and he'd been to the store to get feed for the horses or chickens or whatever. They were going to the same place he was, to the commune—they call it the Lower Farm. The Sun Farm is up this way. And he has five or six hundred-pound sacks of feed, and these three fellows got a ride. He took them right down to the commune. When they got there, these three fellows got out and started up to the quarters. And Ulysses says, "Aren't you going to help me unload?" And the fellows each said, "No, I'm tired." The three of them. Ulysses says, "Well, you're going to be a damn sight tireder if you don't help me, because I'm going to whip hell out of you, all three of you." And he was just positive enough, mad enough, that he bullied them. Well, they should have helped him if he gave them a ride. Sure enough they gave him a hand. They weren't going to tangle with him.

This again is hearsay, but you can check it around. A few days ago, a week or so ago, maybe two weeks, a radio or TV commentator of local repute made the comment that within a few days some startling results were going to be disclosed in the Ulysses S. Grant case. That was after I had made up my mind all wasn't as it appeared to be. Now I don't know what happened any more than I know what happened with the assassination of John Kennedy. You see, I was unfortunate I had a TV at the time and I saw the assassination, whatever of it was shown on TV. Immediately then I said, "There's a whole lot more behind this than whatever reaches the newspapers." And when I heard this about Ulysses, from what I knew about the man and what I could size up of the situation, I was unsatisfied. I don't know what lies behind it, but I know it's not as reported in the newspapers.

End of interview. Shut it off and play it back.

HIPPIES AND HASSLES IN THE TAOS AREA

Although they do so for different reasons, many people from both the straight and hip worlds descend on the Taos area each year. When Consuelo and I were there in 1970, we found the area swarming with hip people. Some of them were seeking out or setting up communes; many of the others, in pairs and small groups, were simply building homes for themselves wherever they could.

Most of these people were too poor to afford good dope (marijuana, as well as acid and other psychedelics) and too wise to get into speed and the amphetamine brain-cell destroyers. But such distinctions were lost on the arbiters of morality and upholders of law among the citizenry. Consequently, it didn't take too many young hoods, alias transient hippies, alias teenyboppers, alias kick-kids (never the permanent residents) who were intent upon wrecking their minds and bodies in order to give all hip people a bad name. But then, dumb brute prejudice and repressed hostility never look beyond the hazy image of casual clothes, long hair, and whiskers (although, in truth, perception is no greater when these same qualities are housed in hip heads peering in the direction of the Establishment).

FIVE STAR, R.I.P.

One of the casualties of the Taos hippie-hassles was a nearby commune called Five Star. Situated in a resort town known for its hot springs, Five Star had consisted principally of a large building in which all the residents lived, a parking lot, and some hot springs. When hippies (from the outside, not the commune) began flooding into the town, the local authorities got very upset. After all, the hippies didn't have much if any money to spend and their presence scared off all the well-heeled citizens of America who were willing to pay well for their vacations amid the town's hot springs. So the authorities decided to harass the commune, and they continued to do so until they had forced it to close — which happened shortly before we arrived in the area.

Meanwhile, not to be outdone in such matters concerning the public welfare, the authorities in nearby Taos called off that town's annual fiesta (an important source of income for local Indians and chicano people) on the pretext that there would be too many hippies in the area and that such a gathering would constitute a health hazard. As a result, greater hostility was generated toward the newly arrived hippies.

MORNING STAR EAST

Among the still-existing communes in the Taos area is Morning Star East, which was founded by refugees from Lou Gottlieb's Morning Star Ranch in California. When started in April 1969, the 35-acre property had about 35 residents. Since then, however, the commune's population has varied considerably, because it is based on the same open-land principle as Morning Star Ranch—that is, no one is denied access to the commune's land.*

The residents at Morning Star East have been active in constructing a number of adobe houses and a communal kitchen. In fact, when much of the construction was being carried out, they were making close to 2,000 adobe bricks per month! However, because anyone can come and build a home at Morning Star East, the commune is, of necessity, loosely organized. This has resulted in some unfortunate occurrences. For example, when we were in the area in 1970, we heard that the community was attracting a lot of people who were interested only in getting high—mainly on cheap wine and amphetamines. But we also got another report that was more positive and optimistic: a great celebration was being planned in which the residents would be getting together with the Indian members of the Native American Church for a peyote ceremony.

NEW BUFFALO

We wanted to visit New Buffalo because it seemed to be the oldest and most developed of the hip communes in the Taos area. The sign near the gate indicated that visitors were not welcome, but we decided to go in anyhow.

We parked alongside several other vehicles in back of a

*For an explanation of open land see the account of Morning Star Ranch, this Chapter.

long, low adobe building. This was a motel-like structure, with several private rooms connected to a large kitchen area and a high, oval living-recreation hall. Behind and nearly adjacent to this structure were two other motel-style adobe buildings. And farther back and off to one side was a community garage, with open car stalls in the front. We could see a mechanic busy cleaning and repairing some parts for a disabled truck. There were two tepees and a hogan or two situated a short distance from the main complex and two or three storage sheds somewhat nearer to it.

New Buffalo, we were told, had recently decided to reduce its population from 50 to 25. True, its population could drop as low as 10, as it had the previous winter, but the number quickly increased with warmer weather, reaching the intolerable level of 50. So it was determined that 25 was the maximum number of people that the land and buildings could support with comfort and good sense. Consequently, the 25 most recent members had been asked to leave by the older ones, for as in most communes, length of residence and age meant authority.

While at New Buffalo, we talked mostly with Bill, a serious-minded resident in his mid-30s. He was the one who seemed to hold most sway in the group. Bill was extremely critical of the transient hippies who were coming into the area and causing trouble for everyone, especially for anyone who stayed year-round.

Bill said that he and his wife and two kids were not going to stay. They had been there for several years and he now felt it was time to leave in search of a better environment in which to raise his kids. He was tired of all the hassles. He had, along with others, only recently learned to say "no." The open-armed philosophy of love that welcomed one and all had been beaten and flogged by every insensitive spoiled kid in the country. So it was now time to discriminate: time to take stock of ideals and decide how to live with the awareness that people are less than ideal; time to realize that love has two sides, positive and negative; and time to realize the ability to say, "no, I do not want to help you, I do not want to relate to you," which can be more loving and honest than saying "yes," and not really meaning it.

A list of projects that had to be accomplished was posted on a door in the kitchen. Most of this work related to farming, for New Buffalo was an agricultural commune. However, as Bill said, "This is awfully difficult land to grow crops on. People come here thinking it'll be so easy. It isn't. Then they leave, oftentimes taking much more than they give. Those who remain are the ones who get hurt. Now we have a rule that visitors can stay one night only."

"The sign by the road asked visitors to stay away altogether, didn't it?" I asked.

"Yes, but who pays any attention to signs? Did you?" he retorted. "You see, people will come anyway if they want to. There is no way to stop them. We appreciated receiving your letter but we never answer our mail. If you want to come, you will, whether we invite you or not."

"Well, you can lock your gate and put up a sign: 'Trespassers will be shot.' And you can write back to inquiries saying, 'Take this paper and shove it up your asshole.' Or you can set up your own tourist bureau and charge admission for a guided excursion of a *genuine* hippie commune. Or—"

"—Yeah, but we don't want to do that sort of thing."

"Perhaps the overnight rule will be adequate for you?"

"I don't know. I'm planning to leave this place in any event.

I felt pained that another idealistic youth had apparently blossomed into manhood at the cost of his ideals. These ideals are not so bad. Great religious leaders from Buddha to Jesus to those of the present time, have preached them, and organized religions continue to pay hypocritical lip service to them.

It is always the problem of how to change an ideal into reality that gets in the way of both the leaders and the people. A thought is not a deed and never will be.

We are not magic men. We cannot imagine something into existence—especially a change of behavior. Just as we have been conditioned to be what we are now—greedy, competitive, stingy, mean—so we need to learn to love, to learn to be free.

Freedom is a difficult thing to handle. How many people given the complete freedom to do whatever they like would die of boredom? No structure, no rules, no compulsion to work from nine to five, no one telling us when to do this, do that—it sounds great until we try it. We've learned to be directed by so many others—by mommy, daddy, teacher, principal, boss, policeman, politician, bureaucrat, etc.—that freedom from all this could be overwhelming. Imagine: balling, eating, sleeping, playing . . . and . . . ho, hum, now what? Where do you go and what do you do when the trip ends?

Give people freedom and they'll do all the things they thought they never had a chance to do. But that won't take very long. And after that? After that, my friend, it'll be time to make your life meaningful.

Can you do it if you're free? Can you do it if others no longer require you to do what they say is best? Authority is only necessary for those who need it. Most of us need it because we've been taught to believe that we have to be concerned about others. For instance: "You're selfish if you think of yourself," or even: "Ask not what your country can do for you, ask what you can do for your country."

Sorry friends, but that's all Christian, authoritarian, manipulative bullshit. You've got to get in touch with what your real needs are before you can begin to be of any value to others. The other-directedness of Americans that is promoted by mom, God, and the flag has pushed us to the precipice of Fascism in this country. We are no longer able to think for ourselves, we think for the "good" of others. "Who am I?" "What do I really want out of life?" These are considered selfish questions. So a whole society goes down the drain. So it is with communes, whose members are too eager to help their curious "brothers," who find it remarkably easy to create all kinds of physical and figurative mess and then leave it for the members to clean up.

Challenges to this traditional, other-directed, do-gooder mystique are met with admonitions and scoldings: "Why are you so selfish? All the time thinking only about yourself? Don't you have any regard for the rights of others?" (The intent and frequent effect of such a question is to make one feel guilty and consequently willing to conform to the "altruistic" wishes of others.) And because we have become so confused about what is really important to us as individuals, we believe these admonitions—and with good reason. Our demands are indeed "selfish." As we are no longer capable of knowing who we really are, we are compelled and desire to be like someone (everyone) else. We feel we must have money, a new car, power, position prestige, and an all too material sense of personal worth.

Consuelo and I gave one of the New Buffalo members a ride to a nearby general store. He had saved a little money and was going to buy some chocolate candy. He told us he was lucky to have been able to stay on at New Buffalo. Before they had taken him in that spring, he and his buddy had bummed around the area and lived at Morning Star East awhile. They got drunk all the time, shot speed, and went to town to have fun. Now he was off all that bad stuff. New Buffalo was home. He beamed and all 18 years of his life lit up. As he got out of the car he said, "I'm taking a lot of acid these days. It's a much better high and no hangover. Bye."

MAX FINSTEIN AND NEW BUFFALO

Edmund Helminski's conversation with Max Finstein, in the summer of 1968, provided me with more information about New Buffalo and also with Max's own views about this particular commune and communes in general. He spoke with knowledge and candor, which may or may not be attributable to the fact that he was New Buffalo's founder and is now one of its ex-members. If the following excerpt from that conversation seems somewhat one-sided, it is simply that Edmund didn't bother about the questions, pauses, interruptions, etc. This is what Max said:

"I left The Buffalo [New Buffalo] several months ago and I guess I have my own opinions. But I'll talk.

"The walls were left after the lodge fire, but they've been tearing them down to make way for whatever it is they're planning to build. Before, there was one 40-foot wing, the foundation of which you can still see, and then there was a big circle. Now, that big circle was two stories. It was a sleeping loft, just magnificent, and then another wing coming out on the other side. The original plan was to start that way and then off of that we could go, extending it and so forth. But the reason they've been tearing down the walls is that, I understand, they're going to put a lower ceiling in and then cut it up into individual areas.

"I don't know much about the rest of their plans, but I'm sure they'll be growing crops. The garden is coming along well this year, but this is the first year that they've been able to grow crops. Last year we got the land too late to plant much more than a small vegetable garden. It looks pretty good, but they're going to have to do a lot of work—people to weed and all. You can't just put seeds in the ground when you're farming organically.

"I had thought that, as long as we did what we set out to do, somehow the place would take care of itself, which is what the name is about. The Buffalo is the provider, as he was for the Indians. But right now they're pretty broke.

"Of course, this idea of being self-sufficient is — well, if you're burning wood and building with some wood, even though we got all our wood from the mountains — well then you have to use some kind of vehicle to bring the wood down and then you're hung on a gasoline economy. You've got to go 40 or 50 miles to get gas. You can't just carry it on your back. To say we're going to be self-sufficient is pretty difficult, unless you really just get a horse and a wagon. Throw the tractor away and use horses, but that requires a whole adjustment in your thinking. I especially don't know how you do it in the face of this landscape. It demands so much of you. It's very hard country. I imagine if you told that to an Indian he would probably laugh. It's just a matter, you see, of how ascetic you want to be. And are you capable of it? If you're going to carry all your wood by horse and wagon, it means you've got to go away for a few days. Now they're into using the tractor as a means of income since there's no money. They barter with people for the use of the tractor. They might plow someone's field in return for a certain percentage of the crop.

"It's hard to get a man to go out and grow a field of corn or something, which he knows is just barely enough to keep him alive, when he can go to the Safeway. I mean, why go hunt a bear, take chances with your life, when you can just go to the Safeway and get some hamburgers? It's not as good, but . . . the human animal is prone to temptation. It takes a very, very strong bunch of people to turn away from temptation. And at a place like The Buffalo you have to work things out in terms of: do enough people agree to do this? For instance, there was a lot of discussion at first about the tractor; shall we just start right out with a horse? And then it seemed best that since nobody really knew anything about farming that maybe we ought to just start with a tractor. No matter how strong you are, when you think back to those pioneers going out and cutting down trees and cutting boards out of trees with just an axe and maybe a saw — they just don't make them like that anymore. Men just aren't up to that kind of thing.

* * *

Max Finstein

"We tried to avoid meetings, discussions — the so-called democratic process. We tried to avoid that because words can be a big hang-up. And if you say, 'Let's have a meeting every Wednesday night to thrash out our problems,' then you get a bunch of people who walk around all week and say, 'What will I talk about at the meeting, what don't I like, what would I . . . ? — You know, so what we did was that anything that came up we tried to talk about it during the weekdays. And it worked. You found out that if you talked about it enough while you were standing around making mud together that you corrected the situation without it ever coming to a vote. Then when it got to a point where it looked like a decision couldn't be made that way — that some people just didn't want to hear that or were grumbling or whatever — then we would have a meeting. But that was very rare.

"When we first started it all it was with a particular group. Out of that original group of twenty-four there are only four or five who are still at The Buffalo. Well, we started talking together before we ever had the land, just trying to see what we had in our heads, seeing what we wanted to do, who was really committed. Then we ended up with a bunch of people who seemed to be pretty much together.

"After we started we decided that for a year nobody could come in until we got those crops up and we saw how many people we could support, and if it seemed we had enough. That's the way we felt for about a week. And then somebody would show up who was very groovy, and then the first thing you know somebody would be saying, 'Oh man, like you know, it'd be great, let them stay.'

"One of the reasons The Buffalo didn't make it for me—and this is as simply as I could put it—is that it didn't sustain its original premise. Somehow people weren't big enough to do what they said they were going to do. Of course everybody had a different idea, but I thought everybody was pretty straight on what it was supposed to be. For me it represented an alternative to the aggressive society that surrounds you.

"If everybody insisted that they would live a good way (however that was defined by the group in terms of how they were to each other) and if they worked hard enough so that they produced an economy pretty damn close to self-sustaining—which is, you know, unless you're really going to be an ascetic, impossible today—then at least it would be a start at getting close to that. Then somehow your living this way would show the rest of the world and the rest of the country that there is an alternative, that you *don't* have to go out and cheat each other and rob each other. It would show them that you can work together and love each other.

"I believe that working together is the way. Trying to think up love doesn't work. Love is a very physical thing, it's not a head thing. It comes out of any kind of discipline you can find to make it become real. And by spending 8 or 10 or 12 hours a day working with a bunch of people you can really get something. Even that kind of love which includes fighting amongst the kin.

"I think that a strict work discipline is very necessary, but you have to find a way to make it human, to allow for 20th-century people—there has to be some way to temper that old work discipline with humanity. If it were possible to just let people walk around, say *if it were possible*, then that's the ideal. If somebody can't make it today, then they can't make it today and you can't say 'Why?' unless it becomes flagrant; when it's so obvious, then it's a lack of communal understanding or something. If anybody doesn't work, then the community is as much at fault for not giving them what they want. And then it's for everyone to straighten their heads about whether they want to be there or not. If not, get out.

"You see, what I think is the difficulty in a contemporary communal scene is that all the communities that have existed before were created because of an intense need on the part of the people involved, you know, out of necessity. And now we have a huge body of people who really don't have to put up with much and whose background tells them, 'Well, if it gets hard, just go somewhere else.' With the extreme mobility that people have today, where most people that are poor are poor out of *choice* (I mean that most of the people involved in this thing are from the middle class), they don't have any background of intense want or deprivation.

* * *

"The outside people, the Mexicans and Indians, saw a lot of internal strife or whatever you want to call it, at The Buffalo. This changed their whole idea about what the people were. Obviously when it started, there was a lot of prejudice. Without anybody knowing anybody that was involved, people would say, 'Well, they're hippies,' and so forth. The insistence on work changed that a great deal. The fact is we made 10,000 bricks last summer and put that whole house up; we didn't even start until July, when we got the land; then we often worked 14 hours a day and, I mean, there were no five-day weeks — we just worked until everybody had to stop, and that gained a tremendous amount of respect.

"But what turned the people off is when the winter boredom set in and all the internal problems started. It's very natural for people to ignore their own hang-ups and say, 'Look at those people!' They may be doing the same damn thing in their own houses, but if you do it, then you're singled out as weak. Half the people said, 'Well, they're not what they said they were, they're just like us.' If you do something like that you've got to be better than everybody, you have to be stronger if you're going to set yourself up as the alternative. You're

196

doing it right in the midst of a bunch of people who know what it is. They know what strength is and they know what community is without ever having lived in something that called itself a community. You go around here and you see those little complexes with four or five little houses. Well, those people have been living there for generations, man, and that's a community. They have never called it that, but in the true sense of the word they're people who are willing to help each other and work together.

"Unfortunately, history, at least on this continent, says all the communities have eventually failed, either by melting back into the culture, like Oneida making silverware and Amana making refrigerators, or by simply falling apart. Those two, they were celibate communities, very religious. The Pueblo Indians here, have endured, but they have a lot of trouble—like gossip and there's a lot of backbiting, people putting each other down. But I guess what's important is that everybody realizes that no matter what happens it's still their home. And those people at that Pueblo stay there because they have to. They probably didn't want to, all these hundreds of years, they probably wanted to split. But there was nothing out there. If there's nowhere to go, you stick with it until you find out you can hate your brother—and that's different from hating someone you don't know. Or you can disagree with your brother; you can fight like hell with him but he's still your brother and that's what tribal life is. No matter how much of a son-of-a-bitch your tribal brother is, he's still your tribal brother and he takes precedence over anyone who's not in the tribe. Now this comes out of that thing that "the tribe's going to succeed,"—that it exists and will continue to exist. When you come up against the rest of the world you're this. So I really think that a communal situation will not really exist until there is a situation of necessity. Of course, in this country, we're probably approaching that situation already."

THE HOG FARM

Yet another commune in the Taos area is the Hog Farm which gained national publicity in 1969 when members appeared at the Woodstock music festival in New York and ended up distributing free food to and caring for the hundreds of young people freaked out on impure drugs.

Driving in the Taos area is not particularly difficult, but unfortunately our directions on how to get to the Hog Farm were rather sketchy. We ended up atop a hill, driving along a road in which the rocks and ruts got increasingly larger until finally we lost the muffler. After finding the way back to the main highway, I drove to a garage. While waiting for the car to be repaired, Consuelo and I contented ourselves with reading about the Hog Farmers in the latest issue of *The Fountain of Light*, at that time the local hip newspaper, but now defunct.

We never did get to Hog Farm, but here's part of what that article said:

"The Hog Farm is about 75 people living on 14 acres of land in New Mexico, all taking care of each other and this one hog and her friend."

I started laughing. "All those people taking care of just one hog?"

"And each other. And 15 chickens that lay 10 eggs a day on methadrine."

"Hmmm. . . . Now let me see if I've got this straight: 75 people living on 14 acres of land, all taking care of one hog and 15 chickens laying 10 eggs a day, and each other?"

From Woodstock the Hog Farm was hired to police a pop festival in Dallas. Again, they set up a free kitchen, first-aid and freak-out tents, ran a light show on the free stage, and gave both physical and spiritual nourishment to anyone who needed it.

From Dallas the Hog Farmers went home to New Mexico, only to find the house full of strangers—some stranger than others. On waves of publicity, seekers from all over the country who had been turned on by the Hog Farm had washed up on the property and pitched their pup tents. When the dinner gong rang, long lines of people

198

stood outside the kitchen with their plates and tin cups, waiting to be fed. Often there wasn't enough to go around.

Overcrowding almost inevitably tends to uptightness. *The Daily Hogtopus*, the Hog Farm paper, ran the following item about a meeting held near the Sea of Krasnakovitch (a small pond):

It was one of those occasions on which everybody got a chance to speak out. It seems that the "family" is split into two different camps, overlapping in various ways. One side, generalizing, feels that the greatest favor we can do for newcomers is to tell them, although nicely, to split. The other side, again generalizing, feels that whoever comes up the hill is here for a reason and becomes family in such a sense that whether he stays here or not, we should be able to enjoy his presence and either help him on to do his own scene, or to become a Hog Farmer. It all sounded sort of confusing, but somehow a greater feeling of benevolence prevailed.

Meanwhile, Hugh Romney—then the Hog Farm's spiritual leader and spokesman—had gone on to California to set things up for a seven-day Starve-In, which was supposed to happen on October 11. With the members' double consent, Romney committed them to be there. But the caravan buses were delayed day after day at the farm by mechanical difficulties and sluggish cosmic machinery. By the night the buses were finally ready to roll, the Starve-In had already begun. Snow in Nevada and bus breakdowns en route made certain that they reached California too late.

Romney was upset. His work had been violated. So, he chose to sever all visible connections with the Hog Farm, even to the point of changing his name. He now wanted to get together a few people, about 20, who could be responsible for their commitments, and a fast bus that could speed to wherever it was needed.

Some members drifted back to the farm in New Mexico, some stayed on in California. Others joined Hugh Romney on his super bus and went on to other things.

Meanwhile, back at the farm, a handful of people decided to stick out the winter, put up an A-frame, and try to make the farm into a real home so that the rest of the family would have something nice to return to. Now, instead of handing out insufficient food to long lines of people waiting outside for dinner, the family could sit down together at three long polished tables, holding hands for a few moments in silence, and dining by candlelight.

Conditions gradually improved during that winter — the winter of 1969-1970. Alberto organized the back room of the information house into an arts and crafts workshop, where he began turning out some very attractive jewelry. Mark Twain got into building adobe ovens. A well was dug on the property, but there still wasn't any indoor plumbing. Meals were cooked over, and houses heated by, wood stove. The farm's animal population totaled three chickens, five rabbits, some cats and kittens, four goats, too many dogs and dear old Pigasus. And, during that winter, the members nurtured their plans for planting a vegetable garden in the spring.

There were now two adobes and a cabin, which together were capable of housing a maximum of about 26 people. The Hog Farm population was down to about 20 people ("no men, no women — all children"), and they kind of hoped to keep it that way. Subsequently, a three-day visiting limit was posted.

Lately the "children" have been out doing odd jobs around the neighborhood, pulling stumps and transplanting trees in order to earn enough money to make the farm's land payment every month. Some well-meaning idiots bought the farm a flatbed truck and half a backhoe, hoping that these would make the farm self-sufficient. The flatbed is presently out of action because it will cost $91 to register. The backhoe keeps breaking down and can't even finish paying for itself, much less anything else. But somehow, with faith in the cosmos, themselves, and each other, the members keep on trucking. They made a deal with a neighbor who fixed the backhoe the first time; in return, the "children" dug him a hole for a septic tank. Hog Farmers would really rather trade services than deal in cash.

DROP CITY

The note we received read: "At your convenience take Interstate Highway 25 into Colorado . . . [turn] 'til Drop City drops on you—Jack."

Because other communes we had visited had been so difficult to reach, it was a relief to have good directions and a paved road all the way to Drop City. Drop City dropped on us like a flash. One moment we were on a pleasant drive on a semi-rural paved highway; the next moment we had a full view of several colorful geodesic domes on a hillside.

I loved Drop City immediately: no hassle finding it; it was compact—all the buildings in a small, neatly arranged complex, and those domes—beautiful domes are somehow much more lovely than the loveliest of suburban mansions. The domes, each accommodating from five to ten members, were usually two stories inside. One double-dome contained an office, library, workshop, living room, and kitchen, along with some second-floor living quarters. A large dome in need of repair was to be renovated for use as a recreation-workshop center. Another dome, about the same size, was partially completed and was intended to be used as a crash pad for the expected hordes of summer visitors.

We arrived at Drop City on a Monday in April 1971 — a day that was promisingly clear and bright. The current residents were extremely open and friendly. Here was a commune entirely different from The Impossible Family in Taos,* yet the people had the same youth and vibrancy; we felt the same comfort and at-homeness with them.

None of the people at Drop City had been there more than nine months. At the end of the previous summer, 1969, things had become so chaotic that everyone had left. And two of the domes had been damaged as a result of accidental fires set by careless residents.

HOW THE COMMUNE GREW

Drop City was one of the first rural commune efforts. It was the first to construct geodesic domes as living quarters and was a recipient of the Buckminister Fuller Award. It had water and electricity and something more — solar energy was used to heat one of the domes used as living quarters.

When I was publishing *The Modern Utopian* magazine from Boston in 1966, I received mimeographed newsletters and flyers from a new community called Drop City. They advertised themselves as a community of artists who were innovating not only in the area of buildings and life-style, but also in a multi-media approach to art.

The Drop City people were the avant-garde of American society and they invited everyone to come visit. They even pulled off a big art festival, which attracted young

*See Chapter VI for a discussion of The Family.

hip types from all over the country. This open-door policy resulted in an inundation by hordes of teen-age runaways, thrill seekers, sightseers, and miscellaneous dropouts — mostly of the irresponsible variety.

At first the permanent residents accepted this invasion as part of their mission to help others get their heads together and move on to creating their own alternative life styles. After awhile they got fed up and threatened to burn the place down. Such threats did not, of course, discourage visitors. Several of the Drop City leaders decided to move to a mountain several miles away. There they formed a new community, Liberty.

Drop City continued to be a place for every transient commune-seeker to crash. But in the fall of 1969 conditions got so bad that even the crashers couldn't stand it (no food, no maintenance, plenty of hostility). So everyone pulled out.

LIVING AT DROP CITY

That same fall, though, two couples came and stayed the winter. Then others began to trickle in. Drop City was coming to life again.

By the time of our visit the following spring there were between 15 and 20 residents. We talked casually with most of them. They were all bright, enthusiastic, and optimistic about the future. None of them were temperamentally or philosophically inclined to settle in and make Drop City their home forever and ever. What was important was that it was their home *now*.

In contrast to the other communes of this nature, Drop City was on surprisingly good terms with its neighbors and the townspeople. The hostility which we had experienced in Taos, New Mexico, for example, was absent when we stopped to check out our traveling directions with a local shopkeeper in Trinidad, Colorado.

204

While we were visiting Drop City, a neighbor dropped by with a pickup truck loaded with goats. He wanted to know if they wished to sell their goats. "No, man, we like our goats. We need our goats."

"Like to buy some goats then?" the man inquired.

"Sure, if you'll take beads and pipes in exchange. We don't have money."

"No thanks," came the reply.

The farmer was congenial but a little freaked out by the barrage of happy and joking comments he encountered. He was used to more serious negotiating, I'm sure. "Besides, one of our goats is going to have kids pretty soon," one member told me. "We don't need any more. Grass we could use anytime; goats, no."

There seemed to be an abhorrence of normal currency transactions. We tried to buy a gorgeous pipe made from a deer's antler. As a cash purchase it was a tiring effort to settle on a fair price, whereas we would have had no problem obtaining it in exchange for a lid of marijuana. In fact, this one encounter was the only negative aspect of our visit to Drop City. We were too anxious to be fair and to encourage the sale of their handmade products. The major creative effort of these people was to make beautifully unique pipes, pottery, and beads.

Still, they needed cash to pay utilities and taxes ($40 per year) on the property. Somehow, in the most unstructured way possible, this money became available when needed.

The terrain of the commune was dry and rocky. Good enough for goats, perhaps, but not for crops. The members had a small garden but it was not productive and no one thought of it as much of a resource. Food stamps were better.

When we finally got the pipe, we lost some of the positive feelings of our earlier encounters. We left too hurriedly and with regret that our business dealings had interfered with the casual friendliness of the commune.

CONVERSATION WITH JACK

Jack's dome looked like a small red igloo, but he was not inside on so sunny a day as this. Seated, totally nude, at one end of a large rectangular space dug in the ground, he was playing a guitar. His girl friend, with nursing child, sat nearby. Consuelo and I sat quietly beside them. Jack began to sing a song about getting back to essentials almost as though in a trance. When the song was done he put the guitar aside, looked us in the eye, and said with a smile, "Hi."

The mood of our conversation was meditative. Jack was no speed freak—he was unhurried and deliberate in his speech. He espoused a philosophy that I did not grasp entirely. It was probably for that reason that I felt him to be far too abstract and idealistic. Yet, he, more than any one else we had encountered on our trip to the Southwest, was deeply involved in a journey toward self-enlightenment. He spoke of energy levels and of man's relationship to the earth in its mystical sense. As he spoke, his finger-tips touched the dry earth over and over, and I felt that somehow he was more at one with that earth than most of us: whatever he sensed in it, the earth simply felt like chalk to my fingertips. In this atmosphere I felt unable to ask the mundane questions I had about Drop City. How are decisions reached? How will you deal with the on-slaught of visitors this summer? Do you eat communally?

THE ESSENCE IS CHANGE

I did find the answers, but Drop City had been through many changes in its four-year history. It was still changing and would continue to change, so for each answer to a question, there is another question — and another answer, and so forth. They took their meals together in the giant double-dome today. But tomorrow? Decisions in a group of this size were by consensus, but what will happen when more people arrive? Income comes mainly from food stamps, outside help, and barter of commune-made products (whatever the maker of a product receives in ex-change for it he shares with the rest of the commune). But how long will these simple economics last; how will they change? The answers are not structured. Similarly, interpersonal relations are unstructured and therefore largely conventional. Couples with children live separate from singles. Males outnumber females two to one.

The essence of Drop City is change. In this respect it is a microcosm of American society, which has moved into an era of accelerated change — indeed so much so that America, perhaps more than any other country in the world, is sinking deeper and deeper into the quagmire of affluence.

Drop City pioneers who have left for the mountains are like race horses put out to pasture and retired from the race. But one must remember that there are at least two kinds of races — horse races and rat races. And it is here that mainstream America and Drop City differ. Main-stream life in America is a rat race because the majority are on a treadmill that leads at best to a piece of cheese that satisfies but only momentarily—then the race-cycle must be repeated. Drop City life, on the other hand, is a horse-race—a race in which there is an attempt to measure the quality of the experience as well. Any old piece of cheese will not do. The perfect cheese is sought after and only it will satisfy the participants' hunger perfectly.

Such analogies can be useful, but I think I could easily carry this one to utter confusion. So I'll stop. In any event, Drop City is appropriately named, for it remains a place for people who need to get out of the Establishment rat race and discover an alternative route. (They may discover that the alternatives are infinite.) Stimulated from their initial experience at Drop City, they may develop the courage to venture forth in a direction of their own.

LIBERTY

In the spring of 1968 I read the following news about Drop City in an underground paper:

At the entrance a large sign reads exactly like those outside the ramshackled Southwestern Indian Reservations: NO PHOTO-GRAPHS, VISITING HOURS WEEKENDS ONLY 8 AM to 8 PM.

"We'll let anyone come for awhile, but only those who contribute, can stay," stated a resident. "It has to be that way. We've learned the hard way, by letting too many come who could only take away."

"We're thinking of burning Drop City down," he continued. "We're going to move; start out new in Canada or Virginia or on a farm near here, but this time we'll keep it a secret."

And so they moved. Peter Rabbit and his friends moved out, not to Canada or Virginia, but to another location in Colorado. It was no secret. They wanted more isolation, perhaps even total isolation. They wanted to get away from the tourists, the crashers, the teenyboppers—all the people they had initially invited (wittingly and unwittingly)

to visit them at Drop City. So the members determined that if their new community was comparatively much less accessible, they would have far fewer visitors. But it didn't work out that way. They still had to confront their own inability to turn people away.

Liberty represents an alternative route for people intent upon getting out of the rat race. But it seems an unlikely one for young energetic idealists, for it is a sort of recluse for hip artists who wish to maximize their privacy but still retain neighbors who are like-minded and cooperative. These artists have attained a measure of success and recognition — one, for example, as a novelist and another as a painter having exhibited his works at a famous New York gallery.

Liberty, a nonprofit organization, actually began when four artists, together with their wives and children, bought 400 acres of land on a mountain far from the main highways of Colorado. Each family built its own unique geodesic dome and did so under an agreed-upon community rule that, for reasons of beauty and privacy, no dome could be within sight of any other dome.

A dirt road, several miles in length and itself on private property, leads to Liberty. Upon arrival, you follow a sign directing you to a parking lot, where only one log cabin is clearly visible. There are two huge gardens lying south and east of the parking area and woods stretching away behind the cabin.

When Consuelo and I arrived, two or three people were working in the fields while another person was trying to repair a tractor. Two campers as well as other vehicles were in the parking area. A lean, bedraggled Scandinavian-type female was hassling with two screaming kids. A bearded fellow in weather-worn overalls sat on a crate eating a sandwich. No one paid any attention to us.

We walked over to the log cabin and knocked on the door. "Come in." The voice came from the top of a staircase, which led directly from the entrance to the second floor. We were not invited up. We sat on chairs near the doorway at the foot of the stairs. To our left was a rustic kitchen with an old wood-burning stove; to the right was a partially elevated living room with fireplace, wood floor, rugs, and cushions.

The voice joined us and turned out to be that of a young girl in her mid-20s. "I don't usually answer the door, but I could see you coming from the window up here and thought you had a nice face," she said, gesturing toward Consuelo.

Most of the conversation revolved around the Liberty community's growing fear of people invading the place. The girl spoke at length: "We thought we could get away by coming up here, but people just kept following us. We've had at least half a dozen visitors this afternoon and it's only early spring and a weekday at that. What will it be like when summer arrives?

"Tell people not to come here. We're interested in maybe a few more people joining us but we're in no hurry.

"It's funny. We were here all winter and snowed in part of the time. Then, we wouldn't have minded visitors. Yes, my husband and I built this place last year. My husband had some help with the heavy work but otherwise we did it ourselves. Got moved in during the fall and kind of hibernated for the winter. I got a lot of reading done.

"We went to Denver to my parent's home once. They thought I was dirty and smelly so I took so many showers you wouldn't believe. I'd come out of the shower and my mother would say 'you still look dirty,' so I'd smile and say 'okay' and jump back in the shower. I loved it. Sure was good having hot and cold running water for a change. But I wouldn't go back to that way of life.

"Some of the places do have electricity here, but we don't. We don't have any money to spend on that kind of thing.

"The community meets about once a week to discuss issues and make decisions on things which affect us all. We don't take a vote or anything like that. We talk until we reach consensus. We'll have to have a meeting pretty soon about what to do about visitors."

She was a lot like her house: very pretty in her own way, charming—yet direct, bold, without decor, and (like the wood in her house) had an old-new or new-old quality. She seemed young in experience with this kind of life style, yet old with reflection on the life style from which she came. She seemed certain of what she could no longer be; uncertain about what to be now.

TALKING WITH PETER RABBIT

We decided to drop in on Peter Rabbit, the main force of Drop City in its early days and now sort of the spokesman at Liberty. Peter lived in a gigantic and elegant white dome—the most modern dome we had seen. When we arrived, he was sitting in the middle of a spacious room, with a typewriter on a tray in front of him and with lots of paper neatly stacked on the floor nearby. He seemed tired and as bedraggled as had the woman with the two whiny brats in the parking lot.

"We know you've had visitors all day so we'll only stay a few minutes," I said apologetically.

Peter also complained of the traffic at Liberty. We agreed that visiting communes and writing magazines about them wasn't really that great a thing to do. The Rabbit noted that we were using too much paper and destroying our forest lands: "It takes hundreds of acres of trees just to produce the Sunday edition of *The New York Times*. Who reads it? What difference does it make anyway?" He paused.

"I am writing a book about the history of Drop City," Peter continued. "I've made a commitment to do it, so I will."

"Yeah. Consuelo and I recently read a paper on how to practice sound ecology in our private lives. One of the points was that we all use much more paper than needed. It's hard to break old habits. We stopped at a drive-in restaurant yesterday and we were drinking out of paper cups before realizing what we had done. I guess it's hard only because we're too lazy and comfortable to make the effort required in order to change. It's much more convenient to forget."

Halfway through our conversation, Peter's wife entered and went directly to the kitchen to the left of us, an open and unpartitioned area. She began working on the evening meal. The level of tension in the room increased considerably.

Peter maintained a quiet friendly composure and talked of Drop City and why they had left it.

"It served a valuable function," he said, "but we got tired of doing the same thing over and over. A bunch of fucked-up kids would come through and we'd take care of them and get their heads straightened out and send them on their way. Then along would come another bunch and we'd have to go through the same procedure all over again!"

Wow—what a relevant ministry, I reflected.

Peter continued: "It gets tedious after awhile so that's why we moved here. We want to help our brothers and sisters get it together and that's why we hate to tell people they can't visit. We have to have our own privacy though and we certainly aren't interested in being home for every stray person that comes by."

"Perhaps you could have people visit only on Sundays like the Lama Foundation," I suggested.

"Yes, that's one possibility. We're going to meet about this soon. We don't like to turn people away but we've got to do something."*

"One thing I believe people have to learn is to say 'no,'" I continued. "Eric Berne has said that the three responses of a healthy personality are 'yes,' 'no,' and 'wow.' If we can't say 'no' as well as 'yes,' then there can't be anything to 'wow' about. Commune and hip types tend to have that problem—overly positive, idealistic. Let's face

---

*Liberty now has a "Sunday only" visiting policy (summer 1971).

it, there are some times when we have to say 'no' not only for our own good but for everyone else's as well."

"You can say that again," Peter's wife curtly joined in.

"What would a person have to do to join Liberty?" I asked.

"Rent a house in the valley for six months or so and get to know everyone who lives here pretty well. At the end of that time we'd take a vote. If he were approved then, he'd have to build his own place out of view of any other place and would become a full participating member."

Dr. Stanley Krippner of the Maimonides Medical Center in Brooklyn, New York, has written a paper* in which

*Published in *The Modern Utopian*, vol. 4, no. 2, spring 1970.

he describes the Liberty life style as the "incorporation of the paranormal into daily rituals." He writes:

Childbirth at Liberty is also ritualized, a local midwife and doctor come to the community. The entire group is present as the baby is delivered. Whenever possible, the delivery is accomplished outside — "under the sun and moon" — with the inhabitants chanting to welcome the infant into his new environment.

Peter Rabbit, our host, does all of the commune's hunting during deer season. According to Krippner:

When he discovers a number of deer, he reportedly talks with them, asking one of the deer to sacrifice himself, vowing that the energy gained from his flesh will be used for creative and constructive pursuits by Liberty. Without fail, according to the hunter, one deer will move away from the others and will remain still until he is shot.

I didn't get these stories confirmed or denied while there. But as Peter mentioned Krippner as a good friend, the accuracy of the report probably cannot be denied. Still, the people there did not seem to behave any differently from middle-class hip types you see in the city.

Peter said, "Up here we learn from the mountain. The mountain is our guru. Time is unimportant. A day, a month, a year passes like a moment in eternity."

Words, words, words. The tension of being unwelcome visitors and the brevity of our relationship impeded my ability to see these people as types who would stand under the moon and chant to the birth of a newborn babe or convince a deer by talking to it. They seemed far too "normal."

As we started to get up to leave Peter's home, I said, "I guess we'd better —"

" — yes," he interrupted, "why don't you go now. Perhaps someone else here who's had less company today might not mind your dropping in."

He remained friendly even as he hurried us to the door. I couldn't help feeling that it was okay for him to push a little. His wife, after all, was not happy with having visitors at that time, and he had to live with her after we were gone.

Despite Peter's passing remark, we didn't drop in at any other of the dome houses, though we walked by two which were so aesthetically pleasing, settled in a clearing surrounded by groves of tall trees, that we were tempted. Liberty was a beautiful place, like Lama, only more personal, less grandiose. Peter and the girl in the log cabin had been enjoyable to talk with, despite the tension of the visit.

TAKING OFF FROM LIBERTY

"Wow — what a bummer," I said as we drove away. "It's like going into people's private homes, not a community. I don't feel like doing that again. Just snooping around in other people's private belongings. Smelling people's clean and dirty underclothes. What a bummer! If I lived there I don't think I could be quite so friendly without getting an ulcer or two."

"They have the same kind of conflict we have, though," Consuelo said. "On the one hand, a desire to help others, to teach; on the other, a desire for privacy to get away from all that Christian do-gooder crap. You can see that in Peter especially, you know. He still wants to do what he did at Drop City, to help people find a home, but he wants to be free too."

"Well," I said, "they better get clear about how to do it. They can't blame people for wanting to visit them. And if they're unwilling to set up some sort of rules for visiting, then they have to accept the consequences."

"It makes me mad that they bitch and complain about our being there after we arrive. We sent a letter with a return stamped envelope. If they didn't want us to come

they could have written 'Please Don't Come' on the envelope and dropped it in the mailbox," Consuelo added.

"Or they could put up a series of increasingly hostile signs from the main highway up. There is several miles of road to their place. Like first: 'Liberty: Visitors Not Welcome,' and 'Turn Back—We Do Not Want Company,' 'Absolutely No Visitors Allowed: This Means You,' 'Trespassers Will Be Turned Away at Gunpoint,' and finally 'Turn Around! Trespassers Will Be Shot.' Maybe this is a little extreme but the point is they've got to take total responsibility for what happens to them. Of course, we've got to take total responsibility for ourselves. If we go there and are treated with hostility, we can't blame them either."

The responsibility is total for each person. There is no blame, only total responsibility. That's a hard concept to explain, to understand, and it's even more difficult to practice. But it's the only real way—everything else is phony, putting it "out there" on someone else rather than dealing with it oneself.

Down deep we all know everything. We just learn to block out this and that so we can go on doing what we want to do and relate to people the way we want to relate—regardless of the truth of the matter. We kid ourselves so we can be indulgent. In the long run only we all suffer. The cover-up, the blocking—the armor as the Reichians call it—is a part of the so-called civilized world in which we live. We couldn't function in this system without it.

Perhaps it's always necessary to block off some of our awareness in order to function at all. It is the emphasis on what is blocked off that determines the kind of society in which we live. Western society has made fantastic scientific and technological progress by virtue of its ability to block off the emotional and sensual nature of its inhabitants and to focus on their intellectual and logical faculties. It is in that scientific achievement that there resides the root causes for reaction today.

Technology has given the middle class people more leisure time. They are using that time in attempting to regain contact with the emotional-sensual self. But it is only a token attempt, represented by the touchy-feely (sensory awareness) groups and by the encounter groups. At best this attempt can only increase the level of frustration and cynicism because those who get turned-on by and in the group usually have to return to a dull daily routine. Most people are too comfortable to go through the changes, the pain, required to really get in touch with their bodies and to really integrate body and mind in the creation of soul. No drugs, no weekend and marathon groups, will accomplish this. It will take a lifetime of re-learning and/or unlearning. That requires us to drop out and create a totally new environment in which to grow. It also requires us to make sure that the environment does not become as stagnant as the one we came from.

Liberty may settle and stagnate because its residents are tired and unwilling to push, reluctant to innovate with their environment. They may not stagnate—though it's hard to be certain. For if they could build a Drop City and then leave to create a Liberty, then they may be able to create something new for themselves when Liberty has taught them all it can and when they have given it all they can. But they are older now; the older we get the more we tend to settle in, to accept the tried and true, not to venture forth any further. Youth has the enthusiasm and the health to risk the unknown.

I'm talking about myself, you know. Here I am, only 33, and I feel like an old man sometimes. I guess I'm more scared to risk than I used to be. More of a coward. And the less I risk, the less I feel like risking because I have less experience at it. I forget. Things which at one time were easy, get difficult without my even trying. We get old by doing less and less and less—until we work routinely every day and sit comfortably at home every night by the fire or the TV, until we retire and sit comfortably at home day and night, until we get weak and are confined to a bed or a wheelchair day and night . . . until we are dead.

It may be that I'm rationalizing my own tendency to be a speed freak, but action is life and inaction is death. All action requires risk; that which we are unfamiliar with seems more risky. If you can drive a car in heavy freeway traffic without being scared out of your wits, then you ought to be able to risk just about anything else, man!

It's hard to keep this in mind. We're such creatures of habit and comfort. Like lazy dogs and cats. We have to force change and discomfort in ourselves if we're to postpone death. The older we get the more effort is required.

Life has no meaning except to be lived. It is not lived from a rocking chair, in a 9-to-5 routine, by staring at color TV.

We need to push for that total awareness, that total responsibility, which we all have in us but which we've killed in order to make things "easier."

Consuelo and I drove on.

MAGIC FARM

Magic Farm is located in a valley of enchanted hippies —or perhaps I should say an enchanted valley of hippies or a valley of hippies enchanted. Anyway, all up and down Talma Road are the homes and communes of long-haired, dropped-out, ex-urban middle-class kids who are intent upon "doing their own thing" on the land, in the woods. Most of them return to the city or some other locale during those long, rainy winter months in Oregon, but settle back into the valley as soon as the sun begins to dry the rain-soaked soil. These people, along with a small but growing number living there year-round, may be considered *permanent* hippies, dedicated to the proposition that going back to the land will make them free — a dedication reinforced by experience.

220

The less dedicated ones — the more searching and confused types — come to the area in increasing numbers as the sun moves higher in the sky. By midsummer the lakes and ponds in the valley are surrounded by travelers from all over the country — hippie vacationers who revel in singing, shouting, splashing, swimming, living in tents and bedrolls, eating dried fruit and cereals and nuts, drinking water and wine, smoking weed, dropping whatever pills and powders become available as people wander in and out of each other's lives.

Although a few die-hard storekeepers try to shelter behind signs in their windows such as "We Do Not Solicit Hippie Patronage," most of the local business people are cordial and friendly. One good reason for this is that permanent hippie residents provide good business. As the summer wears on and the transient population floods in, middle-class American businessmen get anxious and impatient with their carefree and unconventional patrons.

For all the gamboling hippie sprites along the way, the road leading in to Magic Farm is physically unimpressive. However, the parking expanse nestled among a grove of trees provides the visitor with a clue to the hidden loveliness of the area. Farther on, in a clearing beyond the parking area, stands the main house, a log-cabin style frame structure that serves as kitchen, living room, and children's sleeping quarters. Two adjacent frame structures shaded by trees contain adult bedrooms, a workshop, and a kid's playroom.

Halfway between these structures and the parking area is the open-air communal out-house, a semicircular, five-holed structure, partially covered by plastic sheeting as protection from the rain.

On the other side of the clearing near the main house is a garden, which, when I first saw it, was being watered by a member of the commune. And in a field beyond the bushes and a stream lay two more irrigated and well-tended gardens.

Slightly to the rear of the buildings and on a slight rise squats a massive table with long benches — the place where the community eats its meals during good weather. And farther back amid a clump of trees and next to the winding stream is the commune's large sauna bath.

Beyond all of these structures are beautiful meadows with tall grass and a magical forest. A few cabins and a large A-frame house are hidden among the trees. Some members sleep in these. But during the summer, most people prefer to sleep outdoors.

When I was there in June the commune had between 15 and 20 permanent residents. But this figure was expected to change. By August, it would probably increase to 30 or more. And months from now, in those dark, rainy winter months it would probably drop to maybe 10, although the previous winter's residents had numbered only 7 or 8. But changes such as these are normal in a commune. They are part of the rhythm of community life.

Some of the members of Magic Farm were no strangers to me, for I had known them in Berkeley, California, before they had moved to Oregon to build this commune. I had gotten people together who were interested in forming communes. Magic Farm was one of the results.

Paul, Tom and Evelyn, Robert and John were the first to settle at Magic Farm. Their goal was to develop a self-sufficient agricultural commune in which all members shared equally and intimately.

Paul, a free-lance gardener, was now the aggressive force behind the group, although he had attended the Berkeley meetings only intermittently and had not been an early member. Back in those days, his broad smile and his enthusiasm had made him well-liked and sought after in the group. He had developed both farming and manual skills, which gave him confidence about living on the land. When the Magic Farm property was discovered, Paul was ready to leave the city. Although Paul and I got along well, there was hostility beneath the surface of our relationship. Both of us were aggressive and competitive. As we were both too cowardly to get it all out in the open, we continued with the hugs and the facade of friendliness until we got to the snide remarks and the oh-too-hardy backslaps.

REUNION WITH PAUL

When we met again at Magic Farm for the first time in two years, Paul and I managed to express some genuine friendliness. Our hair and beards were much longer. Paul said, "What are you doing here?"

"Oh, I just came by to visit for awhile," was my first reply.

"You still doing that magazine about communes?" he asked.

"Oh, yes," I smiled.

"When are you going to stop writing about communes and start living in one?" he retorted, with a nervous laugh only barely concealing his hostility.

"Maybe *never*," I replied angrily. And then I continued in a more objective and friendly manner in an effort to conceal my anger. "You see, I don't think people should join a commune until they get themselves together, decide what they really want out of life. At present I want to travel and explore alternative life styles, not just communal ones. I do believe that the communal pattern is the best one but it has an infinite variety of forms. Another viable alternative is just being a hermit. Probably we all need to go through several life styles in our lifetimes rather than be stuck with just one. What about you, Paul? I hear you've moved to Talsen?"

"Yes, Magic Farm has become too open for me. I'm still interested in an intimate family-style commune. Magic Farm is too loosely structured, too open-ended. With new people coming in all the time, it's too difficult to really get to know them. People need to spend more

223

time with each other to become an intimate family. It can't happen here. It's too open, not enough structure. This place is OK as a sort of halfway house. But if you're interested in a more intense communal life experience, you've got to get together with a fewer number of people and work through problems together to understand where each other is at. That's where we went wrong here. We *thought* we wanted the same things but we didn't have any experience living together and working problems out with each other."

Despite these negative comments, Paul expressed some sadness at leaving Magic Farm. He had not wanted to leave. "I've invested a lot of myself in this place," he noted. "I would have preferred to have remained."

"But —" I repeated several times, as he dug his hands back and forth in the soil, over and over again.

"But the people who are here like it the way it is," he said.

"Sometimes in the process, people find out that they don't want what they thought they wanted," I interjected.

"And that's all right too."

"Of course."

"So I hope to get together with some friends and maybe move to a 300-acre place north of here."

"You don't think Talsen could be the place?"

"No, Rob wants Talsen to be an 'Ecological Living Center,' which is, again, an open-ended situation — people coming and going."

"But he wants to live in a close-knit group marriage, doesn't he?"

"Yes."

"Aren't the two incompatible unless you first have the group family functioning and operating the center?"

"Yes, I think so," Paul replied. Apparently Rob did not. "Of course, Rob is the only one there who wants that. But my friend and I aren't into fighting over it so we'll probably leave soon."

A DIGRESSION ABOUT TALSEN

Talsen was a group-marriage community nearby. It too had been formed from the group in Berkeley. Against the better judgment of those closely connected with them in the group, three couples, one single guy, and seven children left the San Francisco Bay Area for Oregon. Others promised to follow, but never did, except to visit. The people in the group had very little exposure to each other but nonetheless decided to live communally, sharing everything in common, including each other's spouse. One couple never really got into the sexual sharing and each of the two other marriages was on extremely shaky grounds.

Previously, they had carried on a brutal suburban existence — pharmacist and housewife; college professor and housewife. The men frustrated and the women unfulfilled. The country, the land, intimate friendships — all these spelled liberation, freedom from the old unhappy pattern; they were desperate to start a newer and more fulfilling life style. That desperation led them to move too quickly. Too many years of wrong habits could not be resolved so easily. Instead, seven desperate adults clung together, each shaking from the weight of his own lack of clarity. It was inevitable that that tiny group would be blown to bits.

Rob was one of that group. His wife Connie was also very close to Jim and growing closer to Joe. Rob turned to Mary, Joe's wife, and she to him. They were all together for a time. Then Mary left Joe, returned to Berkeley, and then went on to get a college degree. Rob and Connie also were divorced. Connie and Joe bought a house some distance away from the community. The second winter, only Jim remained at Talsen. Slowly others came. Rob advertised his plans for a community at Talsen through a Free University class in Berkeley. And more people became involved in developing Talsen.

TOM AND EVELYN

In the beginning there had been only one couple at Magic Farm — Tom and Evelyn. They too had been in the original Berkeley group. Tom was a very calm, quiet guy. He always made me nervous, not only because he was so calm and I tended to be the opposite, but also because I felt it was a calmness always about ready to explode — so much held in, held back.

On the other hand, Evelyn was an aggressive and moody and very emotional girl. She was often bubbly and quite joyous. But at other times, she wandered around in tears and deep depression. Occasionally she could be a real bitch, someone to keep away from.

I don't know what really happened to Tom and Evelyn at Magic Farm, but they decided they couldn't hack it. So they moved to a neighboring town. Evelyn was pregnant. Tom cut his hair and got a job. They settled down into the domestic life.

Tom was at Magic Farm on the day I arrived. Evelyn was sick, he told me, to excuse the fact that he was alone. His eyes were filled with sadness. We talked briefly about the changes at Magic Farm. It had been a deeply disappointing experience for them. I wondered if they would ever again attempt an alternate communal experience. Tom's condition at that moment prevented me from asking that question.

NEW MEMBERS

Herb, who had found the commune only a few months ago, told me how a person got to become a member: "You come here; you make yourself at home; you gradually get to know the others. Anyone can ask anyone else to leave. Someone might ask you to leave. Someone else might ask you to stay. We have regular meetings to deal with problems."

The only hostile member I encountered while at Magic Farm was a guy with blank staring eyes who looked at me and exclaimed, "Oh no, another one! There are more new people around here." The second time I saw him I got the same blank stare and the same hostile vibes, "Oh no, another one. . . ." He was totally freaked. That time Jerry overheard and asked him to step into another room to talk for a second. The third time I saw the guy, I walked in a wide circle. I never did find out if Jerry's remarks did any good.

BIG ROBERT, LITTLE ROBERT, AND SUSAN

I was walking on a path near the upper meadow, heading for the A-frame in the forest, when I recognized little Robert, all of six-years-old, in the distance. "Hi," I hollered. "Remember me?" I ran up to him and, catching his look of recognition, held him up and swung him high in the air.

In the meadow little Robert and I saw what looked like a moving black log. Then all of a sudden it stood up. It was big Robert, the boy's father, who had been meditating there — sitting with his head bent down between his legs so that all we had seen was a big mass of hair that looked like a tree stump.

Of all the people in the Berkeley group, Robert and Little Robert were the two I had grown to love the most. The boy was his father's image. The man was quiet, kind, sincere, reliable, modest, and industrious. He was also, like the rest of us, overly idealistic and naive. His main problem was a lack of self-confidence in any area except his chosen work. He was a professional gardener and had had lots of experience farming on the East Coast. But he had had little experience with people.

He met Susan when she was 15 and he 26. For each of them it was a first love. She got pregnant and they got married. Soon after little Robert was born, big Robert's mother became very ill and Susan was left with the task of caring for both her mother-in-law and child. Making matters more burdensome, she became pregnant again. Robert worked long hours as a farm laborer in order to bring in enough money to support the family. After Robert's mother died, they returned to Oakland, California.

During those first four years of marriage, Susan's childish enthusiasm changed to resentment toward Robert. But perhaps, that was no more than a very natural reaction to having had to carry an unbearable responsibility — of being wife, mother, nurse, and mature woman at an age when she should have been going out on dates and to pajama parties.

Now, in the liberal Bay Area, with the two boys getting older and a father nearby who could baby-sit with them, Susan began to explore some avenues she had previously neglected. At the same time, Robert was weighed down by a heavy burden of good old Christian Guilt. (In a Christian society one does not have to be a Christian himself to learn to feel guilty for not being perfect.) Robert felt responsible for Susan's dissatisfaction and consequently allowed himself to suffer from enormous passivity and self-degradation.

The ideals of community and group marriage, sharing and returning to the land, appealed to them both. They were not happy leading isolated lives in the city, being without social contacts. So they advertised for others who might be interested in forming a group. As a result, they became faithful charter members of the group that I began in Berkeley — and that group eventually set them free. And freedom also freed Susan and Robert from each other. Susan is still roaming the countryside living out her missed teen-age years. Robert, however, has found a home at Magic Farm.

There in the upper meadow with his son, he seemed to have a greater confidence than before. He was more at

peace. Still, he had not changed so much, even though his hair and beard were now long whereas before he had had short hair and no beard (much to Susan's distress). The two boys were on the farm and loved it. They too were at home in the forest and meadows, instead of having to make do with a cramped backyard and the concrete city streets. But they too had not changed much. Little Robert was still quiet and passive, being unable to defend himself against the onslaught of a cruel and aggressive six-year-old girl in the commune. And young Woody, like his mother, was jolly and active and nervous.

Magic Farm, it seemed, is a beautiful place to call home, to relax in, to find peace in. But it did not seem to require growth and balance. But then, few places do, for change is difficult. We are creatures of habit; change requires breaking those habits; breaking hurts; we seek comfort, not pain. Yet, paradoxically, we seek balance and equilibrium, and to obtain and sustain these is not at all comfortable.

Still, for all my theorizing about comfort and growth, I knew from my brief renewed acquaintance with Robert that here at Magic Farm, an environment in which he was comfortable, he had gained a new self-confidence that could not help but be evident to those around him, thereby improving his social relationships and allowing others to see in him the kindness and beauty of his nature. How much dissatisfaction he now felt with his life at Magic Farm I could not observe, but I was sure it was much less than it had been in Berkeley.

SAME OLD JEAN

When I walked up to the main house, Jean was sitting in the open side window talking with another woman.

"Hi, remember me?" I asked.

"Who are you?" she replied. "I don't know you. Go away. I'm busy now talking," she smiled and turned back to the conversation.

"She knows me," I said to a young fellow who was coming out the door. "She knows me," I continued to explain as we walked up the path towards the garden. Had my appearance really changed that much in two years, I asked myself in bewilderment? I guess maybe it had. My hair and beard were no longer carefully trimmed and I wore dungarees instead of pressed slacks.

Dear, crazy Jean. I remembered that every time I had ever said hello to her she would break out in convulsive giggles, complete with half-closed eyes behind glasses and a wide smile. I had gotten to the point where I just wanted to give her a big smack across the face and tell her to snap out of it. But I never did.

Later that evening, when I saw her in the kitchen preparing dinner, she looked at me and said, "Are you Dick Fairfield? Are you Dick Fairfield? Well, I'll be darned." And she broke out in that convulsive laughter once again.

Resisting the reawakened urge to slap her, I just smiled and said, "Same old Jean, same old Jean."

Bob and Jean had been dropping out for years before Jean and her neurotic child came to Magic Farm. Bob and Jean were original members of a short-lived commune in Massachusetts in 1966 and moved to California in 1967. In Berkeley, Bob ran Free University classes, while trying to organize a community in his spare time. They both had joined the Wednesday Night Group, as my original group came to be called. And they too, like most of the other couples in the group, eventually split up.

Jean did not go to Magic Farm immediately after their breakup. She wanted to live alone for awhile and get herself together. Meanwhile, Bob began visiting communes in New Mexico. Later he returned to Berkeley and Jean moved to Magic Farm to become one of its most stable members. Bob was supposed to be arriving at Magic Farm the night I was there, but he never showed up. He visited often, though, I was told.

REUNION FOR THE WEDNESDAY NIGHT GROUP

It was a big day for meeting old friends of the Wednesday Night Group. Gary and Vickie, who lived nearby, came to visit the commune regularly. They had been traveling a great deal during the past year and had finally decided to live in that enchanted valley. Vickie was glad to see me. She and Gary had been fighting, I assumed, for her eyes were red and swollen. She explained that she was trying to adjust to living in the country. They didn't have many friends in the area. And as an artist, she disliked all the hippies around calling her work "groovy," which was what they called every piece of handmade craftwork. She yearned for more critical attention.

The last time I had seen her she had been dealing with

five kids and a part-time job while Gary went to cooking school. The five kids were those of Gary's former wife, Joan, also an alumna of the Wednesday Night Group. Joan, like most of the other wives, was out trying to regain something that had been lost in marriage. But Vickie got stuck with all the kids, and only part of the welfare check (Joan got the rest). I had told Vickie to stop being a sucker. And I guess she had, because she and Gary were here and Joan and the kids were back in the city.

Vickie told me that they lived communally for a time in the former home of Robert and Susan. The place became a crash pad, though, and they ended up throwing most of the people out, then leaving themselves.

I had always liked Gary, but that feeling had not always been reciprocated. When all the marriages in the Wednesday Night Group had been about to collapse, he believed that I was responsible so he had resented me. Now, though, I felt he liked me too and I was pleased.

Finally, I met John again. In Berkeley he and his wife Laurie had been dropouts—just two young kids. At that time she still had some neurotic dreams of being a movie star (despite no training or talent) and he was trying to grow a beard, which, to me, looked just like an ugly pointed patch of peach-fuzz scrabbling off his chin. Laurie was an extremely attractive girl, who made every effort to capitalize on her good looks. The time came when she and John split up, with Bud moving in to take John's place.

After that, John wandered around the area living in an old Volkswagen bus that he had bought and repaired for $50. I saw him from time to time, but never really enjoyed talking with him. He'd ramble on and on about this or that experience, which I didn't have the slightest interest in, and then I would have to make a dozen excuses in order to leave. Then he'd be hurt because I never stopped to "get to know him."

I never had the guts to tell anyone I didn't want to get

to know them. Instead, I was always in a hurry. And I wasn't lying. I made sure I was busy. I had a magazine to publish, mail to answer, full-time work in graduate school, a part-time job in a church, and domestic quarrels to contend with. And in addition to all this there was the Wednesday Night Group. I was in a hurry. Trouble is, I liked it that way — running so fast I missed a lot of the scenery. But I found out that eventually, if you aren't awfully careful and alert, the whole scene begins to blur and you keep running smack into walls. So if you don't want to knock out every tooth and both eyeballs, you just have to start slowing down.

John and I met that evening before I left the outdoor dinner table. His beard was really a beard now, and, what is more, he seemed more aware and mature. When he entered into the conversation during the evening meal, I no longer felt the strain of a high-school student making all-too-obvious statements; rather, here was a person who spoke briefly and to the point. John had become a man at Magic Farm.

Only members of the "family" could attend the meeting that evening, so all visitors were asked to stay out. It was getting late as they began to gather for the meeting in the main house and so I made my way past that marvelous outhouse to my car.

The Magic Farm commune may not be magical, but at least it has produced some positive changes in the lives of the people who moved there after those traumatic times in Berkeley. True, communal living is no utopia, but it seems to me that for these hardy souls at Magic Farm life was certainly much better than before. Can we expect more?

OLOMPALI RANCH

The only time I received promotional literature from a commune was in June 1968, when Ralph Silver, then a public-relations man and now a film producer, sent a news clipping about Olompali Ranch to *The Modern Utopian*.

I had already heard that a dropped-out millionaire had started a commune a few miles north of San Francisco, but I didn't have sufficient time or motivation to check it out. Nevertheless, Silver's clipping caught the attention of Betty and Ramon, then editors of the magazine; they had lived at Morning Star Ranch and were much closer to the hip commune scene experientially than I could ever begin to be.

After a two-day visit, Betty wrote a brief summary about Olompali and its founder, Don McCoy:*

Don McCoy has what at first seems a resort for the wealthy. The 750 acre ranch includes an elegant historical mansion with tiled swimming pool and four color televisions. . . . The kids are taught by Mrs. Garnett Brennan, an exciting Summerhillian, fired as principal in Nicasio for saying she had smoked marijuana for eighteen years. Don has long hair and publically says that drugs, if properly used, can be the most valuable experience of one's life. People go around naked

Don McCoy

The Modern Utopian, vol. 2, no. 6, July, 1968.

in and around the pool. Home-grown vegetables are part of the diet. Twice a week 1,000 loaves of free bread for San Francisco communes are baked by nude members of the community and SF Free City people, moving in the hot sun between the outdoor bakery on an octagonal concrete slab and the pool. . . . The driveway has a sign posted that says no visitors unless you feel like negotiating about this policy. The community grows from inside out mostly, having expanded from 25 to 44. (June 1968)

Don McCoy, a big man in his 30s, inherited some money from his father and then, through shrewd investments in real estate, amassed a fortune of $500,000. But accumulating great wealth was not enough for Don; he was looking for something else. He found it in San Francisco, where he discovered the flower-children in the then-beautiful Haight-Ashbury district, turned on, grew a beard, and dropped out. With him went several friends, including Sandy Barton, a successful nightclub entertainer, and the children of Sergeant Sunshine, the pot-smoking San Francisco police officer.

Originally, Don McCoy leased only five acres of the ranch. But after patrons of a neighboring riding school complained about seeing nude sunbathers near the swimming pool, McCoy took over the lease on the entire property and evicted the riding school.

Most members found much to admire in Don, who had assumed the dual role of both leader and benefactor to the commune. However, there was clearly a streak of resentment in some members because of their leader-benefactor's paternalism and affluence.

Don spent his money freely and lavishly. During the first year, beginning November 1967 (when he and his friends first occupied the property), he spent half of his wealth on cars, motorcycles, color-television sets, musical instruments and clothes. In addition, he set up an elaborate bakery, a recording studio, and arts and crafts workshops. As a result his father-in-law filed a lawsuit against him, contending that Don was squandering money that should be set aside to support his children and grandchildren.

After the lawsuit was filed, McCoy and two other members, including Sheyla McKendrick, flew to India to meditate with a holy man. Shelya's former husband, Robert McKendrick, then took over leadership of the commune. He had a background in business, plus unbounded optimism. He wanted the commune to become self-supporting, with income derived from the production of food and crafts. A leather shop and jewelry shop were set up; commercial plans were made for the bakery and organic garden.

Robert McKendrick's enthusiasm was not shared by most of the other family members. They did not wish to be regimented into a work schedule. Some of the people wanted only to look at trees — an activity that McKendrick had a tendency to interrupt with irritating and, to the watchers, incomprehensible, questions such as "What are you doing?" As a result, much friction was generated, but not much work. By the end of December 1968, McKendrick's leadership had declined almost to the point of disappearance. And in January he himself followed suit, leaving for parts unknown.

Meanwhile, on Christmas Eve, McCoy returned from India with an intense religious message for the members. Unfortunately, this neither averted nor alleviated the series of misfortunes that soon befell the commune:

- a visitor was accidentally killed while riding a motorcycle around the nearby village of Novato.
- there were two large-scale drug raids on the commune in mid-January.
- One of the ranch's horses wandered out onto Highway 101 and was hit by a motorist, with the result that the latter was killed.
- On February 2, the old wiring in the main house shorted out and the ensuing fire gutted the building.
- McCoy lost his law suit; his supply of money was cut to a bare minimum; he lost custody of his children.

236

He also spent some time in the Napa State Hospital and the Marin General Hospital, his ailment being described as a physical breakdown.

From February through July the remaining 20 or so commune members tried to pull things together. They wanted to create a working communal ranch with a school and spiritual center. But firm leadership was lacking. They could not decide which of their projects should be

given top priority, nor how to go about implementing them.

Aside from difficulties about future projects, the commune had money problems right then, seriously aggravated by Don McCoy's decline in fortunes. The utility bills alone ran from $150 per month in the summer to $350 in the winter; the rent was between $600 and $900 a month. Getting this much money together was hard although donations, especially one for $2,200 and another for $500, eased the pressure somewhat. Nearly every day it was necessary to appeal for funds from visitors and residents just to get enough money together to buy dinner. There were continued purchases of musical instruments (including a piano), clothes, and other "necessities," yet everyone bummed cigarettes and there was no money to put the pool back in running order when warm weather arrived.

Like many other hippie communes, Olompali Ranch could not agree on how to deal with visitors. Many members wanted the commune to be closed with no outsiders allowed; others felt they should welcome everyone; no one, on either side, had the strength to actually turn visitors away. Guests might insist that they would vanish into the upper woods, but they all had a way of showing up in the kitchen at dinnertime.

The relationships between adults were often strained and abrasive. The pressures and diverse aims had taken their toll; disparaging remarks punctuated nearly every conversation. The most obvious interpersonal successes on the ranch were the relationships the children established with each other and with adults. The ranch's animal contingent — 11 horses, a cow, and a vast number of cats and dogs — no doubt helped keep the children occupied.

But more than that, there was a near total absence of whining and bickering. Children were treated with the maturity they had earned. A 13-year-old could be treated

as an adult on some matters and as a child on others. Breakfast was a free-lance affair, with the older children helping the younger ones.

Ironically, it was with the unfortunate deaths of two of the children in June that Olompali itself came to an end. Four-year-old Audrey and two-year-old Nika were pedaling a tricycle along the edge of the unfenced pool

239

and fell in. By the time they were discovered it was too late to save them. The Establishment press sensationalized the accident, implying gross negligence on the part of the commune. County, health, and sanitation authorities descended on the ranch and produced a long list of code violations. The landlord ordered everyone off the property within 30 days. Within eight hours of these orders and after dinner-time, the 40 residents were reduced to 18: almost all the guests left; all the children were sent away before the impending visit of the probation officer. A few die-hard members remained at Olompali until they were forced to leave by the landlord's order.

So the commune at Olompali Ranch died in the summer of 1969, at the tender age of 20 months.

I regret not having visited Olompali, because it appears to have been an excellent example of all that was good and bad about the original hippie communal life style.* Many hippies, as a result of experiences at Olompali and similar communes, have despaired of communal living. Few have opted for more structure in order to deal with the individual's inability to self-regulate in group situations. Most have settled on a laissez-faire life style, with monogamous family arrangements and neighborhood-living in the vicinity of other like-minds, sharing more willingly and cooperating more generously than most Middle Americans. Nevertheless they cling to most of Middle America's basic standards — private property, autonomous households with separate facilities, traditional family roles, the patriarchal family pattern, et al.

A few other hippies, so-called, have followed a similar traditional individualized pattern, but have at the same time adopted a radical stance regarding land. These

---

*Having failed to get there, I have had to obtain my information from other sources, such as Betty. Much of my account, though, is from an article written by Steve McNamara for the Marin County weekly paper called *Pacific Sun*. This article was reprinted in *The Modern Utopian*, vol. 4, no. 2, spring, 1970.

people believe that the land should be free to all. Practicing what they preach, they live in open-land communes such as Morning Star Ranch. Don McCoy, among others, has become one of them. He now lives at Morning Star, in a self-built home with photographer Sylvia Clarke Hamilton.

GORDA MOUNTAIN, THE FIRST OPEN-LAND COMMUNE

To the best of my knowledge, the first open-land commune was Gorda Mountain, on the Big Sur coast of California. In 1962 Amelia Newell decided to make her land there available to anyone who wished to come and live on it. As the US hippie movement grew, so also did the population of Gorda. At the peak of the 1967 summer there were over 200 young hippies living on Amelia's land. Local residents became quite hostile about this influx of strange, long-haired, dirty, drug-crazed deviants (to use some of the phrases most favored by the press in describing hippies). One local gas-station owner took to wearing a revolver and refusing to service cars and trucks from the Newell community. Other local businessmen placed signs in their windows: "POSITIVELY NO SERVICE TO HIPPIES (Except the use of the public telephone) ON THESE PREMISES."

The health department was the willing tool of the county politicians who decided that Gorda Mountain was a menace to their political positions—given the opposition of older residents and businessmen. The politicians therefore determined that Gorda Mountain should be closed down—an objective in which local vigilantes aided the county authorities. Gorda died in 1968.

MORNING STAR RANCH

Morning Star Ranch is an open-land community in Sonoma County, California. It is based on the funda-

241

mental principal that all land should be available to those who wish to use it—a principal known acronymically as LATWIDN—Land Access To Which Is Denied No One). "Open land means simply that God is the sole owner of the land and that we, as His children, are not meant to fight, quarrel, and kill over the land, but rather to share this natural resource—to each according to his needs.

At Morning Star there are no rules, no regulations, no organization. The land itself selects the people. Those who do not work hard to build shelter and provide for their basic needs do not survive on the land. If the land gets over-crowded, people leave or spread out.

The ideal is "voluntary primitivism," a term used by Ramon Sender to mean "the reunion of man with his greater self—God's nature"; that is, living in harmony with the four elements—earth, air, fire, and water. In practice this means building your own biodegradable home out of mud and twigs and dead branches and old lumber. It means giving up electricity, gas, running water, and the telephone, as well as other modern conveniences. Living on the land also means conditioning your body to withstand cold and damp weather, carrying your own water for drinking and your own wood for cooking. It means planting and harvesting your crops by using muscles and not machinery.

IN THE BEGINNING AND A YEAR LATER

Originally purchased in 1962, Morning Star was initially the private retreat of Lou Gottlieb, a singer with the pop-folk group called The Limelighters.

In 1966 Lou and Ramon Sender, a friend, decided to open the land to anyone who wanted to live there. The property consisted of approximately 32 acres of land. Forest, meadow, and orchard made up about half of the area; banks and inclines too steep for use composed the rest. The topsoil was not fertile, being generally a clay mixture that possessed only marginal potential for crop-growing purposes. There were two wells, both of them usable throughout the year. Buildings on the property included a small, light-framed house (about 900 feet square), a barn, and a prefabricated chicken coop and shed.

Morning Star took on the appearance of an ashram. It began with a half-dozen permanent residents and gradually increased its population to over 35.

A college student in Maryland named Michael Howden visited Morning Star late in December 1966, when the commune was still less than one year old. In writing about his experiences at Morning Star, he reported:

When I arrived it was chilly out, but people were working and it seemed very natural to work with them, hauling firewood to the lower house. There was no pressure to work, nor was I trying to impress anyone. It was just what was happening and it seemed natural to partake of it. Dinner, as with all the meals there, was a communal affair. Each day, different people cooked breakfast and/or dinner; others washed the dishes. Before the meal we all held hands in silence. Some very nice things happened through this, a very warm feeling, becoming part. The meal was macrobiotic, zucchini tempura, rice and greens, though there was milk as well as tea.

If the ashram had centrality, it was about Lou Gottlieb. He is free from pressures, direct, outspoken. The land is his, but no one was really conscious of this; all were part of the community. Whom the land in fact belonged to didn't matter. Lou made this possible; he was never overbearing, demanding. Yet things happened; they happened because of Lou's nonpossessiveness, his tolerance, which created the sense of all belonging equally, which made sharing and work not only possible but enjoyable.

I went back in late January or early February of 1967. The currents had matured. Some people had gone, but there were still about 14 to 18 people around. The atmosphere was calm and free. Chicken coop areas had been cleared away for an organic garden. Scrap which had laid around for months was being cleared. Trips were made to the ocean for shellfish. The weather, too, was better, more sun and a warm wind.*

As spring arrived, more and more people heard about Morning Star. A few moved in to become permanent residents. By late summer there were at least as many semi-residents as permanent ones, semi-residents being people who divided their time between the ashram and San Francisco.

As the word got out that Morning Star was an "open" commune, more and more people split from the city, especially from the Haight-Ashbury. These transient hippie types would visit for a weekend, or sometimes for a week or two, and then leave. By June 1967, they constituted over half the total population; on weekends they made up an even larger proportion. During June and July an average of 90 people per day ate the communal dinner; on weekends this number doubled. One Saturday in late July over 300 were fed (a figure that does not include the ever-increasing numbers of people who elected to eat separately).**

PROBLEMS

The commune was changing, but not necessarily for the better. Mike Howden noted, "Morning Star was no longer an ashram, but an open community. Many people came and went. The food supplies and general quality of the meals fell off. . . ." But it was not only the quantity and quality of food that worsened; the composition of people on the farm became increasingly urban in outlook as well as origin. As publicity mounted, tourists flooded the place, particularly on weekends. At the peak influx, over 2,000

* *The Modern Utopian*, vol. 2, no. 3, January, 1968.
** This and much of the other factual information that follows concerning Morning Star in 1967 was provided by C. P. Herrick, an architect who lived at Morning Star during that period.

tourists visited the farm. Few of them, though, stayed overnight or ate the common meal; but they still needed other facilities.

Chuck Herrick, one of the residents, noted that, "With the greater number of people on the land, the two inadequate toilets are literally inundated by a river of shit. The situation was made worse by the interruption of services

because of frequent stoppages. At one period, neither toilet functioned for over a week."

The commune's problems multiplied as its population increased. One of these problems was that, owing to the lack of toilet facilities, most people used the woods. Many were careless and did not bury their feces and paper adequately. Thus, this lack of sanitation constituted a serious health hazard.

Another serious problem had to do with the limited availability of living quarters. Buildings on the property, including the barn and sheds, provided only 14 small but habitable rooms. Some of these rooms were claimed by permanent residents as "private space" and this space was seldom disturbed. The newest transients crammed into the two small houses. As a result, both houses deteriorated rapidly and their bathrooms, kitchens, and floor surfaces required major repairs. Such crowding increased the danger of disease as well as of social stress.

Then, as Chuck Herrick noted, "The reaction to this stress was rapid construction of individual shelters ranging from carefully designed and environmentally integrated dwellings to tin shanties. None were blessed by the county building department. About two dozen structures were built. Tents also became common."

The scattered locations of all these structures caused still more problems, such as the fact that the tourists began roaming through the woods in search of more real live hippies, thus trampling the vegetation. Three other problems resulting from the influx of all these transients and tourists were that: (1) a considerable number of trees were cut down before community consensus stopped it, (2) the clearing of ground litter and the leveling of campsites broke natural-drainage and water-absorption patterns, and (3) the fire danger from so many transient campers became acute by late summer.

COPING WITH PROBLEMS

As the number of people and the problems increased, a weekly meeting was instituted. It was the only formal and structured arrangement of the community (although informal groups were created around specific interests).

In the meeting, members attempted to reach some agreement about methods of dealing with these problems, as well as about soliciting volunteers for the work involved. Over half of the community weekday population attended.

Chuck thought that these meetings were remarkably helpful in dealing with the problems, in view of the fact that Morning Star had no mechanisms for interim decision-making, no prohibitions on any specific acts, and no organizations for such complex long-range projects as building communal facilities.

Collective concern and coordinated action deriving from these meetings produced a number of successful problem-solving activities. Among these projects were:

1. The regular removal of great amounts of trash and litter; this became especially necessary because of the transient population.

2. Restricting the use of automobiles on the property.

3. The implementation of fire-control programs.

4. The prevention of indiscriminate cutting of trees.

5. Use of composted vegetable waste for soil replenishment. In connection with this project, one man who joined the commune in the spring was particularly influential in developing an organic garden and teaching all who were interested. However, overpopulation drove him off the land before the end of summer.

An ecology class was also organized and taught by Chuck Herrick, co-founder of Ecology Action and a leader of the Peace and Freedom Party's ecology caucus. However, the class was discontinued because the pressure of existing problems was so acute that they had to be dealt with through action rather than just talk.

THE LAND SELECTS THE PEOPLE – OR DOES IT?

To Chuck, the lack of both population planning and control for an ecological balanced community was the major cause for the problems at Morning Star. On the other hand, to Lou and Ramon, control and regulation of the land and people were undesirable and unnecessary — "The land selects the people." When things get bad enough, according to this view, people will leave and the land will be adequate for those who remain. Thus it is apparent that Chuck, Lou and Ramon between them represented and espoused two opposing views.

One view is: regulate nothing. Let nature take its course. Nature knows best. Balance will be restored if only man will stop trying to "fix things." It is only man who persists in trying to foul-up nature.

The other view is: there has to be an ecological understanding of nature — that is, the dynamics of how each aspect of nature relates. Then we must institute certain controls to keep us from indiscriminately destroying nature and eventually ourselves.

The facts are, as I see them, that man has been controlling and regulating and conquering nature for a long time; that he has been doing so for his own short-sighted ends, with no understanding of and no concern for the delicate interrelationships of all things. As a result we are at a state of ecological crisis.

Planning and controlling nature for the benefit of nature and not for individual human profit is essential at this point in history if man is to survive. Lou and Ramon may be correct ideally: nature is wise and will balance herself. But because we have fouled her up so badly, she would inevitably destroy us in order to reach that balance again. No controls after centuries of waste and mismanagement (like extending life and decreasing infant mortality through medical science without limiting births) would be disastrous for man. Technological advances discontinued or continued without controls would result in widespread disease, destruction, and death. Perhaps that's just what man deserves. But being one of the species, I'm a little concerned and defensive for him.

COPING WITH THE AUTHORITIES

County, health, and sanitation authorities, as well as fire and building inspectors, descended on Morning Star and required major changes in toilet facilities, building improvements, etc. So much needed to be done. The county had no patience. Finally, the authorities required Lou to clear the land of all persons or pay $500 per day in fines. Lou made one attempt to comply with the clearance order, but when the county made additional demands about cleaning up the property, Lou balked. That fall and winter found Lou in and out of court on charges of contempt, facing fines of over $14,000, which were eventually garnished from his bank account.

Chuck Herrick and Betty Swimmer left Morning Star and worked on *The Modern Utopian*. Later Ramon also came to Berkeley to work with us as an editor.

LOU AT SANTA ROSA AND SEBASTOPOL

In the spring of 1969 I became minister of the Unitarian-Universalist Fellowship in the city of Santa Rosa, not too far from Morning Star. Lou came to speak to my congregation. Was I impressed. As a guest, he could tell it like it is and that is exactly what he did, turning on the audience that had packed the hall in order to see and hear this controversial local figure.

What a showman. There he was, a huge hulk of a man, tall, with a broad satirical grin and bushy beard. In his worn work clothes and hip rubber boots he looked like the Paul Bunyan of the commune movement. He spoke of avatars and religious practices, sex and dope:

"Everyone thinks that if we discovered that opium was good, mankind would then become a group of angleworms, just copulating and ohhhh, God, it would be terrible! That is the kind of fear we have of the poppy. But it's the only way to fly! I'm serious. I'm serious. A quarter grain—nay an eighth grain of morphine when you got on

250

the airplane and you would arrive in New York with your face a mask of composure. It's a fact! But it's illegal. A little ball of opium is also excellent for Hong Kong flu. . . . That's all they give you anyway, if you've ever eaten codeine, but that's a false opium. Opium is a little sap which has a bitter taste; it will keep you from taking more than you need. It's good, though.

"Now, in India, it is generally considered poor form for anyone to turn on prior to the age of forty. I mean, up until forty you have this world to deal with, children to rear, a business to get into; but after that, then you must try to free yourself from as many attachments to this world as you can. And if the divine has placed some substance here which, if taken as a diet supplement, helps you to do the trick, you're a fool to not make use of it. Anyone who has prayed seriously in his life, both under the influence of the poppy or the hemp, who will tell me that these substances hinder the progress of prayer, I know he is crazy. They were made to pray with, and that is why the devout Shiva worshippers use these substances in a sacramental manner. . . .

"You see, all men are not created equal. All men are created to reflect a facet of His great glory. And the discovery of what your facet is, or as the Gita says, "your own thing," but *really* your own thing, is the principal job of every human being. It may take a lifetime. . . .

During 1969–1970 I lived in Sebastopol, near Morning Star, and Lou and Rena (his "old lady") and Ramon (who was then living at Sheep Ridge Ranch) would drop in at my place, where we would chat briefly about the magazine, the open-land movement, and the commune movement in general.

Although I was much impressed with Lou's speaking ability, I felt that his communication on a one-to-one basis left something to be desired. I didn't feel listened to. He was still preaching his sermon, tripping out on his own eloquence with words and his grandiose vision. His ego apparently matched his bulk.

As I got to know Lou better, though, I found him much more communicable, and personable. Perhaps we were both more relaxed and understanding of each other. I got to the point where I could always enjoy him and his enviable way of making words sound much more important than they are.

While we were talking about communes, Lou blurted out in an authoritative manner, enthusiastically raising himself up on his toes in order to punctuate his remark: "Morning Star is a training replacement center, or rest and recuperation area, for the army of occupation in the war against the exclusive ownership of land."

"Wow," I replied. "Say that again. I must write that one down."

Lou was pleased. "Here, give me paper and pencil and I'll write it down for you." And he did.

DEEDING THE LAND TO GOD

The county had bulldozed all the Morning Star buildings save one in order to prevent them from being occupied. But people still lived on the property. They slept in tents and bedrolls and sleeping bags; they continued to build temporary shelters. Lou never turned anyone away.

There was little publicity for there were now many more communes around the country than there had been in 1967; the hippie exodus from the cities had already taken place, and only a small number of people lived at Morning Star at any one time. Morning Star was not an ashram, not a commune really, but simply and still emphatically "open land." People came and stayed mainly in warm weather and remained transient.

Lou was still going to court. Now, though, in order to solidify his belief in *Latwidn*, Lou decided it would be best to relinquish his legal title to the land and turn it over to a more universal figure, one whom he believed would not be possessive and greedy and restrictive about 32 acres of marginal farm land. So, in the spring of 1969, Lou deeded his land to God.

252

A short time later God became involved in yet another case in the California courts. In June one Betty Penrose of Oakland sued God for the Morning Star property, claiming that God "so maintained and controlled the weather . . . in such a careless and negligent manner as to cause lightning to strike [her house], setting it on fire and startling, frightening and shocking [her]. . . ." At the same time, Paul Yerkes Bechtel, of Tamal, claimed to be God and became the defendant in the case.

County authorities took Lou to court with evidence that people were still residing on the property in spite of the injunction against him. Lou, standing before the judge in his own defense, stated, "Your honor, you have the wrong person before you. I no longer own the property and therefore am not responsible for anything that goes on there."

Lou told the judge that he, the judge, would have to make a decision that would set a precedent, as there had been no similar case in the history of jurisprudence. The assistant district attorney argued that there was a precedent, to which the judge good-humoredly replied that the

case would have to be investigated further. And, with a twinkle in his eye to match Lou's, he admitted that this might just be a matter for the appellate court. The judge, it seems, was in good spirits. He was the same judge who had ordered the county to bulldoze the Morning Star buildings.

Eventually, the judge, Judge Kenneth Eiman, ruled that God, not being a "natural or artificial person," could not legally own Gottlieb's property; thus Lou was still the owner and would have to comply with the court's injunction — that was, no one but Lou could live on Lou's property.

Lou then spent several days in legal research and then prepared and submitted a seven-page brief entitled "Memorandum of Points and Authorities" in support of his contention that God could own Morning Star Ranch and that he, Lou, could deed the land to God as free exercise of his religious beliefs as guaranteed under the First Amendment of the US Constitution.

As of this writing (February 1971), the case continues in the courts.

Interview with Lou Gottlieb

I taped the following interview with the founder of Morning Star Ranch in February 1971:

Lou: The situation with Morning Star Ranch is as follows. Ever since September of 1968 there has been a permanent injunction at Morning Star, which has classified the place as a public health hazard and a public nuisance and it has denied anyone the right to stay there, except for myself. Needless to say, people have been ignoring that injunction ever since it was instituted; and, in the great American tradition of civil disobedience, there have always been people living at Morning Star Ranch. Last June [1970] I went to court on an order to show cause why I should not be forced to tear down whatever buildings on the place were not up to code — that means the structures the hippies were living in. If I failed to do so the county would

254

be empowered to bring in the bulldozer and remove the structures. They had already done this once before, back in August of 1969. Hippies had moved in and built up structures, and naturally the neighbors had complained, and so the order to show cause issued forth from the superior court [California]. We made the defense that I was no longer the real party in interest, because, since May of 1969, I contend that Morning Star Ranch has been the property of God. It was a deed made over naming God as the grantee, and it was recorded in the hall of records in Sonoma County. This was the first time that we had a chance to go into court and make this particular contention. Judge Eiman of the superior court took it under advisement and came out with a decision which is practically famous now, in which he said that the deed naming God as the grantee was not a valid conveyance because—I'll quote the sentence verbatim—"Whatever the nature of the Deity, God is not a person, natural or artificial, in existence at time of conveyance and capable of taking title." That's a little bit of common-law jargon that has grown out of a a number of cases involving title to real property. The grantee must be a person "artificial or natural"; that means a human being—or a corporation, an estate or a trust, any one of the so-called artificial persons.

Well, we applied for reconsideration and introduced the idea that the deed naming God as grantee constituted a valid conveyance if viewed as a dedication of land to public use. The naming of God as grantee merely fulfills one of the primary requisites of a dedication of land to public use; namely, that the grantor, or the dedicator, expresses his intent. It is precisely the intent of *this* dedicator that all land should be looked at as God's property; or another way of saying the thing is that the earth is the mother of us all and we should treat it in that manner, not try to maximize the net. Judge Eiman denied that particular motion and ordered the bulldozers out there, because he said I had never established a firm evidentiary foundation for my contention that my deed, in fact, constituted a dedication of land to public use. Then I instituted an appeal. I filed a notice of appeal. And I got together a record of the case in one of the four approved methods under the rules of court. That means I got together with the DA and we formulated an agreed statement of the case. Well, I sent it down to the appellate court and they bounced it back like a puck, because it was on the wrong size paper. I started to think about that and what I decided was that it must be God's will because in the Year of Tate and Sokel, this is no time for longhairs to be going before the appellate court and looking for some kind of relief. In the meantime, last December I was again ordered into court to show cause why I should not be forced to tear down the buildings (or the county would do so if I failed to) within 30 days.

This time I went before Judge Murphy in the fourth division of the superior court of the State of California in and for the County of Sonoma, and I did get on the stand this time. I laid a firm evidentiary foundation for the fact that naming God as grantee constitutes a valid dedication of land to public use. It's been nearly three months now, and Judge Murphy has not made a decision. . . . This case has many eminently appealable facets: and as a matter of fact I have already submitted to the appellate court, which doesn't even have the case on its dockets, an amicus brief, written by Alan Kagin and Charles Galford, two law students at Yale Law School. Yale has the Jerome M. Frank Foundation in which kids going to law school can do good work in the legal field and get credit for it, and it's an elegant amicus brief. And I have promise of others.

256

Now the principal advantage, it seems to me, for having a deed naming God as the grantee is that we raise the question of jurisdiction. It seems to me that in these days, to mount demonstrations against the marijuana laws, against the draft laws, against the homoerotic laws, is really like trying to cut off the head of Medusa. What I think it is, is that if land is deeded to God, you have what is, in effect, a statute-free sanctuary. Now obviously we couldn't declare that all over the world, all over the country, that'd be anarchy, Lou, people would freak out! But there is need for statute-free sanctuary in the country today. If we are as we say, one nation under God, then whose statutes prevail on God's land? The minute anybody trained in the law begins to meditate on the question of God as landowner, the question of jurisdiction immediately presents itself. And most lawyers of the straight variety give a little dry cough, consult their watch, and immediately find that they are 15 minutes late to a very important engagement. But I believe there will come a time when it will be seen that the history of jurisprudence has an important watershed; the history before God is recognized as the legal owner of land and the time after. Now, open land or land access to which is denied nobody, needless to say, is the hope of the world. If open land is not the future, there isn't any. The best form that open land can take is deeding the land to God. There has been another person, a young man by the name of Gary Ward, who has deeded a quarter acre of land in Lake County to God. When he went to have that deed recorded, the county recorder said, "I must get legal advice on this." They consulted the county council and the district attorney's office in Lake County and they both said that the deed is a valid instrument. . . . I hope I and others will get some money to be able to buy land all over the world and deed it to God. . . . There's one thing about the legal battle I didn't quite cover. And that is: who will administer land which is deeded to God? Fortunately, in the English common law there's a beautiful tradition called "cy pres" which is Anglo-Latin for a French phrase meaning "as close as possible." Now, when a charitable act has been performed, which for some reason cannot meet the intent of the donor—cannot be carried out— there is the English common law which says that the king, as *pareres patriae*, should step in and administer the charitable gift as close

257

as possible to the intent of the owners. Now, *Scott* is the four-volume work on trusts, and he's the guy whose discussion of cy pres is definitive, as far as I've heard. He quotes a very interesting law case in England, that took place in the 18th century, when a rich Jew died and gave all his money to the founding of a Yeshiva. There was a law in England at the time that you couldn't give any money to any church except the established church in England. So the king stepped in and used the money, cy pres. That means, he founded an orphanage where children could be instructed in the precepts of the Christian religion. Well, there was another Jew who stepped in, who intervened, who said, "This *can't* be as close as possible." And then there was a famous double-talk decision by Lord somebody (whose name has slipped me), who said, "No, the king has acted correctly, because it's obvious that the deceased was a charitable man, and how better way to exercise charity than to found an orphanage?" But that's to prove by the opposite. In other words, I will be happy for any judge to administer Morning Star Ranch as if it were God's land, cy pres, as close as possible to God's intent. That would be delightful.

DICK: But then the judge would be interpreting according to his own vision of what God's intent was.

LOU: I would have to respect that as much as I respect my own.

DICK: Yes, but it might be *very* different from your own.

LOU: As He wills. . . . Either that, or we don't have a—look, we're talking about faith. Faith in terms of application to the daily, practical matters of life, you see. How to introduce faith in the existence of the unnameable into the affairs of daily, practical living. That's the trick. Everybody who can figure out a way to do that is helping mankind. I believe that deeding land to God, which by the way was not even my idea although I'm definitely stuck with it. It was Joan's idea [Ramon's "old lady"]. All right, that could be one possible route that the courts could take in the administration of land which has been dedicated to public use. Now, the other way is that the administration of the land would be put into the hands of the state legislature. And again, as long as God is the landowner, it doesn't make any difference who administers it. Because it is His will that will be effectuated anyway.

* * *

DICK: What's happening at Morning Star now?

LOU: The same thing, you know, there's always people there. God's will, that's all.

DICK: How about yourself? How do you spend your time these days?

LOU: Always the same. Playing the piano.

DICK: Playing the piano?

LOU: Yeah, it seems to me that my real job is what you'd call "continuous application of the will." Somebody on the surface of this earth has got to be continuously beaming from between the eyes the notion "open land." I don't know how I got the job, but it is as if the application of the will is involuntary. It's continuously on my mind. It even gets boring. This is the kind of job that Aurobindo did for the independence of India. He sat there for 40 years and willed the independence of India. And naturally India was made independent on his birthday.

DICK: Who was this now?

LOU: *Aurobindo Ghose*, he's the guru of my guru, and he was a very great avatar, spiritual force, and he lived in Pondicherry, India.

DICK: That's where they're building that commune?

LOU: Auroville. It is being named after him. I've visited there and I have great respect for what's going on; but I couldn't live there for over ten minutes because it's an Old-Style community. In other words, they have rules for everyone. That, of course, is necessary in India, but it's exactly the opposite of what's needed in this country. What we need in this country are statute-free sanctuaries, because many people who fall ill in this country fall ill from an allergy to statute; there has never been a society that has been as burdened by statutes. It's just unbelievable. I mean, you go into law libraries and see what kind of laws we live under.

DICK: Yeah, there has to be that opportunity for anyone at anytime, in every section of the country, so you don't have to come to Morning Star Ranch or Wheeler Ranch.

LOU: Right. There's got to be statute-free sanctuaries everywhere. You can say that deeding land to God opens the possibility of reading the tablets that are written on the human heart. The Church way of saying it. Oh, I meant to say also, with respect to the appeals, that courts have consistently avoided facing any theological question, any ecclesiastical question. And the nature of God is the primary theological question. So Judge Eiman, who is a very nice man — well, he overstepped his judicial authority completely, completely; he has to be reversed, you see. . . .

DICK: He stepped on a lot of people's toes.

LOU: You cannot have a civil court deciding the nature of God. It's impossible, in this country. It just revokes everything we've ever had. Separation of church and state and all that.

* * *

LOU: You know Sun Bear? He's a wonderful man. He told me that among certain Plains Indian tribes they have a custom which is that the minute a chief ceases to serve the interests of his people he awakens one morning to find that his is the only tepee on the campground. The rest of the people have just left — voted with their feet. Many people are doing that in spirit nowadays. I mean they do not wish to be informed of Washington's latest step in the direction of inevitable cataclysm. I don't need that. I don't want to be posted on the minute-to-minute basis of the latest count of catastrophic maneuvers.

DICK: It's a real downer.

LOU: Complete. And anyway, the more I view the situation, the only hope I can see for the future is open land. The only hope ecologically. The only hope sociologically. The only hope in any number of areas. Why? Because on open land you have a juxtaposition of people that is devised by the divine. God is the casting director. God is the personnel manager. And it is the people with whom you live that constitutes the most critical factor in your environment.

DICK: Wouldn't that result in a necessary decrease in population? Because there's only so much space people can live on, otherwise they either kill each other, die of disease or have to move, and there's only so many places where people can live — like people can't live in the middle of a desert or on a barren mountainside.

LOU: Well, you see, first of all it's not so much how many people there are. It's who has put them together and what reason have they been put together, you see. If they have been put together to maxi-

Lou Gottlieb with a Morning Star on his back

mize the rent that can be extracted from a given area, it will be a very sad situation.

DICK: High-rise apartments.

LOU: Yes, that's very bad. And particularly as people rise in the life of the spirit. The minute that consciousness expands at all, you become highly sensitive to what's going on on the other side of this wall. It may be somebody having a terrific hassle with his old lady, whom you've never seen before, and the wall is only four inches thick, and you begin to get these terrifically bad vibes, and you don't understand what's happening, you know. That's one of the things that's wrong with living in the city. All cities are obsolete. They must be evacuated, not as London was evacuated during World War II, but the people who are desperate must be tempted out. How? Not by preaching, certainly. But by an ongoing pilot study of an alternate life style which can be visited. Now the only thing wrong with open land, as far as I can see so far, is there's not enough of it. I have a kind of mystical conviction that there is a proper set of coordinates on the earth's surface for every consciousness. You know, the right place for you to be. The right latitude and longitude for everybody.

DICK: Like in the *Teaching of Don Juan*. There's one spot on this floor that's your spot.

LOU: Yeah, and it's true on the earth too. Just because we're born in Bengal doesn't mean that's where we're supposed to be. I feel that doing away with no trespassing signs is a step in the right direction. After that comes state and national boundaries. I really feel they are tremendously artificial and they are lethal in our time, because they perpetuate this horrible old obsolete territorial imperative that's just turned murderous on us now. The territorial imperative on open land has the tendency to transform into its opposite, which is an instinctive *recognition* of the privacy and companionship needs of everyone else on the earth. That is the territorial imperative turned into its divine essence. Or, as Walt Whitman says, "The real toward the ideal tending." Did you ever read *The Song of The Universe?* It's the Gita of the Western Hemisphere. It starts out, "Come, said the Muse, sing me a song no poet yet has chanted. Sing me the Universal." And, you know, it goes up from there.

There has been a good deal of work done in what's called the science of proxemics. Edward T. Hall wrote a book on it called *Proxemics*, and the subject is: how close is too close. "Too close" is different in different cultures. In Islam, "too close" is a lot closer than in Germany, for instance. People in Germany don't touch. If you're standing in line in an Islamic country, people push and shove and pat and touch and one thing and another. In Germany you could be standing in the same line for four days and nobody would even, you know . . . it's just not their way. But this guy, Edward T. Hall, showed me a lot about it. The science of proxemics concerns precisely the interpersonal effects of the territorial imperative. It's a great study. But anybody who's lived on open land knows that there are some people who have a highly developed sense of proxemics, of privacy needs and companionship needs of the other people there. The main point is in assembling the personnel in the new kind of community, it is essential that this be done objectively; you know, in the Gurdjieffian sense: let God be the selector. If the people are assembled on the basis of any kind of a trip, it's old hat. It immediately becomes a sort of 19th century closed community, closed intentional community, and that trip's been done. It's successful and so on; but the point is, the minute you stop the ebb and flow, that symbiotic relationship with the population at large, it becomes very dull. You begin to know when everybody's going to belch at the table. It's too close, you see.

DICK: Yeah. That was the problem with a lot of older Christian communities; they didn't allow enough intake, enough flow, so they stagnate. . . .

LOU: Yeah, the thing I read someplace, I think it was in one of *The Modern Utopian*'s, some Sun Hill community, the guy said that after about five or six months the sexual attraction between the members of the opposite sex dropped, because it becomes immediately incestuous. Ramon even told me that in the Bruderhof community, whenever a boy and girl from the Bruderhof suddenly found that they were in love, it came as a huge surprise to everybody. I've read that in the kibbutz also, in *The Source*, they talk about the fact that these boys and girls live in the same room until they're 18, but the thought of their indulging in any kind of sexual relationship is just not present. Well, I think the heat should be kept up. And the way to do it is change. It's like Theodore Dreiser said, "The only possible aphrodisiac which is effective is variety."

Now, as I say, the only thing that's ever happened at Morning Star Ranch which I feel was not to my liking was when people came there who were seeking open land but the coordinates were not exactly right on that particular 30-acre piece of land. Now I don't

263

think it's right for people to try to pressure the government into turning loose land or giving it to God, because Uncle Sam is not a generous man. The American people are generous, but Uncle Sam is a skinflint. And just ask any foreign country that's come to ask for money and you'll see how they—

DICK: —except such things as anticommunism or military dictatorships and—

LOU: —well, that's another thing. But I think that, eventually, people who own land are going to come to the realization that I and Gary Ward have come to. Everyone wants to give. Everybody really wants to give. But you should give in a way that makes you comfortable. I hate to give away food. I really do. I hate to give food because I know it's meaningless. I mean those five little fishes and so on, it's a beautiful story but it's not my trip. I'm not a free-food cat. I'm a free-rent cat. I think that in our time what's needed is free rent. And I believe that is the most potent lever for the transformation of our society.

Conversation with Rena Morning Star

I also had the opportunity in February 1971 to talk with Lou's "old lady" who goes by the name of Rena Morning Star. This is what we talked about (with Lou also joining in later):

RENA: My best rap is about childbirth. You want to know about having a baby on the land? It's all right? Having Vishnu [her son] at Morning Star—and it's important that it's open land, because I believe the policy is "open land, open cervix"—made childbirth much easier. We started out with a good fuck during labor. I highly recommend it! A good fuck sets the stage for a beautiful sexual orgasm. And that's what his birth was. During contractions we chanted "om," which was really really fine. I just put my head in the right place and kept my body relaxed. I was on my knees when he was born, like this, I was leaning on the back of a chair. Lou was massaging me and caressing me, and he just jumped out— I didn't have to push. He just came diving out. It was incredible. Afterwards I ate the placenta. I ate one bite raw, and the rest of it steamed. A few other people shared the sacrament. Many animals eat the placenta; and I tried it and it was really right, it was perfect nourishment. I was totally vegetarian — completely — no eggs, no fish, no cheese; but I really put away that placenta. Within hours I was running down to the stream, fetching water, doing Yoga, standing on my head. It was really — it was the biggest orgasm of my life. Incredible! I also stood on my head when I was in labor and did some other Yoga postures.

DICK: How were the labor pains?

RENA: It was all bliss, it really was. It was just a sexual experience, the height of which I've never seen before. It was just really fine.

DICK: I can't believe that now; you're putting me on.

RENA: No! It was *really* bliss. It was really, really comfortable. I was in shape; I mean, I walked about 20 miles a week all during pregnancy, plus lots of Yoga every day. Eating right, too.

DICK: Did you do any preparation exercises for labor?

RENA: Just walking and Yoga. Living on the land, I just wanted to tune in to the land and let the trees and the sky and the sunshine teach me how. I've sunbathed naked a lot, maybe that helped. I didn't know I was in labor until 20 minutes before he came out.

DICK: That's far out, I have to say.

RENA: Also, as far as acid babies go, Vishnu was conceived on acid. I had a lot of acid while I was pregnant.

DICK: He seems pretty healthy.

RENA: Oh, he's perfect, he's really perfect. And he likes acid. When I take it now he gets high through my milk, and he's really really beautiful on it. I haven't given him any straight — just what he gets from my milk.

DICK: Babies don't need acid do they? I mean, they already are high most of the time.

RENA: Oh yes, they're really happy. But he is different; when I take acid he tends to laugh a lot more and sleep a lot deeper. He just starts giggling, and then it's just a total pleasure. A very conscious baby. . . . A critical thing is volitional conception. Vishnu was consciously conceived. Another aspect is eating right. If you don't eat sugar you won't get morning sickness. I was totally macrobiotic: no sugar, no honey, no meat of any kind. I never felt so healthy in my life as when I was pregnant. Also, when you eat sugar you get an

Lou Gottlieb and Rena with Vishnu

artificial sense of nourishment. Most pregnant chicks will crave ice cream cones or Hershey bars. I would crave things like artichokes and spinach. . . .

* * *

RENA: I'm used to going to bed at sunset. And getting up at sunrise.

DICK: Ah. Now you're down in the big city. That's a real change. The vibrations—the whole intensity level is much higher in the city. If you get in the country and you live there awhile, the pace slows down. Most of the time I'm on very much of a speed trip. I go to the country and it's like I'm still speeding, but the brake is on. Sometimes uncomfortable, but if I just let myself go with it, it can be OK.

RENA: The biggest problem in the city is the lack of fresh air. Also, people are just packed so tightly together. There are people on top of one another. Also, in the country you tend to live by the sunlight rather than electric light. Sunlight is a source of nourishment for us. When I'm out in the sun all day I need less food and less sleep. That's another reason I don't go to the city much. It's impossible for me to be in the sunlight with my clothes on. So I have to be out on the land, where I can take them off.

DICK: It seems that the open-land thing is a very male-dominated program. What about women's liberation?

LOU: I'll tell you why women like open land. It gives them the liberty to live like slobs. That's right. Women are absolutely slaves to the ridiculous dwellings in which they live. Dwellings that have to be kept neat — the neatness of the parade ground. Women want to live like slobs, without being criticized for it. And that's what you can do on open land. A lot of houses on open land really aren't very neat.

RENA: All I know is that living on the land has given me what I wanted to be when I grew up. My demonstration is in my life style, seeing how much bliss I can tolerate, how much nothing I can do. Inaction in action. I guess Vishnu helps, though. Having a baby, having a family, living with God in the country. Just being free to trip as I want to. That's what Morning Star gives me. That's really fine. On open land you can just about make any scene you want. God takes care of all your needs. All you have to do is will it.

DICK: That's a very good combination. God takes care of all your needs — all you have to do is will it. Which is a combination of: you've got to *do* it, even though God takes care of it. The willing is something that *you* do, right?

RENA: Sometimes consciously. But it's all part of a divine plan. . . .

SHEEP RIDGE RANCH (WHEELER'S)

In the winter of 1967, after Sonoma County officials began bulldozing the buildings at Morning Star, a 28-year-old neighbor decided to open his land. Four years earlier, using money inherited from his father, Bill Wheeler had bought 320 acres of land in Occidental, California. He had built his own house out of hewn timbers and had made provisions for plenty of glass windows to let the sun shine in. He did all this because he wanted a place where he could paint and live quietly with his young wife and their infant son.

When he opened his land, the county authorities were

quick to move in and condemn his home as not being up to code standards. They wanted to discourage another Morning Star.

(Punitive measures are always the first to be used by governments and those in power. The effects of such measures have always been to increase resistance rather than suppress it. I would theorize that authorities wish to encourage opposition rather than extinguish it, as this gives them the opportunity to show power, boost ego, vent hostility. Without opposition, what use is authority? Military men need wars, or the threat of wars, to make their existence meaningful; so too with those who wage other battles.)

After his home was condemned, Bill and family moved into a tent and an adjacent, 12-foot-square shed with old windows as sides. The home became his studio for painting and for building natural furniture; it also became a convenient place to hold community meetings.

So it was that Sheep Ridge Ranch (commonly known as Wheeler's Ranch) became an open-land community. People began to arrive, among them some refugees from Morning Star. Tree houses, shacks, tepees, domes — shelters of all sorts were built at the edge of the woods, on the hillside, and deep into the woods. A few residents acutely aware of the vogue for county harassment took great pains to conceal their homes.

At the present time, most of the dwellings at Sheep Ridge Ranch are small and airy structures made nearly entirely of used materials, such as old lumber, doors, and windows, which are employed for walls. Twigs, branches, and mud covered over by plastic sheeting are used for ceilings. The floor is typically a dirt floor, although a few of the better shelters have wooden ones. There is, of course, no water, no phone or mail service, no electricity. A few shelters have stoves. The climate is mild, sunny, and dry in the summer, but it tends to be damp and rainy in the winter.

268

It is a two-mile hike from the center of Sheep Ridge Ranch to the county road; then another five or six miles to the nearest small town. The last half of the trail into the Ranch, or The Ridge, as residents call it, is so rutted that only four-wheel-drive vehicles (and hikers) can make it to the parking area without danger. Still, there are always several vehicles and an occasional trailer on the property. Bill Wheeler, like Lou Gottlieb, preaches against the evils of the automobile and mechanized equipment but such opinions have not prevented him—until recently—from owning several vehicles, including a tractor used in the community garden. Cars are always available to take residents to town for shopping, to the city on business, or to court. Cars are among the harsh realities of modern life, even if one practices "voluntary primitivism."

Like Morning Star and other open-land communities, Sheep Ridge Ranch places its emphasis on people's relation to the land rather than their relation to each other. As a rule, there is little departure from traditional standards on the interpersonal level. Women retain their subordinate roles as homemakers, childbearers, cooks, and bottlewashers. Men roam the land in search of food, dope, and occasionally other women. The double standard, monogamous family units, separate housing and cooking, private property (except for land) prevail. Following the territorial imperative, each family unit usually stakes out its own space. Others are welcome to visit that space but not to occupy it.

No doubt, the concept of "Land Access To Which Is Denied No one" requires this separation of units on the land in order to avoid overcrowding in any one space and to maximize individual freedom. It supports and encourages the do-your-own-thing hippie ethic, which is very closely tied to the good old American tradition of rugged individualism, although the hippie way is in fact a rugged *cooperative* individualism rather than competitive. The ideal is for people to relate to each other as they feel the need. The problem is that individuals come together on the land with most of the hang-ups they acquired from the society they left. Little improvement in the depth and quality of human relationships can occur under these conditions, as the need for individual freedom takes precedence over the need for community. "Community" means working problems out with others, not just doing what you want to do. It means having to compromise and to do some things that may be disagreeable. Openland people, like Bill, Ramon, and Lou, are highly individualistic, preferring to spend a lot of their time working on the land, reading, meditating, and tripping. Although they espouse personal change and personal enlightenment, they see this coming about in man's relationship to the land more than in his relationship to people. In part, I subscribe to this perspective, for it contains an important truth. Each individual needs the awareness and experience of his roots in nature in order to reach his personal nirvana. But I strongly doubt that a full actualization of potential can occur without exposure to a heavy

270

load of interpersonal stimuli and conflict-producing/
problem-solving situations as well.

Regardless of the cerebral baloney about enlightenment and self-actualization, the fact is that we cannot
settle for less than everything without chronic personal
dissatisfaction (the plight of humanity). We *need* fulfillment. Where there are holes, we will have aches as long
as the air passes through our beings. It is a perpetual and
fruitless search, which ends in death anyway. But we are
doomed and blessed with this dilemma.

Those on The Ridge who feel a greater need for community form loose-knit bonds with other residents and
share a number of resources; also they occasionally eat
together.

Residents, as well as transients and visitors, convene
each Sunday for a communal feast and sauna bath. Wood
is chopped in the morning and a fire is made to heat rocks
for the bath. By noon, naked bodies are running into the
plastic sauna tent, which is sealed off on all sides. Old

271

wine jugs filled with water are poured on the red-hot rocks inside the tent and the steam permeates the enclosure. After a few minutes of sweating on the mud floor, naked bodies dart out to a cold shower.

This was the scene when Consuelo and I arrived at The Ranch in the spring of 1970. I was impressed with the fact that Bill had installed six chemical toilets and that they were all in good working order. Although it is true we can use the ground and start recycling our wastes directly, I'd rather sit than squat (even if it means sitting on a cold outhouse seat). I admit to being lazy and well-indoctrinated into the "evil" ways of modern technology. Besides, I rationalized, this way Bill avoids problems with the county sanitation officials. As to whether it's the great outdoors or a perfumed chemical toilet for him — that's his business.

Anyway, we sat down on the outer edge of the larger circle that was gathering near the outdoor communal kitchen. Big steel pots of food were being prepared. A gong sounded several times. Presently everyone stood up, joined arms, and began to chant and sway in thanksgiving for the food that was about to be served. Then lines formed and the food was passed out on paper plates. It was a tasty macrobiotic meal of rice and vegetables. Most of the residents adhere with varying degrees of fanaticism to a macrobiotic or vegetarian diet.

I had never met Bill Wheeler, but I quickly spotted him in the crowd, because I had published his picture (taken by a friend and professional photographer, Bob Fitch) in *The Modern Utopian*. Bill is a very young-looking man, and very Anglo-Saxon — blue eyes, light blond hair and beard. He talks with vibrant enthusiasm. He is not shy and seems glad to answer all inquiries and share his opinion on whatever subject is being discussed.

The subject we discussed most that day was his forthcoming trip to court. He had two or three cases pending. One was an assault charge, another had to do with the

272

rights of way on the road, and the third was the usual harassment by county health and sanitation authorities.

Actually Bill and the other residents are quite conscious of sanitation: food scraps are buried for compost, paper and trash is collected and burned periodically. Yet it is easy for officials to find fault if they want to do so.

Early in the morning on October 31, 1969, a 25-man army of policemen, narcotics agents, juvenile officers, FBI agents, et. al., had descended on Sheep Ridge Ranch without benefit of either invitation or search warrant. They said they were looking for juvenile runaways and Army deserters. When they arrested one of the female residents, Bill objected. Without warning, an officer swung around with handcuffs in hand and gashed Bill's forehead with them. This led to a melee of hitting, shoving, and pushing, and the subsequent arrest of Bill and four others on felony charges of assaulting an officer.

When the testimony was all in at the trial, Bill and friends were found not guilty on three counts. The jury could not agree on four other counts, so the judge declared a mistrial.

Bill Wheeler Bathes for an Interview

Going to court is a regularly scheduled event for Bill, which is why every time I see him he's either on his way to court or just finished with it. One such time was in February 1971, after I had moved to San Francisco. Bill came in to visit and be interviewed while taking a bath in my tub. We talked of many things:

DICK: What's happened in the last six months? I haven't been on The Ranch since last July.

BILL: Well, physically the place is growing, there are more and more people coming on. It seems to be the general consensus of opinion that the place is higher than ever, and there are just some really really wonderful people there. It's also the general consensus that we're more together than we ever have been. The sort of organic evolutionary process that we're founded on is bearing fruit now, in terms of a real group head and a feeling of a real group purpose. We're all in a learning process and experimenting and trying to find out what will work, trying to find out in our own heads how we really fit in. I find I become more and more enthusiastic as time goes on.

DICK: That's good. Especially with the open-land concept. Because that's a pretty heavy trip on a person, to have people come in without kicking them off. Do you have any provisions for eliminating people if they get too troublesome?

BILL: Well, in the first year or two I had to kick off one or two people in a very—I didn't really kick them off—I merely said to them, "Look, we have a real personality problem here. The planet earth is a very large place. And we're not supposed to be in the same place." In the last two years, now, there's been no problem. With one exception—one kid who came up here whose mind was completely blown, I guess on speed or something, and was totally psychotic and was a case ideally suited for Marat-Sade. You see, there's sort of a fine balance on the land between private property and communal property, and people soon learn when they come on the land that just because it's open land doesn't necessarily mean that you have the right to go into anybody's place. A person's home is private and this boy couldn't comprehend that. He went in and tore places apart, and

274

started getting automobiles and tearing them apart. At first the more devoted maniacs for open land would say, "Oh, he's all right," and then after a while said, "Something's gotta be done about that kid."

DICK: And *you* had to be the one to do the something about it, no?

BILL: Well, it got to the point where it was more than me. It wasn't a personal thing. . . . But in general we've had a very very beautiful sort of people, and I really see that the open-land concept — you know, all of Lou's theories of the divine casting — is true. When there's a need and when something has to be done, if you've got open land, that person appears and the job gets done. I've seen it happen time and time again. . . . As time has gone on there have been people who have settled there, who have adjusted to the open-land concept and have become dedicated to it. They've also found their own niche, for what they do on The Ranch. We have one person who takes care of the water. We have one person who will do a community run of some kind or other, and we have another person who takes care of the livestock. Each person seems to have found a thing. It's really an incredible thing just to watch it happen, sort of unfold before your eyes. We've been very fortunate that the legal problems, although they're still very critical against us, have been somewhat resolved.

DICK: There was a time when you were worried that the road access to the property would be cut off.

BILL: Yes, absolutely. See, we've had a real hard time legally. We've probably had as hard a time as any commune could possibly have. The county is trying to close us down, the access is being denied to us by a neighbor: two major lawsuits. That's a pretty heavy thing to fight.

DICK: Why do you think that the county has been so opposed to this open-land thing?

BILL: There are many reasons. But I would say one of the primary ones is economic. Naturally, there are elements of politics involved. "The hippies are living off welfare, living off the fat of the land. Why are they having such a good time while us people have to slave in factories 8 hours a day?" That's part of it. Another part is that we depress land values in the area.

DICK: People don't want to buy land next to a hippie commune.

BILL: Sure, unless they're hippies themselves. Also, the access road is through the property of a man who is very influential politically, and has, you know, made a major contribution to the DA's election fund. So, he's able to bring force against us.

DICK: I have theorized that maybe some of the local, rural teen-age girls come out there. Then their parents get uptight because there might be a bad influence on them and so they go to the DA to try to get rid of you. Is that a valid reason?

Bill Wheeler, Zen Jack, Heather, & Claudia the cow

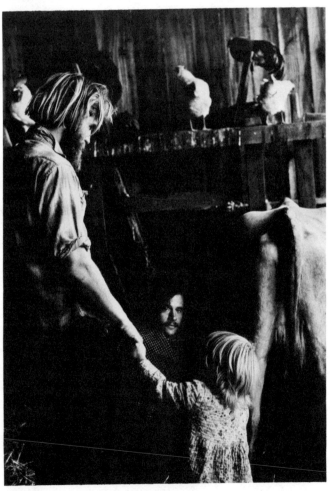

BILL: No, not really. The high school was coming there. A couple of them, maybe five or six, were up there sitting around. Actually I was very nervous about it. But, our thing, our ace in the hole so to speak, is the access road, which is such a miserable road. It's the old Marshall McLuhan thing, the 20th century is communication. Well, we are living in the 19th century. That road buffers us. Primarily because of automobiles. People do *not* want to leave their cars. This is slightly off the subject, but speaking of automobiles, it's been a problem which has bothered me for a long time . . . the whole problem of exclusive transportation. My vision had been that The Ranch would have strictly communal automobiles, no private cars. As it's worked out, The Ranch is so large and there are so many people, it's really hard to have a policy like that. But we have gotten a school bus on the land, a 32-passenger 1950 International school bus, and we squeeze in about 50 guys. And we've got a ton-and-a-half flatbed truck. I've sworn myself never to own another automobile as long as I live.

DICK: That's a hard thing to do.

BILL: Yeah, well, it's where it's at, though. Because the air's becoming unbreathable. With the bus, we pollute much less. Like 1/32nd of a pollution per person. Less than that actually 'cause we often have 50 or 60 people riding in the bus at a time. The whole point of The Ranch up there, or a lot of it, is that we are learning new life styles. Part of that alternative life style is a low consuming way of life. So private transportation, which means more pollution, is out. We combine forces for communal transportation, otherwise just hitchhike. It's amazing what a wonderful way of getting around hitchhiking is. Lou has found it out. He says he loves it. I told him last year, "Get rid of your car, Lou, like, you gotta hitchhike."

DICK: Has he gotten rid of his car?

BILL: Oh yeah. He doesn't own a car anymore.

DICK: How does he get to court?

BILL: He hitchhikes.

DICK: Isn't that a problem? Hitchhiking is not a time-oriented thing and if you've got a time when you have to be there. . . .

BILL: You'd be amazed at how easy it is to get rides. Incidentally, we now have our own food conspiracy on The Ranch — we order food in bulk about two weeks before we're going to buy it. We send out a list of available stuff and people order what they want. My wife adds it up, and then someone goes into San Francisco. We try to get about $50 worth extra for the free store, so that people on the land who don't have any money can get free food. We do this once every month. People are very excited about it; it's a real getting away from health-food stores and getting real participation in the commune. So that's been a really nice thing. We've also set up a church, the Ahimsa Church, which is tax-exempt for California, and we hope to get federal exemption soon. The ownership of the land will be in the church and the ownership of the bus and truck will be in the church.

DICK: You're not going to deed the land to God?

BILL: No, the land is going to be in the Ahimsa Church. It's written in the deed that it's "land access to which is denied no one"; the land cannot be sold, nor can it be used for exploitative purposes. There always has been a funny dichotomy between Morning Star and The Ridge, in that, well, you know, we love Morning Star, it's our spiritual home, it's our Mecca so to speak. But we see also that we're in a New Age and we've got to get together. A lot of it has to do with the nature of the land, a lot of it has to do with who's there—who originated it and stuff, and we've fought hard for our alternative kind of status. The reason we've been as successful as we have is because we're isolated. Appropriately isolated from straight society. Whereas Morning Star is so close and so exposed, it's like a raw nerve. This is one of the reasons why they've had such a hard time. Tourists in general are very debilitating to a community. I think most places have found this and it's really a drag. People coming in with cameras and people getting uptight. The reason we don't have to get uptight is because we're isolated enough that anyone who cares enough to walk in that far is cool. Also, if a person is uncool, there's enough of us and so few of them that we're protected. And they know it. There are a lot of people down there. Very rarely do we ever get any really bad trouble, in terms of drunks coming in and stuff like that. We had one scary thing happen up on The Ridge. One guy just opened up one day with a rifle. It scared the shit out of everybody. Some drunk came roaring in, you know. But this could happen anywhere. It could happen in San Francisco, walking up Haight Street. I'll say this, that

Lou Gottlieb (lower left), Ramon Sender (with accordian),
and Bill Wheeler (lower right)

The Ridge is maintaining its record of lots of babies and no deaths.
And no major injuries actually. We've had a few illnesses but . . .

DICK: I'd really like to ask you about the difficulty of living on the
land. If you have a trailer, or a house that's fairly well insulated on
the land—no problem. But if you're living on the land, almost literally, like Ramon was doing, that's another thing. Ramon had to leave
because the baby got pneumonia, I guess. . . .

BILL: Well, that wasn't quite the reason why he left, but it is hard.
It definitely is harder, and especially those couple of weeks of steady
rain during January.

DICK: A young person living on the land like that might be able to
stand it better than someone who's older. But when he himself gets
older, if he's there long enough, it might take effect on him—rheuma-
tism, that kind of thing. I was wondering if there is an awareness of
the possible ill effects of this. Obviously there are good things about
living really close to the land, but most of us are not *geared* to that
kind of thing.

BILL: I suppose this is one of the ways that open land has a built-in
population control.

279

DICK: You either build a suitable place or you leave.

BILL: Yeah, it's not all a bed of roses. You see thousands and millions and millions of people in the city and you say to yourself: why aren't they all up on The Ranch, free land and all? But it's hard. And, I don't know, it's kind of a mystical thing. The thing about it is we are the avant-garde, we are the, if you will, the future. We are learning new ways of living. I was just reading—it's a ridiculous book but—Leon Uris's *Exodus,* the Israeli thing. Like, I'd never really read too much about Zionism and all the things they went through in Israel. But I see real parallels between what happened there and the young people who are moving from the cities and on to the land here. The parallels are alike in a lot of different ways. For example, much of the early experiments of the Israelis were very disappointing and they needed support from the world Jews to keep them going. They couldn't support themselves. In this sense I feel that the welfare trip which goes on at The Ranch is really just a subsidy from the government to help us get going. Because agriculture things take years and years and years to get going. Home industries take a long time to get going—to support themselves. Most people *want* to support themselves. I don't think there's really anybody on welfare who doesn't want to support himself. But it's going to take time for us young people to find out where we're at, to know exactly what we want to do. The energies are there. There's *no* doubt in my mind about that. The imagination is there—*no* doubt about that. What I've seen of what can be done, it's *incredible*. But it's going to take time. The real insight which I had on this was the Bolinas thing—the Standard Oil disaster in the Bay. I was out in Bolinas, and just to see thousands and thousands of young people out—most of them longhairs—doing a really beautiful thing cleaning up.

DICK: Yes, and the older people there were Standard Oil employees. They were getting paid for the work, and the longhairs weren't.

BILL: Right. Therefore the experiments, such as Morning Star and such as The Ranch, are of critical importance to this country. We are finding ways—ecological ways—to live in harmony with the earth. It's not easy. Time's gone on and a lot of communes have fallen by the wayside; others are still there—like Morning Star is still there—

280

in spite of everything that's happened. The Ranch is better than ever, you know: it's going great guns. And the authorities know it.

DICK: Do they still come onto the property to check you out?

BILL: No, they haven't been on the property for, oh God, well they came up maybe three or four months ago, to deliver a message — some girl whose mother was dying or something.

DICK: I've been getting the feeling that there's getting to be an awful lot more tolerance of longhairs — at least in urban areas where people have had more exposure. It seems the media have picked up on the positive aspects as well as the negative ones lately.

BILL: It goes in cycles. There was a cycle like this about a year and a half ago, in which it looked like communes were the up-and-coming thing, you know. *Life* magazine had their *beautiful* article, all those pretty, you know, apple-pie photographs. And I mean, it's just yummy! It looked like: "Oh my God, we made it! They've *accepted* us. Wonderful!" Two weeks later what happened? Manson. And the honeymoon was over. My feeling is that it's very similar to the Army, like Manson was the My Lai of the hippie movement. The Manson thing has blown over; people really don't have much interest in that anymore. It's hard to really gauge movements — it's hard to gauge exactly how far along they are. All you can tell is that more and more kids are turning on, and the kids are growing older. The lawyers have been turning on and they're going up the ladder. So things irrevocably are changing. But there's no illusion in my mind whatsoever that there are many hard times ahead. We are very much like the Vietcong. We're an underground movement. We're going to take some very hard blows for sure. It's not inconceivable that the county will succeed in tearing down all the buildings on The Ranch. But one of the things that I'm envisioning — I'm sure will happen — is that the movement is above material objects, is above physical objects. It will transcend them, and it will go on from there. We'd hate to see the place torn down and we'll actually fight to our dying breath to prevent it. But we are a form of guerilla warfare and we're going to take our losses. People have said that The Ranch is the most revolutionary place in the United States. I mean, there are all kinds of postulations which you can make, in terms of solving the urban ills, solving the social ills, solving the physical ills — you can go right down the line.

281

But it's an idea, the thing is an idea—it's a simple idea, it's capsule. It's so simple that you will overlook it . . . it's new. That's what's nice about it too.

DICK: There's not too much that's new.

BILL: Well, what's new? It's presumptious to say that. Perhaps it's new within our social context. Lou was able to articulate it. He was able to really put it down in words. I think a lot of us felt, believed, that the earth is common, is owned by all the people. I'm sure that open land would have happened, but maybe not quite like it did. As far as The Ridge went and what happened, it was a real leap of faith to open the land. Originally, my wife and myself were living on The Ridge, and that was it. Then Morning Star started getting closed down. I admired Lou and I believed what he was saying. I didn't particularly want the gig, but I didn't have the choice in the matter. The land was there. . . .

DICK: You originally lived in the studio, didn't you?

BILL: It's a very funny thing concerning that, because the studio was going to be the landmark case to challenge the building code, to take it up to the Supreme Court. Halfway through the case I told my lawyer, "I don't want to live in it anymore. I want to move out onto the land." And he says, "We've done all this work! My God! We've prepared the case! And here you tell me you want to move out of it!" And what was even funnier about the whole thing was that the judge said to me in effect, "You've got to move back into the studio." They wanted to continue the case, and they didn't want me living in any hippie shack. They wanted to fight over that one studio. The judge just recently signed this order to destroy all the buildings on the land. And the only building that isn't being destroyed is the studio. *I* can live in the studio. It's strange.

DICK: It's kind of the precedent set by the case at Morning Star, right? They leave one building for you only to live in. Their decisions reinforce the private-property trip.

BILL: And so they don't get too guilty about what they're doing. The judge has signed the order, the decision has gone against us on the local level, for tearing down the buildings. Next week we find out some very critical things as to whether, pending appeal, they're going to allow us to stay on the land.

DICK: Next week? You're always having these crisis weeks. I remember the last time I was up there it was next week they were going to decide if you'd have access to the road. I have no doubt, from my feelings about it, though, that you're going to be there. Still, it's a very far-out thing, that next week, again, you're always being pushed up against the wall.

BILL: Yeah, it's a real brinkmanship kind of thing. . . . There's this supervisor in Sonoma County — I oddly enough met him at the tax window a couple of years ago. He's actually a fairly nice guy, and he's fairly friendly to me. And he said a very wise thing. He said, "You know, we've *got* to fight against you. Every revolution that's ever happened has had resistance against it, and if you think this one's going to be any different, you're crazy." I thought about it. And he's right — we need it. It's got to happen that way. For us to come together we've got to fight for what we believe in, in the same way the Israelis fought for what they believed in. The way every other tribe has fought. Anyway it's pretty exciting. We've got our food conspiracy going and we've got our school bus. We've got a craft shop happening. It's a very well-stocked craft shop — band saw, vice, table saw, cleaner, sander.

DICK: Is someone in charge of it?

BILL: Let's put it this way: there's a couple of people who know the combination of the lock.

DICK: So they make sure that anyone who's in there knows how to use the tools.

BILL: Yeah, right. There's one person and you'll go in there and he'll be working and other people will come in. We have a rule that no tools can leave the shop. If you're going to do something, you have to do it right there. Otherwise the tools would be spread out all over The Ranch.

DICK: Yes, or just disappear. Not everybody who comes on property like that has the consciousness that it should be shared. So they rip things off. I had this happen when I was in Berkeley. I mean, I just put my records out. You know, anybody could play them, anybody coming in. And I lost dozens of them before I realized we weren't all ready for that. So what you've done on The Ridge is opened the land to everyone; *but* in terms of specific, functioning things, there has to be, at this point, some sort of control —

BILL: — it's not that there *has* to be . . . there *is!* It's happened. This is the way it's evolved into — it's what the people want. Lou says himself, open land is just open land, and that's all it is. And anybody that has any comprehension that it's anything else is very sadly mistaken.

DICK: Whatever else happens on the land evolves from the people who are there. Whether it's structured or unstructured, or whether it becomes a crash pad, or an ashram, or whatever.

BILL: Right, that's correct.

DICK: So what's happening on your open land, is the creation of an ashram.

BILL: Yes, but to experience it you just have to go up there and see what's happening. I can say it's a very nice place to live. I'm happy, and my wife's happy.

TOLSTOY FARM

Late in 1968 I received a communication, either directly or indirectly (I'm not sure which) from Huw Williams in Washington State. I published it in *The Modern Utopian.*

My wife and I have 80 acres which we would like to use as the basis for a community of homesteading families and a cooperative free-learning school. We can also rent more land nearby to use for a cooperative cattle business. We have homesteaded on this land for three years and supply our monetary needs through farmwork and a small leather business, making moccasins, sandals, papoose carriers and saddles. Our current desire is to get in contact with other families who need land and want to homestead and participate in a cooperative school, cattle business, and/or handicrafts business.

Later, when I reread the old community news digest in back issues of *The Modern Utopian,* I realized that the

284

80-acre tract of land Huw was talking about was none
other than a portion of a commune called Tolstoy Farm. I
had already heard from and about Tolstoy Farm earlier
that year, having received a letter from someone there.
That letter, too, had been published in *The Modern
Utopian*, although as an anonymous piece:

I am writing to request a favor. We would really really appreciate it if
you would absolutely not print ANYTHING about us in your magazine. Nothing against *The Modern Utopian*. We read it with interest
and pleasure. But we have a serious (for us) population and transient
problem and we don't want any publicity at all . . . for us it is a matter of being able to survive here.

This is a problem I am continually running into — first a
group wants publicity in order to attract new members;
then they holler "we can't handle all the visitors." Or vice
versa. It's a very changing scene. But then, growth requires change.

In time I got to learn more about Huw Williams and
Tolstoy Farm. I discovered that Huw's parents and grand-
parents had owned over 800 acres of land in the State of
Washington. And it was Huw's mother who had given him
80 acres of the land after he dropped out of the University
of Washington and started a nonviolent training center.
Huw rented a building, near his land, called Heart House,
for the center. More than 50 people passed through the
center during its first summer of operation. Huw married
one of those visitors, Sylvia, and the two of them decided
to form an intentional community based on the anarchist
principle of voluntary cooperation: no rules, no structure,
people helping each other because they saw a need and
wanted to be of service. The community would be open to
anyone and no one would be asked to leave.

Heart House became the center of and living space for
this communal experiment. But without any rules or

structure, so many people living in such close quarters were doomed to chaos. Constant interpersonal frictions rubbed people raw, as could be expected.

People who are new to each other and refuse to develop any sort of structure, group consensus, or methods of dealing with problems inevitably become enemies rather than friends. The larger the size of the group, the worse the problem, and the greater the need for structure. If they are reasonably compatible, two people may be able to live together well without structure. But five or ten or more people will need some sort of framework for dealing with the inevitable variety of problems that will arise. Three basic rules of thumb for new communes organizing are: (1) the more people, the more structure; (2) the less thoroughly members know and understand each other, the more structure; and (3) the less time members spend together, the more structure.

In 1967 there was a mass upsurge of nation-wide interest in rural living in the hippie subculture. Tolstoy Farm was among the places invaded by wandering nomads from psychedelica. As publicity grew, there were runaways, speed freaks, and all varieties of teenyboppers looking for a home on the land, where they could "do their thing" without being hassled by parents and authorities. These transients wanted to be free of responsibilities that were forced on them at home, yet they still wanted to be fed and clothed by "mommy" and "daddy." At Heart House, the permanent residents were forced into the role of parents. And because their resources were limited, the transients considered them uptight and stingy. Dissatisfaction grew so intense that permanent members of the group pooled their resources and bought 120 acres of land located at the far end of the same canyon, some two miles away. These people, including Huw and Sylvia, then moved out of Heart House and built separate living quarters on the newly acquired land. (It was around this time that I received the plea to stop publishing their address; they had really had it up to here with "guests.")

There was a lot of talk about burning Heart House down. This mood must have been strong for the house was mysteriously destroyed by fire in the spring of 1968. (We always get what we want — if we want it badly enough; so it's important to know what it is you *really* want.) It seems that most of the serious-minded folk at Tolstoy were prepared or nearly prepared for the fire. They completed their separate housing, while those transients who were not really serious about the community soon left. A few lean-tos or makeshift structures were also built for temporary shelter during the warmer months which followed.

Since mid-1968 Tolstoy has settled into the individualistic community pattern. It is open "land access to which is denied no one." Huw's North 80 and the South 120 are now cooperatively owned by the Mill Canyon Society. Each family unit establishes its own household by building its own dwelling, tending its own garden, and furnishing its own supplies. Each family usually owns at least two vehicles — a car or motorcycle plus a truck or tractor. Families who live near each other work out cooperative arrangements regarding babysitting, household and farm chores, and, on occasion, the sharing of a meal together.

On the North 80, residents gather in the evening at the cowshed. The two dairy cows give nine gallons of milk a day. Any food produced for communal use is stored here. Mail is delivered to this location, for distribution. The cowshed is, in fact, the gathering spot for people living at this end of the canyon.

There are no modern conveniences at Tolstoy Farm — no electricity, no flush toilets, no gas heaters; no clocks (and therefore no regimentation of time and dates). The people tend a communal garden, as well as their many individual ones. Many of the residents get food stamps and unemployment compensation or welfare. A few of the permanent people take parttime jobs to earn extra cash to support their families. Huw makes and sells leather goods; some residents make wall hangings, pottery and jewelry, and other craft products.

During the warmer months of the year, 50 or more adults live at Tolstoy. There are at least two dozen year-round residents and almost as many children. Besides Thanksgiving, which all families celebrate at the schoolhouse, there is a communal celebration on the first full moon of May. This is a corn dance festival, adapted from the ceremonies of the Hopi Indians, during which the families have a huge feast. They dance, sing, get stoned, and take turns beating on a homemade drum. It is a nightlong event that lasts until dawn, when everyone falls asleep in exhaustion.

Like most homestead-oriented, individual family-unit communities, Tolstoy retains traditional sex roles: men do the heavy work—haul that barge, tote that bale (of hay); women do household chores—cooking, cleaning, sewing, childtending. The roles are more clearly defined here than in contemporary suburbia. For those who can accept these traditional roles there is a great deal of satisfaction. This seems to be the case for most of the men and women who live at Tolstoy, as well as for the people at other open-land communities and hippie-style communes.

In my view of human growth, adoption of such a pattern represents one step forward and two steps backward. Having to settle into culturally conditioned roles in order to get back to a more reverent and natural relationship to the land has to be a most dubious form of progress. When, under the circumstances, individuals decide that they must forsake the advantages of modern technology in order to avoid its evils, they also forsake the notion that men and women need to expand their potentialities beyond traditional sex roles. Men need to cook and women need to chop wood; men and women all need to start defining themselves as human beings capable of diversity and beyond categorization. When we return to the land and the necessity for heavy physical labor, such as baling hay and digging ditches and cutting trees, the tendency is to let brute man function here and to let soft woman nurse the child and stir the pot. Man develops muscle and woman develops tears. And how far is it from here to the outside world? A few steps to one side and we have the Land of Establishment Men: men's houses — men's bars — fights — military — patriotism — Pentagon — war — American Legion. And a few steps to the other side brings us to the land of Establishment Women: women's quilting bees — sewing circles — gossip — mother — country — apple pie — Daughters of the American Revolution. We then, alas, come full circle.

By 1969, a total of 13 homes had been built at Tolstoy Farm, many of them with livestock and outbuildings. At present, Huw is trying to develop a free school for the children at the farm as well as for outside children who would like to attend. As Huw envisions it, the school would be a place where the students are "free to choose their own projects and pursue their particular interests at their own speed."

The community already has the facilities, having built an 18-sided (nearly round) schoolhouse made of pumice block, concrete, wood, and glass. It is designed to support a geodesic dome as a second story. The cost to date has been approximately $1,300.

Huw and the other members emphasize that the entire farm can be the educational environment not only for the children but for the adults as well. They hope to cooperate more and more in the future to provide everyone with a wide range of cultural activities, drawing on the resources and talents of all the members.

There are several different points of view at Tolstoy about what the ideal community should be. Huw still holds firmly to his anarchist philosophy. He'd rather do all

the work himself and not impose any rules upon others
(the good old American pioneering spirit). Others feel that
there needs to be some authority and organization in any
situation where people live together. And a few others feel
they would like a much more intimate community, forming a group marriage with six or more adults. As a result
of these differing viewpoints, a certain amount of unre-
lieved tension is generated among these people when they
come together. Fortunately, there are 200 acres at Tolstoy.
Perhaps as each group comes closer to its own ideal or
mellows in its position, the tension will diminish.

CHAPTER SIX

GROUP-MARRIAGE COMMUNES

HARRAD WEST

GROUP MARRIAGE can be defined as a voluntary association to create a family group, in which there is sexual
sharing, consisting of four or more adult members with
at least two of each sex. Such a group-marriage community, called Harrad West, was started in Berkeley, California.* I published their public statement in *The Modern
Utopian* magazine:**

Our basic idea at Harrad West is that perhaps six, eight or even a
dozen or more adults can form "marriage" relationships with each
other as a means of attaining far more than monogamous marriages
can offer. (There are presently six adults, three male and three female, plus three children living here.)

The six adults at that time were Don, Barbara, Bill,
Karen, Jack and Molly. I had known all of them (except
Molly) for some time, since before Harrad West, so that
I had had the chance to observe a group marriage in the
making. But that sounds too objective and impersonal.
As it happened, their lives and mine became interwoven,
first in a group meeting and then in a communal experi-
ment I started.

THE EVOLUTION OF A GROUP
MARRIAGE

It was back in 1968 that I organized a weekly meeting
that lasted for about one year and was known in the Bay
Area simply as the Wednesday Night Group. The group

*The name Harrad West is inspired by a book, *The Harrad Experiment*,
written by Robert Rimmer. Bob Rimmer is one of the foremost proponents
for group marriage in the United States today. In addition to *The Harrad
Experiment* which is a fictitious account of college students who evolve a
group marriage, Rimmer has several other fiction and non-fiction books on
the subject to his credit, including *The Rebellion of Yale Marrett*, *Proposition 31*, *You and I Searching for Tomorrow*, *Harrad Letters* (see bibliography).
** *The Modern Utopian*, volume 4, no. 1, winter, 1970.

meeting was intended for people interested in the possibility of setting up one or more intentional communities. What I wanted to do was to get a commune started with *The Modern Utopian* publication as the basic working project. I too was personally interested in group marriage. It seemed like a positive alternative to the unhappy marital situation in which I found myself at the time.

Don and Barbara began to come to the meetings regularly. At first there was something about Don's behavior I didn't like. He seemed an insecure show-off. Barbara was very thin and very quiet — I wasn't too impressed. It was two months before I learned from them that they too were interested in a group marriage. I was surprised: Barbara appeared unlikely to be that liberated or experimental. Don and Barbara had been married 14 years before deciding that a group-marriage community was right for them. They had tried and tired of the "swinging" (mate-swapping) scene and wanted relationships with more depth.

Eventually I rented a big old 12-room house in Berkeley and decided to live communally. Peter, a friend of mine, held the lease, but now he was splitting up with his wife and heading for the country. None of the other people living there — hip Berkeley types — wanted to pick up the lease so they also decided to move. They promised to be out by September. Since that was only two months away, I consented to live in their communal scene and bring new people in later. But September came and only one couple had left, although not before storing most of their gear in the basement and a few closets. Another couple went to visit friends in the country and promised to return to move out by September 10.

In the meantime I arranged for Don and Barbara to move into the house on that date. Don, a commercial artist, was enthusiastic about the prospect of working on TMU magazine. He had dreams of quitting his regular job and working within the commune movement full-time. I had grown to like him and Barbara a great deal. We had driven to Iowa to visit Don's mother, so now I felt positive about having a stable family move into the house. Their three children—Lynn, 12, Ken, 10, and Joyce, 8—were very bright and also good company. They had been educated mostly in free schools. They were kind, cooperative kids, willing to help on the magazine or in decorating my room; I, in turn, enjoyed helping them with their schoolwork.

By September 10, Don and Barbara had put their suburban house up for sale and were ready to move in. Which is why the couple that should have returned found all their belongings in the basement when they showed up two weeks later. Another carry-over couple moved out of the house in October, disappearing one day while still owing us $40. We agreed to let the last couple stay on one more month because of their "extenuating" circumstances. Meanwhile, three single friends—Andy, Walter, and Ruth—had taken the vacant rooms.

This was not really a life of togetherness yet. All of us, except Barbara, scattered in different directions during the day and evenings. Don continued to work at his job in San Francisco. Andy worked nights, Ruth had an irregular schedule, Walter and I were going to theological school during the day and working with a Unitarian fellowship on some evenings. This commune was an example of what can easily occur in an urban area: too many outside diversions or commitments, too little internal commitment, no real task in common. Everyone had agreed to help on the magazine one night a week. As it turned out, though, only Don, Barbara and the kids could be counted on to do so regularly.

We did set up an effective housekeeping, dishwashing, and cooking schedule. Each of us cooked one communal meal a week and signed up for household chores. As Barbara was around the house most of the time, she ended up doing most of the work herself, out of habit acquired in those suburban days. None of us were particularly satisfied with these arrangements. True, it was inexpensive to live in one house together ($30 for rent plus $25 for food were the shared monthly expenses per adult). But that was not enough. Don and Barbara wanted a group marriage to get started. I preferred more communication through regular meetings, but these were impossible to set up. None of us communicated very well; nor were we very clear about what we really wanted or how we should accomplish it.

In December, 1968, after a six-month marital separation, I had decided to see if there was any chance for reconciliation. When Jonathan Prince, a St. John's University (Minnesota) student, asked if he could come to live in the communal house for a month and learn how the magazine ran, I gave him my room and moved out on what I thought would be a temporary basis. In February 1969, I turned the lease over to Don and Barbara. I was divorced in March and subsequently I moved to Rohnert Park (near Sebastopol), where I became the minister of a small Unitarian church.

Don and family continued to work on the magazine with me one evening a week since I kept an office there as well. Now that I had moved, though, the possibility of our getting back together in a commune was left undiscussed until finally one day I opted for facing the issue squarely.

"I really care a lot about you folks but I don't want to live with you," I said. "We should function independent of one another and yet try to cooperate in those areas where we can be of mutual benefit. I don't want to take advantage of you and I don't want you to put any expectations on me."

"Let me do you a favor," Don replied.

"That's just the point—I don't want you to do me any

favors!" I exclaimed. And Don walked out of the room.

Bill and Karen moved into the Berkeley house soon after I moved out. Bill, an early advocate of group marriage, had been the principal founder of Walden House in Washington, D.C. back in 1965.* After a group marriage failed to develop there, Bill eventually moved out. After that (April 1967), Bill started to compile a list of people around the country who were interested in experimental marriage systems. Many people contacted him because they had read his article entitled "A Utopian Answer: Walden House Plus Group Marriage," which I had run in the first issue of *The Modern Utopian* (September 1966).

In October 1967 I published another article by him, "Utopian Ethics," which was an updated version of his ideas on group marriage. Bill described Utopian ethics as:

positively reinforcing someone because he is a fellow man, not because he is a man of a particular type, but simply because he is part of all being . . . not a simple idealized love of all humanity, but the concrete positive reinforcement of the other real person . . . unconditional positive reinforcement. . . .

Boiling down all Bill's verbiage and excessive jargon, I came to believe that what he was really trying to say was: Any girl whom I want to fuck, should fuck me; any girl who wants me to fuck her, need only ask me. Bill's was a heterosexual approach. He hadn't extended his idea to all persons.

Committed to his ideals and ethics, Bill became interested in swinging, a phenomenon that was fast becoming a well-known, popular pastime for middle-class plastic America. When marital boredom sets in and your partner's eye begins to stray, how do you hold the marriage together? How do you keep mommy or daddy from abandoning you? How would it be, being alone and on the mar-

---

* See the section on Walden House in Chapter III.

riage market again? And the answer is: compartmentalize the "threat" of extramarital sex and conventionalize the rest of marriage; that is, become a swinger.

Bill, however, really did look upon swinging as the first major step toward group marriage. Many of the people he corresponded with had been swingers and were now interested in living communally.

Bill eventually met Karen and together they moved to California. In Berkeley, Bill and Karen appeared super-straight. I remember the first night they came to the house: Bill in his suit and tie, very stiff and formal, his words well guarded; Karen, in her best party dress, more conversational, but very proper. Even after several visits, they remained basically unchanged in their formality of dress and composure. Bill, especially, found it easier to join the Sexual Freedom League than to relax his manners.

The other two adult members of Harrad West were Jack and Molly. Jack was pushing sixty, a past member of the Wednesday Night Group, separated from his black wife, and overly sensitive to the feelings of others ever since his mind-blowing encounter weekend at the Esalen Institute. He was a man who could be counted on — honest, sincere, no bullshit, anxious to be a friend.

Then there was Molly — recently separated from her husband, seeing her analyst, and wearing the gaudiest colored dresses you can imagine. She joined the Sexual Freedom League and became the life of the orgy — trying, trying to stay young, and doing quite well at it in a comic sort of way. Molly always made me feel a little uncomfortable, but perhaps it was only because of those lustful glances she used to give me.

THE CREDO OF HARRAD WEST

These, then, were the six adults who started Harrad West in early 1969. And it was from the old 12-room house in Berkeley, now the home of Harrad West, that the group issued its credo which was part of the public statement mentioned earlier:

We feel that a larger number of concerned persons learning and growing together often can deal with stresses that would overwhelm two individuals. In addition, children in a group marriage can be more certain of the continued existence of their families and have more than two adults to rely on.

All adult members of Harrad West are considered married to all other adult members of the opposite sex. "Pair bond" relationships do exist since most of the members entered the community as couples, one with three children. These couples and those who have entered as singles do not demand exclusive rights with each other. Relationships are on all levels. . . .

We believe that sex is vital in a successful marriage. We find that our more ample number of loving relationships helps us to become more affectionate persons. We feel our friendships deepened, our capacity for warmth and understanding increased, and our lives enriched as a result of this community. The development of this rational and agreeable means of helping fulfill our social and sexual nature has enabled us to become more honest with ourselves and others. . . .

We share a certain number of possessions while reserving an ample amount of individual private property. . . . Most of us hold full or part time jobs and we pay monthly sums for housing and food expenses.

Since we are a growing community, we would welcome as new members those who share our aims. . . . Couples who are unsure of how they feel about mate-sharing can find out by first "swinging" with other couples before applying to any group marriage community.

We sponsor weekly meetings in the Bay Area for those interested in exploring group marriage communes. . . . For those who join our community, these weekly meetings and other get-togethers are absolutely necessary. No one may move into Harrad West until we know each other very well.*

*The Modern Utopian, vol. 4, no. 1, winter 1970.

In my opinion, the advice about swinging was very unsound, for it seemed to me that the Harrad West members' ability to relate had not been improved through mate-swapping. As I understand the notion about the swinger route to group marriage fulfillment, group marriage is an intimate personal *relationship* among people; while swinging is essentially sex among people. Now, if you don't know the difference, you're a swinger, and if you do, then maybe you're ready to go from swinging with others to living with them.

Their advice, I think, is like telling a person that if he wants to be sexually free, he should have sex with a donkey; the only thing that happens to the person who follows such advice is that he gets a piece of ass. Swingers and sexual freedom leaguers I've met do not appear more free than others, often quite the opposite — controlled and reserved. Sexual freedom is determined, I believe, by an attitude, an emotional state, rather than by a person's ability to "freely" couple in a room full of couplers.

NEWS FROM JEAN AND SAM

Two people accepted by Harrad West were Sam and Jean, a married couple. However, this apparently did not work out well, for Sam and Jean left Harrad West within a month of having joined. Subsequently, they went to live at Crow, up in Oregon. It was there that I met them and had a chance to find out what had been happening back in Berkeley.

"They used to write little notes to themselves," Sam began. "Saved up all their complaints and hostilities for the Sunday night encounter session — going around all week with that tension inside, unwilling to say anything — waiting for that Sunday evening meeting. The vibes were very heavy there."

"And that woman who ran the encounter sessions," Jean joined in. "A professional therapist, yes, but I don't

299

know if she handled things very well. Don had some serious problems. You knew he quit his job, didn't you?"

"No, I haven't been in contact with them for quite sometime now," I replied.

"Well, he quit his job and then locked himself in a closet for two weeks," Jean continued. "They ended up taking him to the mental ward at Herrick Hospital."

"And the whole thing has split up now," Sam concluded.

"Hold it—back up a bit. Why did he lock himself in a closet?" I asked.

"You know Don was having some pretty heavy experiences in that house, in those encounter sessions," Sam said. "There was an aspect of himself he just wasn't willing to face, and that whole experience just got too much for him. Especially after quitting his job."

"Yeah, the job was a kind of escape, a crutch which he needed. Then, because he was always so busy doing his clown act for kids on weekends, and writing little notes to people, the pressure was on to spend more time relating to others," Jean added.

"So he figured if he quit his job he'd have more time," Sam noted.

"And then he locked himself in a closet! Whew, heavy . . . that's heavy, man," I exclaimed. "How come everyone split? Who's left?"

"Bill and Karen moved out. And Molly too. Jack stayed with Barbara and the kids," said Jean.

"Bill was pretty tight," Sam introjected. "He was always pushing for everything to be on a schedule. They had this elaborate rotating-partners schedule. You had to sleep with whomever you were assigned on the list, whether you felt like it or not that particular night. Bill liked this system. He was afraid if it were done more freely, he might get left out."

"Still, I think Bill opened up a great deal as a result of that experience," I came to Bill's defense. "When he first came to Berkeley, he wasn't very social. He softened some, let down his guard and became much more human and likable."

"Yes, that's true, but he didn't like doing the dirty work very well—housecleaning or anything like that," Jean added.

"Didn't he, Don and Jack do the evening dishes?" I asked. "When I was there last, they decided the women preferred to cook and cooked better than the men so the men did the cleaning up."

A LETTER FROM DON

It was sometime later that I received a letter from Don, bringing me up-to-date with his group marriage:

We are doing rather well now. Barbara went down and ripped off some welfare for us. And now I'm beginning to get some commercial art to do.

Molly and Bill have both moved. We have stopped having Wednesday evening meetings too. Now we have people over if they really seem interested (and interesting). I have talked at a few places too. The idea is to get the whole Harrad West thing out of the house.

A NEW PUBLIC STATEMENT

Meanwhile the members of Harrad West had prepared a new public statement, which was duly distributed as a flyer to the world:

Harrad West is a group of half dozen adults and several children who live together in a big old Berkeley house. We function as a family; joyful, angry, helpful, turned on and turned off. Our children are cared for, we care for each other.

Physical needs that are provided for as a family include housing, food, some recreation and a variety of things related to the home. Our economic structure is similar to that of a cooperative. While employment, transportation and most other things are individual responsibilities, there is a great deal of non structured (spontaneous) sharing within the family. We do not see ourselves as a commune.*

Emotional needs are met (much of the time) in ways that make us different from ordinary families for we believe in multilateral relationships between adults. Our shared ideals include a belief in openness and honesty between people, responsibility for one's own feelings and concern for others. Our family has had regular group therapy sessions within the house and most of us have been involved with individual therapy.

If you are interested in multilateral relationships, we suggest reading Robert Rimmer's books, *The Harrad Experiment* and *Proposition 31*, as well as *Stranger in a Strange Land* and *The Moon is a Harsh Mistress* by Robert Heinlein. These books each contain fictional accounts of multilateral marriages. An excellent series of articles, based on information gathered from existing multilateral marriages, has been written by Larry and Joan Constantine, 23 Mohegan Road, Acton, Mass. 01720. Send a stamped envelope for information. Two good books on therapy are *Gestalt Therapy Verbatum* by Fritz Pearls and *Don't Push the River* by Barry Stevens.

In two years we have come up with an alternate to the existing family structure. It isn't exactly what we planned, but it is us. If you think something similar might fit you we would like to hear from you. We have no big organization to join. We are just humans who want to know and enjoy other humans.

A PERSONAL REACTION

The Wednesday Night Group, the communal start at my Berkeley house, the people involved, the conversation

---

*Many groups do not consider themselves a commune by their own definition of that word. They might, for instance, define "commune" as a group which shared all things in common—no private property or private space, etc.—and oppose this idea. As I mentioned in the Introduction, the term is used loosely by myself and others who do not care to deal in precise definitions.

with Jean and Sam — put all of these together and then try to reconcile the result with Harrad West's new statement. It won't be easy. The experience and the statement are separated by the yawning chasm between reality and fantasy, public propaganda and private practice, posture and perception.

Translating ideals into actuality is damned hard. But simply intimating on paper that it has been done is to bridge the chasm with a mythic structure that can't possibly bear the weight of real people trying to cross at your beckoning.

Read all the science fiction you want, read all the articles on multilateral marriages and gestalt therapy and modern utopias. But just forget about *doing* your thing until you've got enough self-awareness and courage to be able to deal with revealing your failings as well as your successes.

Pep talks and propaganda have no place in positive interpersonal relations, for they sell only products or images, not human beings.

By telling only the best part of the story or pretending that utopia is finally a reality, how many people will believe you. I'll bet the only people attracted to such a story will be those who love to fool themselves. These are the people who, when confronted with the problems of attempting to actually live their ideals, either run into the closet (seek refuge in beliefs) or run out of the house (escape from reality).

Until these people can face the ugly as well as the beautiful, the cycle will simply keep repeating itself — another broken marriage, another dose of incompatibility, and another load of blame dumped on somebody else for one's own failings.

I hadn't been back to visit Harrad West for quite some time when that mythic manifesto appeared. I felt that if they had been more frank, more honest — especially with themselves—their statement would have begun something like this:

"We are attempting to be a group marriage but it's not easy. Each of us is fucked-up as a result of our previous conditioning and hang-ups, which we cling to like grim death. But despite the pain and the difficulty of sharing and growing toward a new family structure, we keep at it. Why the compulsion, why the need? Lots of reasons. But what's really important is that, whatever the reasons, we have made the choice to go ahead in this direction. We know there are no absolutes and that group marriage isn't the ultimate answer to anything. But group marriage is what we're attempting to explore now. . . ."

Of course, I realize that these words, or any others, can be dismissed as just verbiage. In the long run the best thing to say is nothing. However, words are a valued part of our cultural heritage-hang-up, so the alternative may be to say everything. That, of course, ends up being nothing and everything and so forth and so forth.

The way we say something is important, though, because it will attract the kind of people who dig it. And if we don't dig the kind of people we're attracting, we've just got to try saying it another way. . . .

Harrad West is still functioning and living in the same place. I'll bet (and hope) they've come a long way as a result of their early experiences.

THE CRO RESEARCH ORGANIZATION

Before I visited the Cro Research Organization in Oregon, commonly known simply as Crow, I heard at least a dozen rumors about the place. Seven of them, just to give you an idea, were as follows:

—"There are about 50 people who eat, sleep, and work inside a gigantic dome-like structure."

—"Everything is shared totally, including sex. There is no private space. It's just one big open dome."

—"It's mainly an agricultural commune, with lots of land and a large herd of cattle."

—"There are actually two groups with two differing life styles living on the land. They keep separate but are friendly and cooperative. They're encouraging other groups to come there and settle."

—"Don't go to Crow. They have a lot of interpersonal tension to work out and aren't open to visitors now."

—"Cro Research Organization. Yes, I know about them. They just got burned out. Had a big fire over there. I think everyone has left now."

—"A fire burned down one of the houses near the road. All that remains of it is a big stone chimney. They have another house back up the road."

Then there was the information I received directly from the group. According to a prospectus I received from Crow, "CRO represents a radical new experiment in 'total involvement' living. . . . Its overriding goal is to create a total immersion community in a rural environment that combines creatively the advantages of farm living with those usually associated with the urban setting."

I visited Crow to find out for myself. At Crow, I learned, the members are not the slow, pondering easygoing ranch types. Rather, they are active, aggressive, and forward. They tend to impose themselves on the land, rather than blend with it. They earn enough money to make the $1,200 monthly payments on their 65-acre farm site. Most of the cash income is derived from outside contractual jobs, such as crop-picking, house painting, and other short-term projects. By hustling, this 28-member commune has an income and expenses that balance out at approximately $3,000 per month. This does not prevent these people from eating well. The night I visited, for instance, dinner consisted of steak, mashed potatoes, asparagus, lima beans, salad, and various assorted drinks.

305

Crow has several head of beef cattle (not a herd as reported in one of the quotes) grazing in pasture. They hope to add more cattle gradually. They had purchased a pregnant dairy cow, Bessie, two weeks before my arrival. One of the women, Lillian, was made responsible for Bessie's care. She explained in some detail what this chore entailed. While most women at Crow are happy in the kitchen and the nursery performing traditional female roles, Lillian finds greater satisfaction in minding the cows and also in learning to be a midwife. She is studying with a woman doctor and hopes to learn midwifery well enough to be able to travel from commune to commune helping pregnant mothers deliver at home.

A worthy service, I thought. Yet, somehow, I looked at that pregnant cow contentedly chewing her cud and felt sure that in this day most expectant mothers were about as dumb as she, especially those who were working on their second or third "calf." I could forgive the cow. Her mental and emotional capacity is limited. Pregnant women, on the other hand, are capable of understanding the dangers of over-population.

According to the CRO prospectus, "Communication among members, children and adults, must be established at all levels, verbal and nonverbal, to an extent far beyond that usually deemed 'acceptable' in conventional society. This means that the traditional 'right to privacy' is consciously and voluntarily surrendered by all members."

I was told soon after I arrived that this is a radical experiment in community living. There is no right to privacy. Although each member has his own sleeping area and space for personal property (clothes, toothbrush, and the like), anyone can occupy that space, at any time, day or night. No rooms are private. In practice, though, this is not always the case, much to the dismay of some — and the relief of others.

TWO HOUSES

Actually, there are *two* houses at Crow, rather than one, and, correspondingly, two major opposing life styles.

The larger house is not a dome, but a dormered two-story structure, which serves as a communal kitchen and provides space for dining, living, sleeping, and recreation. Adjacent to the living room are the children's sleeping quarters. Besides bunk beds, this room contained two or three boxes of toys. Upstairs there were two large bedrooms. One of these has an alcove, which serves as an office where correspondence is handled and the commune's business and financial records are kept. An annex to this building holds the large communal washer and dryer, the deepfreeze, and bags and cans of food bought in bulk.

When I was there, the living arrangements in the large house were as follows. Two couples shared a downstairs bedroom: one couple was unmarried and flexible in their sexual relations with other commune members; the second couple was married and preferred remaining strictly monogamous. One of the two large upstairs bedrooms (the one with the alcove) was shared by two females and three males, who all slept together in one large mattressed bed. The other upstairs bedroom, known as the "men's dormitory," accommodated five males. These men, the excess after all available women in the community had been matched up with men, occupied this room with varying degrees of dissatisfaction or resignation. None of the members with whom I spoke felt this to be a very happy arrangement—neither for the five men who were without sleeping partners, nor for the three "liberated" females who were being continuously propositioned.

The other house resembles a prefabricated one-story bungalow yanked straight out of the middle of suburbia. It is a white frame building situated on the hillside overlooking the large house. When I was there, the couples who lived in its four bedrooms were all monogamous and quite traditional in family structure. There was no formal attempt to communally rear the children—that is, with all adults acting as parents. This was espoused as an ideal but the reality of the situation was that the biological parents retained primary responsibility for their own children.

THE CRO SYSTEM OF GROUP MARRIAGE

I learned that, some time before I visited Crow, the commune had undergone a major ideological division. Although the commune began with a definite set of ideals, the male/female relations and sex roles were not clearly defined. As new members arrived with ideas of their own, a division was inevitable—this is not an uncommon experience in new communes. It was a split that ran right down the middle, between those who favored communism of persons as well as property, and those who wished to pursue a more traditional family style within a communal structure. When the confrontation over group marriage

308

arose, differences were so strong that the proponents threatened to leave. This did not influence the opponents, who would neither leave nor change their attitude. Two women who favored group marriage did, in fact, move out but only as far as a neighboring city where they set up their own commune. Meanwhile, the remaining five group-marriage proponents stayed on. They, even more than their opponents, had an investment in Crow amounting to many thousands of dollars and a great deal of time and energy. In staying on, these five hoped that in time the others would be persuaded to share more totally as relationships within the commune deepened.

When there, I did not see any signs of progress in this matter (as I have already indicated in effect by describing the two houses). The people in each house still tended to communicate among themselves rather than with those in the other faction (house). There were two separate communes, eating together and sometimes working together, but essentially distinct — one living in the large brown house, the other in the small white one. Thus Crow, for all its espousal of radical experimentation, was on one level a communal economic venture, but on another level was simply a cautious social and personal project.

FAMILY AND COMMUNAL ROLES

Even those who favored group marriage, however, were not clear in their definitions of family roles. They still felt that it was permissible for women to do the bulk, if not all, of the housework, while the men did the outside jobs and the so-called heavy work — building construction and repairs, tractor and vehicle operations; etc. But true communism of persons means more than everyone balling everyone else. It requires an obliteration of rigid or habitual role behavior. It requires, instead, that no person be restricted to one set of economic tasks and social roles, that no person should have to repeat actions so

much so that his or her behavior becomes categorized
and defined. This does not mean that a person may not
have a preference for certain activities, only that such a
preference must not be rigidly or restrictively adhered to.

While I was at Crow, the meals were prepared mainly
by the tradition oriented females, while clean-up jobs—
(doing dishes, mopping floors, etc.) were the work of the
more "liberated" ones. After dinner, I recall, the men retired to the living room or sat leisurely around the huge
dining-room table, but the women who had done the cooking seemed to disappear. The following morning, though,
those women were almost the only people around. The
reason was that in the morning, most of the men went off
to work, some to outside jobs, some going to their own
fields in order to cut and bail hay, one or two staying
around the barns helping to care for the chickens and pigs
and cattle. They had just butchered a 250-pound hog the
day I arrived.

The Crow people hold no meetings as a group. Each person is responsible for creating and maintaining whatever relationship he or she has with another person. Meetings, I was told, accomplished nothing. No one is interested in heavy encounter scenes. They feel free to speak up to another person to express a gripe or a desire on a one-to-one basis without the need for a group. If a person does not speak up, then that's his tough luck.

"This is a commune for aggressive-type people," Lillian admitted. "If a person is passive or slow, he probably will feel very uncomfortable here. You have to be pretty forward and make your need known."

Despite this admission and despite the fact that these are active, hardworking, aggressive types, a lot of feelings are obviously not communicated and many relationships, even if cordial, tend to be superficial.

All of the men are required to work on weekdays. Most of them had their own special jobs. A few, mainly the newer members, help the others. They leave at varying times in the morning and return at dinner time, 5 or 6 P.M.

Mike, a new member, explained it to me this way: "Yeh, it's kind of a drag sometimes. Today we're haying and I don't like it, but sometimes I work with Sam on the truck and I like that better. Some days I don't feel like working at all so I just try to *look* like I'm working."

Bill, another member, said, "By the time I get home at night from working all day, I don't have the energy to try to relate to everyone on a one-to-one basis, if that were possible. I'm not interested in playing all the games required to get to take a girl to bed."

Later when I was talking with Jean and Sam, one of the couples in the group marriage, Jean told me: "I don't like guys to play games. If a guy wants to make out with me I just wish he'd come right out and say so. Some of the guys around here think they have to go through all kinds of maneuvers to get a girl to bed."

"Well, that's a pretty standard expectation, isn't it?" I asked.

Sam, Jean's husband, added, "Yeah, all a guy really has to do is say 'Have you got 20 minutes to spare?' Then she can say 'Yes' or 'No.' Simple as that. I think too many guys fear rejection, as though it was some sort of put-down to him personally. It may be she just doesn't feel like it at the moment."

Jean continued, "We need more women now. I could spend all my time in bed. Especially when most of the women here won't sleep with anyone besides their mates."

"Like Marion, for example," Sam said, pointing to a dark-haired girl who was putting food in the deepfreeze.

"She won't even undress in front of anyone. 'Fraid we might see her *body!*" Sam added, partly to cover up his resentment. "She does a lot of good things around the place, though; she's the treasurer and I trust her with the money more than if I were handling it myself."

Now, I'm one of those rare birds who likes to wash dishes, so after dinner I volunteered. "You must have visited communes before," one member commented, noticeably pleased with my contribution. I replied, "Oh, I like to do dishes." An hour later I remarked, "Man, there sure are a lot of dishes. You need a dishwasher. You sure there was only 40 people for dinner— I've washed at least 100 plates."

And then came the pots and pans. Hell, I really do like to wash dishes. But in moderation, man, in moderation. I hoped my soft shriveled fingers would someday return to normal.

Jack was in a jolly mood. He came up to Lillian and began to make pelvic gestures against her buttocks. "I'm hot! I'm hot!" he exclaimed. Then he rushed over to Jean, repeated the performance, and moaned. Shortly

312

thereafter, he went upstairs to the men's dormitory, read for awhile, and went to sleep.

Henry and Susan, the monogamous couple who lived in the larger house, came into the dining area where several of us were talking. Henry was in a bright velvet robe, preparing for bed. He and Bill joked for a bit and then Henry exclaimed, "Presto, Chango!" and threw his robe open to expose his naked torso.

Everyone laughed. "Encore, Encore," several shouted. Henry turned toward his audience and repeated his performance. "Bravo, Bravo." Henry laughed and then made his exit. "Good night," he said.

VISITORS

Along with other aspects of Crow life, the rumors I'd heard about their treatment of visitors turned out to be less than accurate. Visitors are asked to make a donation of $3 for each day they stay. They are provided with meals and, in general, are told to make themselves at home. On the other hand, if visitors are not welcome (say because of overcrowding or any other circumstance), there is no reservation about turning them away. On one occasion, I was told, a fellow showed up and announced to all that he had come to live at Crow permanently. When gentle persuasion did not result in his leaving, three of the more husky men in the commune threw him to the ground and physically and verbally scared him so badly that he immediately got his belongings together and left.

In former times, visitors (those of them made welcome, that is) stayed in a third house closer to the highway. But that building, part of which had served as the communal school, had been lost in the fire, a rumor, for once, being at least partially correct. The commune members, I learned, had decided not to rebuild at that location, as it was too far from the other houses. At that distance, the school had tended to be a separate entity; also, visitors staying at the third building had been little inclined to participate in the primary activities of the community. The members now feel that the school and visitors' quarters alike should be an integral part of the main community complex. They want visitors to involve themselves as totally as possible in and with the community.

A unique opportunity for such involvement came my way the day after Henry's elegant torso performance. An eight-year-old boy standing near the shed with a shovel asked me to help bury the hog's head. "Well, Ahhh . . . ," I said. "Let me see. . . ." Backing off smartly, I rushed indoors, got a whiff and a taste of some yeasty homemade bread for breakfast, and then drove off in the flashing sunshine to find still another glorious commune.

THE FAMILY

"We're a commune of about fifty people and we live in a four-room house together," Lord Buckley began.

"We're a group marriage," the typist joined in.

"Fifty?" I inquired incredulously.

"Yes, more or less — we haven't taken a count in the last day or two," Lord Buckley laughed.

GETTING TO LORD BUCKLEY

We headed for the northern part of New Mexico — high mountains, cooler weather, more greenery, less dryness and desert. We were on our way to Taos, once the Hippie Mecca, but now, according to the roundup of late state news, no longer congenial to longhairs. Two hitchhikers whom we picked up along the way told us of a hip general store and information center in Taos that would provide us with a map of all the communes in the vicinity. It was mid-afternoon and we had only eaten a few handfuls of raisins since breakfast and hunger was catching up with us. Also, I had a headache from a need to shit. So we decided to get the information on the communes and then find a convenient restaurant and rest room.

It was such a relief to see a large, well-stocked, hip general store complete with health foods that I completely forgot about my physical discomfort. After wandering around the store and buying some sunflower seeds, we went next door to the information center, which also published a local hip paper, *The Fountain of Light*.

We could get little information about communes because, apparently, the communes got upset about the center giving out directions on how to reach them. Too many tourists. So there were no more maps.

We were encouraged to meet Lord Buckley, who was, I guessed (although I was probably told), the editor of a commune magazine which was being prepared. With some sketchy directions on how to get to Hog Farm and New Buffalo, we offered a ride to the new magazine's typist. She was going to the local free school, where we could probably find Lord Buckley.

We were ushered into the spacious living room of a large and elegant house in the center of town. This large room had to be the free school, for its crates, toys, playpen, plants, and general appearance strongly suggested that lots of kids had been there recently. Our typist, whose name I had missed up to this point, disappeared into another room. Shortly after that, a young guy in his early 20s with rosy cheeks and lips appeared. He told us about the school—that it was attended by the commune children and a few kids belonging to local hip types, and that the commune members took turns running the school.

Our typist entered the room with a radiant guy sporting a red beret and a broad grin. "Hello," he said, "I'm Lord Buckley."

We were led to the back of the house, where Lord Buckley seated himself behind a desk while we took chairs in front. Our rosy-cheeked friend Dave and two other guys joined us.

"We're a commune of about fifty people and we live in a four-room house together," Lord Buckley began. . . .

LORD BUCKLEY AND FRIENDS

There they were—four guys and a girl at a free school, sitting in a small room discussing the beautiful life of a turned-on service commune consisting of 23 girls, 22 guys and 9 kids in a two-bedroom bungalow and a school bus.

"How did you hear about us?" Lord Buckley asked.

"Oh, just now. We were at the information center inquiring about communes and agreed to give her a ride here," Consuelo said, gesturing toward the typist.

I added, "We're really interested in knowing more about your commune, though."

"One thing—you publish a magazine about communes, right? Are you planning to write about us? We aren't interested in publicity that'll bring more people into this area. There are too many already. Some of us are even thinking about moving and setting up a branch elsewhere."*

"Of course I want to write about you and let people know of alternative possibilities," I replied. "If you don't want publicity, I won't give out your address. The main thing is to let others know. I personally think people should do the commune thing where they are anyway, rather than visiting or joining others."

I talked much too long about my good intentions instead of letting them begin to explain their life style. All five of them were proud, enthusiastic, and excited as they started to tell us what some 50 people were doing sleeping

---

* Yes, dear reader, don't go to Taos looking for this commune. They have *all* moved elsewhere. I am told they are either in Colorado or Jamaica.

in four rooms together. Actually, the nine children plus one or two adults slept in a converted school bus next to the house. "Only" about 44 adults slept in the four rooms.

Crowded? A key to their success was having to deal with impossible situations. They deliberately chose the crowdedness. It required them to be *together*. "We are people-oriented, growth-oriented," they said. "We are flexible, we have no elaborate structure, rules, requirements—such organization evolves as the group evolves."

"Today," Lord Buckley mentioned, "I'm editor. Tomorrow it may be someone else; or one person in the morning, someone else in the afternoon. Inefficient? Time-consuming? That doesn't matter. We've got plenty of time. It's people that count."

LORD BUCKLEY: We've tried every type of decision-making method except democracy (majority rule) and the method changes from situation to situation. An individual may write an article for our new magazine, but he reads it to the whole family and, maybe, to others individually for criticism and suggestions for improvement. Then he may rewrite it. But it's still his article.

LADY JANE (the typist): Music? When we did have records at the house and someone didn't like what record was playing, or if it was too loud, he would just turn it off, change it, or whatever he felt like doing.

DICK: And if someone else objected?

LADY JANE: Well, then, he objected. He did whatever seemed right to him at the time. We don't have a phonograph at the house anymore: We used to, but we moved it to the store.

LORD JOHN: Yeah, someone broke "John Wesley Harding." Sure wish it hadn't been that, but it's only a record. I was too hung up on that record anyway. One of our basic tenets is no hang-ups on material possessions. When someone joins, they come in with all their personal property. If we think they're too attached to something, they have to give it up.

LORD JIM: Like the girl who loved her down sleeping bag so much.

Or like if someone is reading too much, someone will point it out. 'Hey man, what's with you?' We're a product of a thing-oriented culture. To live with people you have to get over that hang-up. That's why we have the rule. It's better to break records, even "John Wesley Harding" than to break up people.

LADY JANE: Sure, I've been hit a few times. If someone feels the liberty and is open enough to give me a good wallop, I feel like we're really communicating. I probably deserve it anyway. I can act like an ass sometimes.

LORD BUCKLEY: So what we're saying is that anything that interferes with people communicating with each other gets the axe. We don't use drugs anymore, either. Up until a few months ago we smoked marijuana and occasionally used LSD or mescaline or stuff like that. But we found it interfered with communication. Now we have a no-drug rule.

DICK: You're not talking about alcohol — wine or beer, right?

LORD BUCKLEY: No, but we don't bother with liquor much.

Money? Our attitude towards it is to turn it over — spend it, put it back into the system as quickly as possible. We just finished making a movie about the communes in this area. It's going to get mass distribution and we expect to make a million dollars with it. Two of us are in Hollywood finalizing distribution plans right now. It's not a short, but a full-length film.

We had rented cameras and film provided to us by a corporation and we'll split the profits 50–50. With rented equipment we don't have any possession hang-ups regarding what to do with it now that the film is completed.

With the money from the film, which we made collectively, we plan to set up a research foundation. It will explore extrasensory perception, dreams, psychic phenomenon, that sort of thing.

We are open to new members. But frankly, we have reached our limit here. Some of us may move to a city in the Northeast. There was a branch in Michigan, but last winter they broke up and a few of them moved in with us.

Most of the hippie communes around here think us a little weird. They can't believe what we're doing, either. It does sound fantastic but it's real.

318

LORD JIM: Sometimes I wake up in the morning and just lie there in amazement. This is the greatest, most unbelievable experience in the world.

LORD EARL: Hordes of people aren't flocking to join us, not because we've been secretive (although we don't advertise ourselves) but because most people aren't willing to go along with the situation.

LORD JOHN: Like, sleeping 44 in four rooms. And a guy would have to cut off his long hair. We decided a few weeks ago that the long hair had to go. Too much importance was being placed on it. Now that eliminates most of the hip types right there — especially with the no-drug rule.

LORD BUCKLEY: What holds us together is a collective urge toward individual growth and self-realization. This is best achieved through others being mirrors for us. The idea that the individual gets submerged in the group or has to conform to group pressure is hogwash. I feel like more of an individual, with more freedom, than ever before in my life.

LORD JIM: Privacy? Another silly notion. Who needs it. I've never once felt the need for what is termed 'privacy.' Privacy, or the view that the human needs to be physically and completely alone without anyone else present, has no validity. Privacy is in your head. You can have 'privacy' in a crowded room if you like. What if you want to be alone in your head and someone is jostling your body? Maybe you need to be jostled. It depends on the circumstances. Are you communicating or withdrawing, spending too much time or too little time in your own thoughts?

LORD BUCKLEY: Meditation? Not much now. Used to. Now we're into movement — dance as a way of communicating feeling, of expressing ourselves. We have a movement class once a week.

LADY JANE: We used to have encounter sessions every night but it's not as frequent now.

LORD JOHN: We have business meetings whenever they're necessary. Anyone can call one if there's something important to discuss.

LORD EARL: Our ages range from a new birth to about 35.

DICK: What do you do about the tendency to couple? (Laughter)

LORD BUCKLEY: There's a whole lot of coupling. We encourage it. (More laughter)

DICK: I can dig it, but what I meant was the tendency for a guy and girl to pair off and get possessive and jealous of each other, you know. (But I wasn't sure they did for a moment.)

LADY JANE: Oh, we had a problem with that awhile back but it worked itself out okay.

LORD JIM: Yeah, every now and then. But our specific goal is to eliminate possessiveness and *unhealthy* attachments. Everyone has that in mind and so we work at it.

LADY JANE: I have six husbands here. There are a few others that I relate to fairly well. As time goes by, these relationships and others will develop even further. (Lady, incidentally, was full of child, about five month's worth.) We're a group marriage.

DICK: Group marriage, what does that mean?

LORD BUCKLEY: Oh, it's just a term we've latched onto in the last week or so to describe ourselves. Next week it might be something else.

LADY JANE: Once we were all going around talking about being 'mystical.' A few days later it was another term we liked.

LORD BUCKLEY: Again, you see, we don't want to get hung up on words. They're only tools we use to communicate. Inadequate ones at that. That's why we're into movement classes. Bodily-control, movement exercise has been emphasized by Sufi masters and other teachers for ages.

It was easy to see that the commune handled the quantitative aspect of human relationships pretty well. But what about that elusive thing called quality? My own relationship with Consuelo has so much depth and meaning for me that I was suspicious and doubtful of the possibilities of that kind of involvement other than on a one-to-one basis.

"Are there any people in the group that came into it as a married couple, with a history of a monogamous relationship?" I asked.

Lord Buckley said that he had been married previously. The others had difficulty remembering who had come in married and who hadn't. Recently they had all married each other symbolically.

And the quality of their relationships? The question is difficult to answer. Each person felt good about his particular set of relationships—different people related in different ways, in different degrees.

Buckley expanded on this: "If someone is not willing or able to relate to someone else, the group encourages them to spend more time together. Usually, they are not relating for a reason, which, if discovered, will aid their personal growth and break down the barriers between them. What you don't like in someone else may be something you don't like in yourself, but fail to admit.

"If Joe, for instance, can't stand Jane, we might ask him to sleep with her for a few nights. We mean *sleep.* They don't *have* to make love. Usually that solves the problem. By the second night they might want to make love. Physical intimacy then would enhance other aspects of the relationship.

"Somehow I still believe that you have to give up something in order to get something else. You have to pay a price for all this but I can't for the life of me figure out what it is."

"I think you only give up what you don't want anyway," Lord Jim added.

"We may not have material possessions, new cars, fancy clothes," said Lord John. "But we don't want them. That's no price to pay."

I was still skeptical. "There's a law in physics that for every action there is an equal and opposite reaction—which I believe applies to the realm of human and all living matter, as well as the inanimate."

"Maybe so," Lord Buckley said reflectively, "but if a reaction is created which we expect, anticipate, even want anyway, there is no loss—right? We think we've got the right formula. Things work out the way we want them to—

it's not all wine and roses. That's not what I mean, not what we want in fact. The struggle, the conflicts, are part of the whole, which moves us closer together as a group and makes us stronger and more fulfilled human beings."

BEGINNINGS

The Family, as they called themselves, got its start in Berkeley, California, in early 1968, when five men and women from an encounter group decided to live together. In the encounter group they had learned to utilize various techniques, including ideas from the writings of Gurdjieff and Ouspensky. One of the five was considered the leader, a sort of guru to the group.

With only $100 between them, they set off for Las Vegas where they took their chances at gambling, and subsequently won several thousand dollars. With this large sum they moved to southern New Mexico and settled in for the winter. There they picked up additional members. And before long the money ran out. Throughout the spring and summer, they obtained their food and other basic necessities on a precarious day-to-day basis. When food was needed, several of them (by now a group of 20 or more) would go out and sell newspapers to earn enough money to buy the evening meal; or they would check with local supermarkets for free spoiled food, part of which might be edible. Their emphasis was always and fanatically on interpersonal relations — on each other's growth rather than on possessions. They had seemingly instinctual awareness that acquiring possessions and object-attachments would cause disruptions within the group.

Their zeal for opposing such attachments was and is unbounded. As a result, they moved around a lot. In the first two years of their experience together, more than a thousand people related to the group in one form or another. Some of these people stayed for only a few days,

unable to adjust to an environment of such material austerity and interpersonal passion. Finally the family settled in Taos, where they began helping to run a health-food store, medical clinic, and information center for local residents. They soon began a free school and then went on to make that full-length movie about other communes in the area. As of 1970, they were confidently hoping to eventually distribute 40,000 copies of the film. Perhaps they will, for not only are their plans ambitious, but their enthusiasm and optimism are at a peak.

HOME IS A BUNGALOW AND SCHOOL BUS, UNDER GUARD

The commune's relations with the town (when I was there) seemed precarious. True, they were on excellent terms with the fire department because members of the group had helped the department set up a shortwave radio system. But the police were, at best, medium cool and the residents were suspicious, though not overtly hostile.

The recent shoot-outs and hassles from local rednecks of other communes in the area (a Hog Farm schoolbus had been dynamited and two long-hairs were wounded by gunfire while sitting on their front porch one evening), had made the Family extremely cautious. At night windows in their free school had been broken and someone had fired bullets through the general store window.

"It's going to get dark pretty soon," Lord Buckley began. "We better close up and get out of here. I'll call the house. Will you stay for dinner?" he asked us.

We accepted as it slowly dawned on us that the free school was *not* the commune's living quarters. (The school in fact turned out to be larger than the bungalow where they all lived together.)

Lord Buckley and one of the other fellows went to a front room, from which the chatter and buzz of a shortwave radio came back to us. When they returned they announced that the house was notified that we were coming and that someone would be sent here to the school to stand guard after dark. Windows had already been broken; and they now feared someone might try to burn or bomb it.

Shortwave radios were in operation at the information center, the house, and the free school, as well as in several of the commune's vehicles. This radio network provided swift communications for emergencies and also for the daily routine. So, when people at school wanted to return to the house, they simply called and asked for someone to drive over to pick them up.

In this case, though, we all piled into the Plymouth station wagon. The two girls up front with me and the four guys in the back.

"I hope it's not too crowded back there," I yelled. Then

I laughed at my own remark and added, "Guess you're used to it, huh?"

We drove several miles before turning onto a winding dirt road that took us to the top of a hill, from which we could look down over the town in the distance. Then we turned right, down a one-lane driveway that led to the house.

"Blink your lights a couple of times when we get close," one of the fellows instructed.

There at the foot of the drive, in a small clearing, was an equally small building with several parked cars in front, an old school bus to one side, and what appeared to be two or three old sheds on the other side. I parked in the first available space and we all piled out. The entrance to the house was on the side near the bus and it led directly into the kitchen, where several women were bustling about preparing dinner. Two little kids, aged five or six, were running about underfoot while several people were standing around, just talking.

Consuelo and I were left to make it on our own as our

original hosts disappeared into other rooms. We stood there somewhat awkwardly and I began reading a bulletin board which listed the names of current residents. Most of the people were Lord this or Lady that, but some of them did not have any such illustrious prefix by their names. One guy, who looked like a cross between Mickey Rooney and Mickey Spillane, was standing nearby so I asked him what Lady and Lord meant and how come all the names didn't bear these titles. He smiled brightly and remarked cheerfully that he didn't know and couldn't care less—it was just fun and games. And he added that his name, Mickey, was one of those that was Lord-less. Mickey went on to say that he had only lived with the group for four days. I surmised that a certain length of residence was required before a member could assume a title.

At that point I knew better than to ask if my assumption was correct. No title or rule was so rigid or absolute as to warrant a fixed answer. The few exceptions to this generalization appeared to be the following: (1) no drugs; (2) no attachments to material possessions; (3) no long hair on men; and (4) required individual flexibility and openness to group demands (if the group felt that an individual was hung-up about one thing or another, that individual should be willing to change his behavior).

Finally, I looked into the next room. It was rather small, about the size of a double hallway. But the room was crowded, buzzing with the noise of conversation. In one corner three or four people were talking together. Nearby, a few people sat quietly on the couch or floor. Everyone seemed in good spirits—the vibrations were very high. We entered the room and sat down on the couch. The open doorway to the front room revealed more people sitting on bunks and standing while engaged in conversation.

I noticed that one mother was nursing her child. Lady Jane sat down next to us and I asked her about women's liberation, as it seemed to me that the women here were playing pretty traditional roles — cooking, doing other household work, caring for children, and having babies.

Lady Jane explained: "We get help from the men sometimes in the kitchen and with the children. It's just that I don't want to chop the wood or do the heavy work and the other women don't either. We could if we wanted to. We feel liberated, and that's what counts, isn't it?"

"I'm not so sure," I replied. "Most Americans would think us insane if we told them they are not free. They *feel* free. But what is the freedom to discuss and argue over tons of misinformation disseminated to us by the government, the military, big business, financial and advertising interests, all using the communication media of radio, TV and mass circulation newspapers."

"Anyhow, what about overpopulation?" I added. "I think there should be some sort of moratorium on having kids until we provide a minimum health-care standard for everyone who's already alive. What's your rationale for having a kid?"

"Well," she replied, "we think any woman who wants the experience of having a child should be able to have it. This is going to be my first and I'm excited about it. If a woman wants more than one child, well, that depends on the circumstances, I think."

"Will it be a natural childbirth at home or will you go to the hospital?"

"Oh, I'll use the Lamaze method and have the baby in the local hospital. We are on very good terms with the hospital. One of the girls had her baby there just a few months ago and the fathers were all able to watch. They're getting used to our coming in like that. We believe everyone should have the opportunity to witness the birth of a child."

"Like Aldous Huxley recommended in his utopian novel, *Island*, huh?"

"Exactly!" she exclaimed.

Our meal looked simple but nourishing—a bowl of hot potato soup and a sort of egg roll-burrito. Famished, I started to eat. Lady politely stopped me saying, "No one is supposed to begin eating until everyone is served."

Somehow, although hungry, I was pleased with that rule of courtesy. It was immensely reasonable, almost ritualistic, for a group that large, seated as they were on chairs, on the floor, on couches and beds.

Before we ate, I happened to go out to the car. Through lighted windows I could see the front room and a portion of the first bedroom. These were crowded with two- and three-tiered bunk beds. So that is how 44 people could sleep in four rooms!

After dinner, a brief meeting was held. A map of the house and surrounding grounds was shown, indicating the angle at which rifle shot could enter the house if hostile outsiders staged an ambush. In the event of such an emergency, a warning alarm would sound and people would be expected to immediately take shelter according to the pre-arranged plan. A practice drill was to take place that evening.

Because of the fear of harassment, the commune had begun posting guards to watch over the house at night, taking turns in two-hour shifts. One or two women were also among the volunteers.

Gazing around the room during the meeting, I was struck by several things about the people present. None were too fat or too skinny; indeed, a few were physically beautiful. Most of them seemed in good spirits, though one girl with a furrowed brow and an angry look to her kept me from feeling that everything was a billowy cushion of love. One fellow whom we had sat next to on the couch before dinner had moved to the other side of the room, but I didn't feel any bad vibes from him; of course, it may have been that I was too hungry and too distracted by other things there for me to pay close attention to him.

On the whole, the atmosphere there made us high. And when it was time for us to leave, we excused ourselves reluctantly. Dave, who had greeted us initially at the free school, said good-bye to us at the car. As we drove away, our headlights paused momentarily on two of the family's members walking up the road, rifles in hand, to stand guard on the hilltop that overlooked that amazing 44-member, bungalow-and-bus commune.

CHAPTER SEVEN

THERE ARE A NUMBER of service-oriented communities active in the United States. Privately financed, self-supporting, or associated with some large organization, they exist in order to provide certain services for various segments of society. Inevitably they all involve some form or other of communitarianism — sharing among those who serve, sharing among those served, sharing by all within the community. This particular characteristic makes them part of the world of the commune although some of them in practice do not care to actually be called communes.

CAMPHILL VILLAGE

Camphill Village, located in Copake, New York, considers itself to be part of a movement rather than a single community, for it serves and receives support from a much larger and widespread population than resides at its own location at any given time.

The Camphill Movement, begun in Scotland by Karl Koenig, is based on the work with mentally retarded adults that was done by Rudolf Steiner (1861–1925), the founder of anthroposophy. Steiner's ideas about what he called Curative Education are based mainly on the principle of accepting the retarded person as an individual, caring for him as a total person — body, soul, and spirit — and concentrating on his potentialities (rather than his liabilities), however limited they may be.

Camphill Village, which was established in 1955, provides a warm and supportive environment in which the handicapped can work and support themselves as much as possible, thereby increasing their self-confidence and self-respect. For young people between the ages of 18 and 21 the community also provides a progressive-education program.

The community, which has a population of approximately 150 (as of early 1969), is divided into families. Each family consists of a staff member, his own immediate family, and five to nine retarded adults. Each family, which lives in one house, manages its own finances in order to encourage a maximum of shared responsibilities and the greatest degree of individual flexibility.

There is a wide variety of both workshops and occupations available to the villagers. The people work in teams — on the farm, in the bakery, and at construction and such crafts as doll-making, woodworking, and making enamelware. In addition, the villagers are expected to do the usual tasks of housekeeping and taking care of the grounds.

In order to qualify for admittance, applicants must be able to take care of their personal needs; that is, they must be able to wash and dress themselves as well as not require constant medical supervision. They must also have both the ability to work under guidance and the incapacity to earn their living in the outside world. In addition, their families, if they can afford it, are required to pay as much as $200 per month. This cash income, together with that derived from the output of the farm and workshops, is responsible for the community being almost self-supporting.

Recently the US Government has offered the community a $20,000 grant on a matching basis. If the community can raise an equal amount from private sources, it will qualify for the grant. And that will enable the Camphill Movement to expand its facilities and perhaps even to develop new community locations to accommodate the applicants on its long waiting list.

There is also another Camphill community in the United States. Called Beaver Run, it is a community that specializes in the treatment of retarded children. It is located in Glenmoore, Pennsylvania.

THE CATHOLIC WORKER FARM

The Catholic Worker Movement originated in New York City in 1933 during the depths of the Depression. When begun by Dorothy Day, it consisted solely of *The Catholic Worker*, a radical pacifist newspaper. Soon after that a House of Hospitality was opened in the city to help feed and clothe the poor and unemployed. And in 1936 the movement bought a farm at Tivoli, in the Hudson Valley, New York, in order to start a Catholic Worker community. It was only the first. By 1941, there were well over 25 Catholic Worker rural farms, most of them connected with hospitality houses in various cities. *The Catholic Worker*'s circulation climbed to more than 100,000 but Pearl Harbor made pacifism immensely unpopular throughout the country and the paper's circulation subsequently decreased to 35,000.

Today, *The Catholic Worker* and the New York City House of Hospitality are still flourishing. So is the Tivoli farm, where Martin J. Corbin co-edits the paper with Dorothy Day. In addition, several other autonomous CW farms and hospitality houses still operate in various other places throughout the country.

In December 1970 I paid my first visit to the Tivoli farm, which represents the Catholic Worker Movement's principal rural effort. I found that the farm consists of a 90-acre tract of land, most of which is left uncultivated. There are three main buildings, which provide space for sleeping quarters, kitchen, dining room, chapels, and library. The community's population is between 25 and 35 people in winter, and a good many more during the warmer months. In the summer the farm also serves as a center for conferences, which can mean the presence of as many as 150 people on a weekend. The farm depends primarily on donations for support. All able-bodied members share in the routine maintenance and repair work there. In spite of its title and origins, the

Catholic Worker farm houses people of all sorts of religious persuasions, including not a few unbelievers. The purpose of the Farm itself is still, as it has always been, to provide a home away from the city for the poor and needy regardless of religion, race or creed. Work and facilities are shared in common, without structure, and with most members having the privacy of their own room when needed.

CONVERSATION WITH STANLEY VISHNEWSKI

Among the people I had a chance to talk to about the Catholic Worker Movement was Stanley Vishnewski, who had been one of the movement's early members. The following is a transcript of part of my conversation with Stanley:

STANLEY: Running the paper is our main work, see. Communities like Twin Oaks, they make hammocks. Other communities, they make organic foods. Our main work is the paper.

After we started the newspaper back during the Depression, people came to us for help. A woman came to see us and said, "I heard you people write this paper and I'm out of a job. What are you going to do with me?" So Dorothy says, "Well, the only thing we can do is rent a house." We rented a small apartment and we were able to take care of about 12 ladies in our first House of Hospitality. The paper's circulation increased to 20,000 and our staff slowly increased. Then we moved to Charles Street; we got a bigger house. We got this bigger house because our staff increased.

The third part of our program was to establish communities. This seems to be a much more popular idea now than then. When *The Catholic Worker* movement started it was completely, well . . . utopian, looked down upon, crazy—"How are you going to work it?" People put up all kinds of objections. None of them were valid. None of them were actually the kind of problem you actually met, you know. It's funny, because the problems that you do meet are alto-

336

gether different from what people think you're going to meet. It wasn't until we got a staff of people who had skills that we were able to start our first farming commune.

DICK: Have you personally been involved in the city mostly or did you spend most of your time in the country?

STANLEY: I worked a lot in the city through the Depression. I always had a love for the land, so when we got the farm I worked there a lot. But we alternated back and forth, because we actually were one unit — the farm and the city house. We were one staff and so we'd alternate back and forth. We had the ideal of a beautiful farming commune but we were always taking care of lots of sick people. We were always sort of a house of hospitality on the land, more than the ideal farming community that we envisioned. We had to face reality, you know, that's the one thing you can't escape. You have to realize that you're living here, now, and if a man comes to you in need, what can you do? It's only a matter of space. There's always food for people, you can always share food, but space . . . that's the problem. Summertime, people can sleep on the ground, with their sleeping bags; but it's wintertime now. And also, you can't overcrowd a commune because people's nerves, they get on edge; people need space. Privacy is very important in a commune; that's one of the very important things in order to establish a successful commune.

Another mistake people make is they think all they have to do is get a group together, go out on the land, and start a farming community. They fail within nine months, unless they have an underlying principle. People have to have a reason for their existence. Not only a reason for their existence, but also they have to realize that in the beginning they have to sacrifice more than they would if they were working at a regular job. They have to give up creature comfort. They can't expect creature comforts in the beginning; they're working towards a better life. If they're willing to sacrifice, then eventually they will get together. It won't be forced. You see, you can't force a commune. You just can't take 12 families from the city and say, "There's a house." It's not going to work. My advice to people who want to start a commune is to get together for about 12 months in a city, meet twice a week, and have common meals.

Pool your interests, go out for walks, and maybe have a trial run by renting an old abandoned farmhouse and spending a vacation up there for one month. And then see.

My own experience, and I have been 35 years with *The Catholic Worker* movement, is that communes based on a religious motivation seem to succeed, whereas the ones based on a purely economic motive fail. Because a man who's got talent suddenly realizes: "What the heck am I doing here? I could be getting $150 or $200 a week with my skills, and this other guy here is just living on my work, he's not contributing half as much." So he leaves. In a group with a religious motivation, there's a common reason for being together. It works out that way.

Our farm here is not really like a farming commune because we work so closely with our city place. We take care of a lot of sick people; I have joined the list now. And for the first time, I tell you, I came to realize the value of community when I got sick with this heart disease; I mean, people take care of me. They cook my meals for me, they see my bed is made, that I'm comfortable. Suppose I had been living in the city? Making money, all unhappy, stuck in an abandoned old room, social worker to see you once a week? A community has its blessings which far outweigh its faults, but people have to sacrifice for that in the beginning and have to work towards that goal.

DICK: You don't get something for nothing.

STANLEY: Oh no, you don't get something for nothing. You have to do it because you *want* to do it, and then you really will have a beautiful commune. As a way of life it's very rich and very rewarding and satisfying.

A Community of Need:

INTERVIEW WITH MARTIN J. CORBIN AND MARJORIE HUGHES

While visiting the farm at Tivoli, I also interviewed Marty Corbin (co-editor of *The Catholic Worker*) and

Marjorie Hughes (one of the central figures at the Farm). This is a good portion of our three-way rap.

MARTIN: During World War II there wasn't much opposition to war, only on the part of pacifists and Trotskyists.

MARJORIE: It was a very uncomfortable boat to be in, you know.

DICK: Your philosophy is also anarchist, I believe. Is there any easy definition of anarchism?

MARTIN: Yes. The basic idea is that it's a movement which calls for the abolition of the state and its replacement by a federation of communities. This federation would gradually usurp the function of the state and perform the same functions the state does now, but on a decentralized basis. Of course, there are other schools of anarchism, but this is the one we subscribe to. Some anarchists are syndicalists — for example, the IWW. They favor the idea of one big union which would perform the function of the federation of communities.

DICK: That idea has gone done the tubes with the "one big union" almost a reality today.

MARTIN: Yeah, although it's funny, there's a revival of the IWW among many people at the University of Chicago. There have also been extreme individualist anarchists based philosophically around a guy named Max Sterner. At the turn of the 19th century he wrote a book called *Ego On His Own*. It's pretty much forgotten now, except Marx wrote a couple of hundred pages attacking him. Sterner's anarchism was that you don't accept any law outside yourself.

DICK: I'd like to change the subject to what's going on here. You've started to have meetings on Monday nights, I hear.

MARTIN: We don't have formal community meetings. We're very informal. We have little talks once a month on Sunday afternoon. We invite a guest to speak. For example, tomorrow a priest from India will be here. These aren't really concerned with community problems, just information. Mostly the decisions are arrived at quite informally. Plus, Dorothy Day is the leading person who has most of the say about both the paper and the farm. She just returned from Africa, India, and Australia. She was also just out in the Midwest on a speaking tour. She divides her time between traveling, the House of Hospitality in New York City on the Lower East Side, and here.

* * *

339

DICK: Are you taking all the people that get sent up from the city?

MARJORIE: No. We take in people that arrive on our doorstep. Very often the ones who didn't bother to call are the ones to get taken in 'cause we don't have anything else to do with them. We get a lot of visiting kids in the warm weather, even in the winter. It's surprising how many turn up with their sleeping bags. That's never a real problem because they'll sleep anyplace, you know, and they'll eat whatever's there. If they don't show up for meals they'll eat bread and peanut butter and not complain. The real terrible thing is the families. We get so many calls from families that have no place to live and that are being evicted, or that have a run of bad luck, and we just don't have any place to house them. All summer long, there were families on the move, and not all poor either. Many were middle-class, college-educated people who'll go back to their jobs in the fall if they don't find what they're looking for. On the move with their children, looking for a community.

DICK: A lot of people who subscribe to *The Modern Utopian* are the type of people who read about communities and get interested in them that way. Many younger people tend to get into communes more experientially while older people get into them more intellectually. I get a lot of white-collar, professional-type people writing and asking, "Where is there a community I can join, I can't stand my present situation." Like one time there was a doctor with ten children. His wife had already left them a couple of years before. And he said it's time for him to do it. But I thought to myself: Where is he going to find a place that'll take ten children? Ten children! You have people here of all ages and types. Don't you have any hassles with such diverse people coming in?

MARJORIE: We do from time to time, but generally speaking, if you're patient and wait, people who don't really fit in will take themselves off — maybe not as soon as you'd like them to, but eventually. Or else they'll change. Once in a great while you get somebody you can't cope with at all. That doesn't happen often.

MARTIN: We've only had two people who could be really violent. Both psychotics, I would say, but psychotics given to physical violence. Boy, that's a really sticky problem, because you have your children to think of and you're opposed to calling in the police, at

340

least in principle. We have occasionally used the threat, and in both of these cases the threat was enough. We have occasionally called the state police to take people to a mental hospital, people whom we couldn't capture and take care of ourselves when they really freaked out. But then, they'd come back when they were over that, so . . . so far, we haven't had any serious violence; we had a couple of close calls.

MARJORIE: We have a lot of conflict but it generally stays at the level of shouting and grumbling and doors slamming.

DICK: What is it that makes you who have been here these last six years willing to tolerate that conflict?

MARJORIE: Well, I don't know about Marty, but I know there have been many times when if I had had the money I would have gone. At the same time, I can say it's lucky for a person if he can't leave, because there's so much to be gained if he can stick it through. You learn so much. One thing I've learned is that conflict is inevitable and not to duck it. Conflict can be creative if you don't let it be completely destructive. For me that's a big lesson, because I tend to just walk away from things. The more aggressive people learn to simmer down a little bit and learn that other people have legitimate points of view. But it's hard. It's terribly hard. We are a community of need here, we're not an intentional community. Which means that we avoid some problems but we also get problems that could be avoided by weeding people out. The other thing is that we don't support ourselves from the land, and that makes a big difference. Many communities fold because the economic problem is too much. I still think it's desirable to support yourself, because I don't think it's a very real experiment as long as you're having outside support.

DICK: But then is small farming viable any more?

MARJORIE: I don't think it's viable by itself, but I think that the combination of farming, crafts, and part-time jobs is viable. And you probably need a center where you can give hospitality and take on as many people as you can cope with. You also need some private scenes, some separate buildings, for people too, because I don't think everyone can survive under one roof, plus support themselves; you're loading yourself with more than you can do then. On the other hand, if you start by excluding other people and saying, "Well, once we get prosperous enough, we'll help other people," that's like being a little bit pregnant, you know?

DICK: Because you never get prosperous enough. But the fact that you are a community of need does bring in the outside donations, which makes it so that you do not have to rely on outside jobs, because your job is here.

MARJORIE: Yeah, although ordinarily we really do, because we have quite a mixture here, and several people go out and teach or take part-time jobs because we don't have the money. The money we get from New York simply pays for basic things, it pays for food and laundry, so if we want our own money we have to either get checks — social security or retirement — or we have to work for it.

DICK: Do you have a requirement that each person has to pay so much?

MARJORIE: No, but most do. For instance, the other day the check didn't come from New York, they forgot to send the check, and we've had unusual expenses this month too; we had two people in the hospital and —

DICK: — do you have to pay that out of your community funds?

MARJORIE: No, that's Medicaid. But it still involves money, like it involves special diets or getting somebody a bathrobe that he wouldn't get otherwise, and that sort of thing. There isn't any stretch in our money for that. But what happens usually is that just when you're worrying about it, from an unexpected source someone will give you money. Like Cathryn handed me $75 'cause she heard me griping about how forgetting to send the check was going to foul things up. She gets social security — so she handed me $75 just like that, you know, and S—— gives me a dollar from time to time. I don't know where he gets it. Maybe old friends mail him a dollar and he doesn't spend it. Or H—— will give me $5. It always seems to come out, somehow, even when we have unusual expenses.

DICK: Have you had any problem with this volunteer setup as far as doing the cleaning?

MARJORIE: We don't really have a problem. A lot of people gripe. Like some of the older men gripe at the kids. Lately things have been going very well, because we've been having those meetings, and we have a wonderful bunch of kids here now. Normally they're young and selfish and careless, and they get a lot of hassle from the older men. They've really taken it very well without fighting back. Now it's begun to really dawn on them that these older people are doing what they call the "shit work." So they've been taking on more of it. At the same time, they've been careful not to just take it over because then that deprives the older men of their feelings of worth and participation. While we have a lot of day-to-day conflicts, things do improve. Just about the time when you're celebrating, they'll all leave and we'll have to start all over again. Usually it's little things, though, like the milk's been put in the wrong place or somebody forgot to put his plate in the sink.

MARTIN: It gets more abrasive in the winter.

MARJORIE: Yeah, that's why I'd like a decentralized place. Also, the young ones like health foods and the older ones like meat and potatoes. And the young ones want to sit up all night and sing and make noise; the old ones have a hard time sleeping. I would never choose a place like this, a big structure. I'd prefer a comfortable fairly large house for sick people and older people, and then a lot of outbuildings.

MARTIN: Also this building is really built for summer occupancy. The walls are paper-thin.

MARJORIE: It really can get pretty tight if there are a lot of people sick and we get snowed in.

MARTIN: If you cough in here they can hear you in the next room.

MARJORIE: We've been really lucky this last year. Two years ago we put in a terrible winter because we got overloaded with psychotics and alcoholics, and then a lot of people got sick, and boy, it was really heavy.

MARTIN: But of course that goes in cycles.

SYNANON

Perhaps the best-known service community in America today is Synanon. Although there was only one to begin with (in California), Synanon is now a collective name covering the several Synanon communities that exist in various parts of the country. Synanon began as a communal approach in treating drug addicts. As a result of its subsequent overwhelming success, Synanon expanded its therapy program (the core of which is the Synanon Game) to include alienated middle-class Americans. The Synanon Game is not unlike the Twin Oaks (Oneida) practice of mutual criticism; but, it is geared to expressing more overtly and passionately one's hostile feelings toward others. From these beginnings have developed the present Synanon community complexes which, although still very middle-class and comfortable, are highly communal in their organization and operation. Within each complex there are separate facilities for children, communal dining and recreation activities, and the pooling of income. Adults, though, do have private rooms.

Synanon has a sort of tribal structure, patriarchal, with Charles Dietrich, its founder, as head chief. The main criticism I have heard of Synanon is that it takes a person off hard drugs and makes him dependent on Synanon. This criticism sounds too much like a rationalization which allows the critic to dismiss the group's value in order to smugly continue old biases and attitudes. Certainly even the critic who reflected ever so slightly would have to admit that the Synanon alternative to drug addiction is no worse than dependency on a methadone program and far better than continued addiction. When it comes to some of the middle-class addictions which are dispelled through Synanon, the critic might very well feel his case was stronger, but then he would perhaps be defending his own addiction. Nevertheless, it is the patriarchal, somewhat less than democratic, structure of Synanon which is worth a most deserving critical reflection.

GOULD FARM

A community that specializes in serving the emotionally disturbed is Gould Farm, which is located near Great Barrington in the hills of western Massachusetts. Gould Farm's objective is to help people through their period of emotional stress and then return them to the mainstream of society. The staff that runs the place is paid, which is a somewhat rare phenomenon among communities. But then, Gould Farm's board of directors does not consider the place a "community."

345

AMMON HENNACY

Another place that more readily lends itself to being called a community (and doesn't object) is Ammon Hennacy, or Peace Action Farm, which is situated in upstate New York. This place is cooperatively owned by three member-families. Its principal activities and interests are in providing a place for disadvantaged urban children who come for summer vacations and in attempting to provide accommodations for the families of conscientious objectors who are in jail.

CHAPTER EIGHT

YOUTH COMMUNES

AMONG THE HUNDREDS of thousands of young Americans who are experimenting with cooperative and communal living ventures, there are not only the somewhat stereotyped, dropped-out hippies, but also the degree-seeking college students as well as the more conservative young professionals and working secretaries and typists. Even people who previously restricted their sharing to an apartment in the city (and this because of exorbitant rents) are now experimenting with an increased degree of sharing, both of living quarters and household expenses. Still more radical changes have taken place in attitude. Instead of such unspoken agreements as "I keep out of your way, you keep out of mine" or "You help me and I'll help you," the trend has been toward a commitment perhaps best expressed in the phrase "From each according to his ability, to each according to his need." This saying is hardly new, having long served as the slogan of an effete Communist ideology; but what is new is that it has become a basic and widespread humanitarian consideration. Mainstream America, or at least its youth division, is edging rapidly toward alternative life styles.

YELLOW SUBMARINE

On the side of a hill in the suburbs of a city in Oregon, there is a large yellow house, hidden from the highway by a bank of tall trees. The residents, Beatle fans, had come to call their dwelling Yellow Submarine, not because it is near a body of water (for there is none nearby) but because of its obscurity from the road. I must agree that the name is an appropriate one for this commune.

In terms of longevity, Yellow Submarine probably has few equals among communes existing in an urban-suburban setting. The commune got started in 1968, when several friends moved from Colorado to Oregon. Some made the move to attend college, others to be with their friends while dropping out and trying a new life style. When I visited Yellow Submarine in the summer of 1970, four of the original members (two brothers and their girl friends) were still there, together with six or seven newer members (of whom only one was female). A few of the other original members who had left lived nearby and remained in close contact; "They just found they'd rather live with their families in separate dwellings," Tom told me simply.

Yellow Submarine supports itself primarily through the sale of Granola and Familia, two popular and tasty grain mixtures, whose ingredients they purchase in huge quantities from other suppliers. These products are sold to the hip and college community through the local co-operative. The income from the commune's business is divided equally among the members after deduction of the amount necessary to pay for rent, food, and other household expenses. This usually leaves several dollars of spending money for each of the residents. Additional income is obtained through some outside work. When I was there, for instance, one or two of them held outside jobs and contributed an equal share of their earnings to the house fund.

Yellow Submarine is not a unique community. Rather, it is one of thousands of typical urban-suburban residential houses being used as something more than a college co-op, and something less than a revolutionary commune. Its members are satisfied with an easygoing low-income economic arrangement for the time being. It takes care of their basic needs and allows them a great deal of free time, which would not be possible if they worked at straight jobs, lived in a straight environment with separate apartments and transportation. (When I was there the commune had one truck as well as a car, although the truck was actually in a garage undergoing repairs amounting to $200, no small sum of money for a group of this nature.)

MAKING WINE AND CHARTING
POSSIBILITIES

The large living-room table was partially covered with empty bottles. Several crocks of dandelion wine were being prepared under the kitchen tables and counter, while finished crocks of wine and beer were being stored in the cellar. I helped Tom and Bill pour bottle after bottle of corn syrup into one of the wine crocks.

"It takes nine pounds of sugar to make one gallon of wine," Bill's girl said.

"Fattening, huh," I repeated.

Tom got a big pitcher of homemade beer from the refrigerator and passed it around. A few friends had dropped in and we all sat in the kitchen, listening to the rock music playing continuously and loudly from a phonograph in an adjoining room. Around went the beer again; then someone passed a joint and we smoked that. It was a cheerful gathering, and I enjoyed myself.

While there at Yellow Submarine, I had the opportunity to find out more about the residents' activities. After getting up in the morning, they often would proceed to narrate and discuss their dreams of the previous night. Then they would chant and meditate. A huge chart hung on the wall of the kitchen outlining the possible activities of the forthcoming day. It told of going with friends to the park where they would dance and sing, chant and meditate, hold sensitivity groups, do psychodramas and sensory awareness exercises in the afternoon, and have an early, potluck dinner. After dark they would light a huge bonfire, take a little dope to expand their consciousness and then dance and sing and make music together. And before leaving, they would pray for good crops and the good health of all present in the coming year, and then each person would burn something from his past in the dimming bonfire. "Those are only suggested ideas," Tom noted, when he saw me reading the chart, "we may do all of them, or none of them, according to who's there and how we all feel at the time."

These are after all a new and better breed of youths. They are not hung up on plans and schedules and rigid structures. They are able to adapt, change, modify, and eliminate a plan if the mood and tone of the moment does not fit the pre-described plan; they are now-oriented and yet able to project toward the future—that is, to organize and plan without disregard for the reality of the moment. Thus, they are not continually trying to impose a system on a situation simply because it had been planned.

A COMMON SENSE OF PURPOSE

After my visit to Yellow Submarine, I contemplated the group's way of life and its commitment to an alternative life style. This commune was no band of pioneers living in lean-tos at the end of a semi-impassable mountain-goat trail. This was suburbia—or rather, a commune in suburbia—where the members made no great efforts to isolate themselves from the outside world. In fact, many of the group's interpersonal and recreational activities took place outside the commune. As the male-female ratio was about 3:1, and as each female was involved in conventional monogamous pairing, most of the guys had to seek female companionship elsewhere. This kind of arrangement tends to make the membership in a commune more transitory; it also reduces depth interaction and interdependence—characteristics that, if present, can create a more satisfying and permanent community.

But should every member of every commune be intent solely upon the purpose of developing depth interaction and interdependence? There are now many people, especially the young, who are content with a yellow submarine type of situation.

These people are not ready to make a permanent commitment to any one endeavor while there is still a whole world of alternatives out there for them to explore — a universal wall chart to choose from. Only after a broad and satisfying experience of many diverse possibilities can a person really hope to find the place where he really wants to be — the place he can grow with, rather than beyond.

Few of us ever find that place. Some continue the search for quite some time, struggling bravely against exhaustion and exposure. But most of us take only a few steps before spotting what looks like a comfortable niche and snuggling safely within; thereafter, we confine our explorations to vicarious experience derived from newspapers, magazines, books, radio, television, and occasionally people.

In a world like ours, where the environmental stimuli run high, we are plagued with constantly gnawing feelings of discontent, dissatisfaction, boredom — feelings which can be traced directly to our inactivity. We cannot escape the fact that the search for self — for the true and total place (in all its physical, psychological, emotional, and social aspects) — where we *know* we ought to be — is as basic an urge in man as is any automatic body function. We play all manner of games in our efforts to ignore this urge, because it offers no guarantee of fulfillment. But it hounds us throughout life and can only be outrun by death or nirvana; there is no in-between. Direct consciousness of this fact, combined with a total personal commitment to the search (not just intellectual — you must get in there with your hands and feet), constitute the only way to deal with this urge. Although some people have postulated that this urge is "the religious instinct," organized religion has no recognizable connection with it even if most clerics would like to claim it as their exclusive province (yes, including today's liberal-cum-social worker-cum-do-gooder-cum clergyman).

I discussed no such weighty matters as these while at

the Yellow Submarine. Nor did I studiously sit there thinking Important Thoughts and speculating about the ultimate meaning of it all. There was no need. My visit was relaxed and casual. It was *fun*. I emerged from that landlubbed Yellow Submarine much fuller than when I had entered. One useful and practical generalization was possible after my visit: homemade beer is a good fuel with which to keep a commune brewing.

GREENFEEL

Greenfeel, a commune in Barre, Vermont, was begun by two young bisexuals who had been working on an underground newspaper in Monterey, California. One of them, Ron, wrote a short article called "Something Positive," in which he said:*

There are many undiscovered ways to rebel that are honest and constructive. It is your job to find such methods and to change your goals if you are self-destructive. No one else can be your saviour . . . be joyful and painful and miraculous, never ever dull. Fate doesn't control you, you do. Try harder. Please.

Ron and his friend began publishing a magazine, *Greenfeel*, presenting this positive point of view. Ron wrote to me saying how *The Modern Utopian* was such an inspiration to them. I replied by asking for an article with details and photographs about their commune (also named Greenfeel) in rural Vermont. Ron sent several typewritten pages of very general comments about his place. It was not what I wanted. Everyone can write beautiful words and philosophy about the ideal society. But what is really going on? What is the nittygritty reality? What about the inevitable human interactions and conflicts? How are problems dealt with? Most people interested in communes have too naive and idealistic a view of the day-to-

* Published in *The Modern Utopian*, vol. 3, no. 2, spring 1969.

day realities of communal living. They do not need to have this view reinforced; rather, they need more awareness of the difficulties.

After editing Ron's article, I wrote again and asked for details. This time I received a handwritten reply, along with the comment that he didn't think the details too important. With them, I was impressed.

The original article said in part:

Greenfeel is a vision, two people, now eight, and a forest. We come together to live as a community of lovers. . . . Greenfeel is not a romantic utopia, it is a very real place of growing, joy, much pain, hope and effort.

Our most beautiful creation will come: kids, alive, spontaneous, sexual[ly] . . . unrepressed, free from hang-ups, not stifled in school. . . .

No one believes words anymore, too much bullshit has been written. . . . But try to believe this is where Greenfeel is at: Sensuousness all day long, including full sexuality, spontaneity and nakedness. Good psychoanalysis . . . intense, honest relationships of many loving beings. . . .

And despite the disclaimer, have you ever heard such utopian romanticism? Then there is Ron's awareness that "too much bullshit has been written" accompanied by the compulsion to produce still more of it!

I sent Ron some critical comments: "Greenfeel is messed up—still talking about some utopian reality *out there*." Ron was unhappy and replied:

I write "No one believes in words anymore." You called my words bullshit words. You don't believe words anymore either. That is sad. You called us messed-up idealists, but we're neither messed-up nor idealists. We don't philosophize—We Live, We Feel, We Grow. We are together and never feel uncomfortable about the way we are living, if we live our beliefs.

You are a reactor—you react and criticize and judge before you allow someone to reach you deeply. You must miss out on much real beauty and humanness. Please consider this and us.

Feelingly, Greenfeel.

My response was: "Oh, hum—write on, brother. Now really, Greenfeel, I'm on your side. Why must you insist on how much you Live, Feel, Grow?"

I really get put off by people who say they're honest and loving and beautiful, even if they do admit they have some hang-ups too; it all sounds like one big glorification of the ego. When "Greenfeel" (meaning Ron) talks about pain and self-destructiveness and loneliness, it all sounds so romantic and lovely. Like the whole phony-baloney encounter-group scene, which wallows in talk about expressing and emoting and feeling so that everything becomes one great big exaggerated feeling—a form of compensation, of acting-out, for those who are afraid they may wake up one morning and not be able to feel anything. So, relax, man (meaning Ron), we all know you've got feelings; we've got them too. Yes, and we've been fucked over and conditioned not to feel ("Only babies cry—Be a big boy/girl now"). And now you're relearning to experience how you feel about people and animals and nature. Cool. Dig it—no need to talk about it. Like one gal said to me, "I don't read pornography, I do it."

I thought the details concerning Greenfeel were interesting. Covering a total of five acres of Vermont land, the commune had "600 square feet of livable space in winter, plus another 600 square feet of usable work area." Its population fluctuated; throughout the summer and fall of 1969 it had a seasonal total of about 20 members, ages 11 to 40, as well as visitors. Members contributed at least $12 a week (without therapy) or $20 a week (with therapy). The money was earned by taking outside jobs. Greenfeel, of course, hoped to eventually build an income from work done within the community. The girls tended to do most of the cleaning and cooking, although everyone was expected to participate in all chores.

The ideal held by the commune was a belief that every member relates totally to every other member in an open, spontaneous and loving manner (including sexually) regardless of age, sex, or relationship. In actuality this did not occur, though they struggled to make it happen. Ron noted that "we frequently feel sexually free." That impressed me, for he did not claim to be sexually free "all day long" at that point. Those who wish to, go naked when it's warm.

In February 1971 I received the following note from Ron Norman:

Greenfeel magazine is sold out and won't be reprinted. AND the community in Vermont no longer is together. Please save people false expectations and take our name off your lists, o.k. Will explain more in detail later—Thanks for everything beautiful you've done for us, and are still doing! Peace and love. . . .

Too bad. Greenfeel's demise was not a great surprise but it did make me feel sad. I would like to have written about it here in the present tense.

CHAPTER NINE

THE WAY TO ONENESS

If outer space is now the province of the scientists and bureaucrats, and inner space the province of mind-expanding drugs, rock music, and religion, then interpersonal space is the province of the communal movement. Growth centers, encounter groups, sensory-awareness weekends, these are the testing sites for people too timid to make interpersonal living a full-time reality. But it is the several thousand communes of all kinds — religious and ideological, hip and group-marriage, service and youth — that are the avant-garde in exploring interpersonal space.

Just as the forward thrust of this movement does not depend on the continued existence of any particular commune or communes, so a commune's own contribution to the movement isn't necessarily measured by the commune's longevity or survival. If, through participation in the communal experience, individuals feel more alive and fulfilled (greater awareness of self and others, etc.), such a commune must be deemed a success — a contributor to the great fund of communal experience being accumulated.

Viewed through my eye(i)sight, then, the communal experience in America today can only be considered a positive one, both for the individual and for the collective consciousness of the society. It marks the beginning of the only relevant and necessary revolution that needs to take place here — the revolution of consciousness that will carry people upward from the private, intolerant, grasping, solitary self toward the cooperative, sharing, loving, universal self.

The physical gap between people has been closed by the interactive effects of transportation, communications, media, and population expansion. It is now time we caught up on the emotional-psychological level by whatever means we can develop. The communal movement is both the response to that need and the innovative expression of those means. Communal members are the explorer-pioneers and the initial beneficiaries.

IDEALS

People in the commune movement have innumerable points of view about not only how to create the better society but also what the ideals should be fore their various utopias. Some general agreement, though, does exist, and the following are five basic ideals held by perhaps the majority of these pioneering utopians:

1. GETTING BACK TO ESSENTIALS

Real Needs: What are our real needs anyway? We are a society filled with gadgets and junk and Madison Avenue ad men. Haven't you gone into a discount store or supermarket intending to buy only one or two items and come out with a bundle in your arms? Next time you go to that same store, refrain from this impulse-buying. Don't buy anything you didn't originally intend to buy. During the following week, you'll realize, I think, that *not* buying those extra things makes no difference in terms of your basic needs. You're just as well off without them; no, *better.* We get satisfaction out of so much buying and consuming of goods because these activities seem to fill a gap not being filled by extending ourselves into other areas of our potential. We need to develop all aspects of ourselves other than the dubious ability to buy and use. Fulfilling one's basic needs does not, of course, mean leading a life of abject poverty and penury. Each of us needs: (a) living quarters that reflect and fulfill the group's and the individual's ecological awareness and basic needs, which means ignoring the ticky-tacky tract house, the dehumanizing standardized apartment, and the multi-garaged, gadget-filled suburban mansion;

(b) clothing that expresses self-individualized dress (including hair style and length)—whatever feels right to the individual, including no clothes at all perhaps; and (c) healthful, natural food, rather than junk—a need based less on nurturing a food fetish than on having a concern for additive-free foods and a balanced, inexpensive diet.

Dependence on Things: As the Peace Pilgrim asked, "Do you own your furniture, or does it own you?" Perhaps you are working as hard as you are chiefly to make the car and house payments, or in order to finish paying for that new TV or stereo or. . . . One way we can stop being run by things is by giving up the practice of pretending that everything we buy is an essential acquisition.

Consolidation of Resources. Through cooperation with one another we can consolidate resources. By sharing material goods, such as cars, television sets, furniture, etc., we would not have to work so hard to pay for what is essentially a superfluity of private property. Instead we can work on the less tangible things in our lives that are far more important—personal and spiritual growth. (And, it so happens, the most efficient way of sharing material goods is to adopt a communal way of life.)

Ethical Considerations. Then there are the ethical considerations. How many restful nights can you spend in your warm, comfortable bed before being jolted awake by the horror of a woman and child sleeping (or dying) in the gutters of Calcutta? How many steaks can you consume before your appetite is taken away by the realization that a child is dying of malnutrition in Mississippi?

Most of us North Americans (and West Europeans) flaunt ourselves as the modern pharaohs, while the other peoples of the world generally live like slaves, having to spend their lives building pyramids—pyramids of economic wealth for our use, not theirs. If, as many people believe, there is a law of karma, our affluence in the face of suffering humanity will surely result in our being ac-

corded a truly horrible and well-deserved destiny. It is not good enough to say, "I can't do anything about it; my not eating steak is not going to feed that poor child," and then go on eating. It is mistaken for us to try to rationalize our behavior in such matters. After all, if men refused to fight, there would be no wars. So, too, if we refused to eat so much, there would be less starvation in the world.

But, beyond this "practical" consideration of starving people, what about you and me as individuals; what about conscience and principles? We march on the picket lines and participate in demonstrations against the war in Vietnam, knowing full well that these small protests of ours cannot possibly end the war. So why do we join in? It is for the sake of our souls, our sense of right, and our need to declare this sense to the world. What is more, there is the principle of being willing to translate principles into action; high-minded thoughts are not enough. Ideally, all of mankind should be moved to participate in bettering the human consideration. That being improbable we can at least actively demonstrate our own sense of right by sharing with and giving to and caring for at least some if not all people.

2. GETTING BACK TO THE LAND

Man has become alienated from his natural habitat. Communal people want to get away from the pollution, the congestion, the foul odors of the cities and freeways. They want soil, not concrete, under their feet. They want to breathe clean, fresh air and feel the sun on their bodies. Why, you ask? Next time you're outdoors in the country, reach down and take up a handful of earth or grass. Feel it, experience it, touch it to your face; open yourself up to it completely—even get down and roll in it. You'll experience a part of yourself, the deep inner you, that you have almost forgotten.

And it hardly needs mention that we are destroying the land by our lack of ecological awareness of it, caused in part by our living most of the time on concrete and freeways. Experiencing nature first hand, learning to grow the grass, the plants, the crops in harmony with the soil, these may help us to save the land, and ourselves who are as much its products as are the trees.

3. GETTING BACK TO THE PEOPLE

Do you realize that this is probably the first time in the history of man that society has been deliberately structured to alienate people? A mood of separateness, isolation, loneliness is everywhere. Only the last generation has grown up in the most isolated environment ever created: the nuclear family and television.

Last week I heard a radio talk-show in which the participants were trying to discover the reasons for so much student unrest. One person speculated that one reason may be a "racial memory of the extended family"—that is, young people are unconsciously experiencing dissatisfaction with the lack of extended-family participation. Whether or not the explanation is valid, America certainly does suffer from a lack of full family life. One remedy for this deficiency is offered by the communal movement: a realignment and restructuring of human relations to allow for more sharing, whether it is simply a strong sense of neighborliness or the evolution of an intense and involved group marriage. In anthropological terms, the extended family consists of people related by blood and marriage ties. In communal life, it consists of unrelated people who have come together as loving friends.

Loneliness and isolation gather together in the cities, where people tend to remain cut off from one another even in the most physically crowded situations—as the rush hour on New York City's subway system so aptly and sadly illustrates. "All the lonely people, where do they come from?" is a line in the Beatles' song, "Eleanor Rigby." Why ask? Just listen. They are there, all around you. The need for human contact stands out on the surface of the skin (what do people really go to church for?). Right now, if you are not alone, grasp the hand of the person on either side of you and say "hello." Is it a little embarrassing for you to do? Embarrassing? Do you understand what it means to be embarrassed just to hold a person's hand and greet him, be he stranger, friend, or acquaintance? It should be easy. We should be able to put our arms around each other and sway and chant together. Commune people want to get rid of the interpersonal isolation, rid themselves of the things that separate people. So they plead for cooperation, for people to live and work together so that each can benefit more fully from life and one another.

If there is to be any continuity to this process of bringing people together, there must also be a concerted effort in the field of education. This means fostering the development of the whole person, not just the intellectual function of the brain but also the body. It means teaching children and adults so that they can experience the joy and mystery of learning new things. And it means *not* having to rigidly follow a text, to sit straight in rows of chairs, to keep quiet until spoken to (by the teacher); it's so much better for kids to learn in a free and informal atmosphere—to sit on the floor, to talk with each other, to yell and sing.

4. SEARCHING FOR SELF

People in the communal movement also seek self-actualization—finding out more fully who they are and realizing as many aspects as possible of their potential. They are tired of specialization, which creates dehumanized intellectual machines. Life is not getting a college degree, a good job, settling down, and raising a family. It's more, much more, than that. It's developing as a fully functioning, sensitive human being.

5. SOCIAL CHANGE BY EXAMPLE

Commune people do not wish to escape from society or pretend it doesn't exist. Rather, they want to set an example that others may follow. They believe, most of all, that we learn from what a person does, not from what he says. If I call out to you to "sell all you have and give to the poor" from the open window of my new Cadillac, I doubt if you'd listen. And why should you? A commune, though, provides a real example of an alternative life style—a persuasive message from the nonwealthy to the Cadillac drivers.

The commune people intent upon change-by-example are disillusioned with the revolutionaries who wish to destroy the system and set up their own, believing that they would be as bad at ruling as the forces they oppose.

Although a gutted bank building is a dramatic example of revolutionary action, it is a very small dent in the system. Such action, although an understandable response to an insensitive and uncaring society, only provokes more controls by the Establishment—hiring additional police, stocking more riot guns and other weapons—all with the approval of a frightened and confused public. The communal movement takes a much more positive approach to social change; ideally, *everyone* in society can participate in the revolution of consciousness, the rulers as well as the ruled. And communes can help to show the way.

MATTER OVER MIND

The utopian pioneers are not without their own hangups, if only because they, as Americans, are the products of an overly competitive, over-intellectualized, individualistic environment. The most sound criticism of these new dropouts is that they are too idealistic, given the cantankerous nature of man; they are far too naive about the possible results of their endeavors, and they are overly cerebral. That last point, which bears directly on the other two, has been elaborated upon by Robert DeRopp:*

When it comes to creating a stable community, they [these more adventurous intellectuals] have a hard time. The "intellectual" is poor material from which to construct a stable community. His weakness for theorizing, his fondness for argument, his habit of losing himself in the jungle of his own verbiage, the power of his false ego, all render him unfitted for the practical tasks involved in building and maintaining the new society. He argues about the nature of goodness, truth and beauty when he should be milking the cow or gathering the hay crop. His whole outlook is distorted by the overactivity of his intellectual brain.

Out of my experience with communes and groups and life, I have learned several lessons during the last few years, sometimes directly, sometimes indirectly.

One such lesson, repeated many times, taught me that to have a great idea or ideal really is meaningless in and of itself, and can even be personally harmful. For example, a friend of mine, after reading Heinlein's novel, *Stranger in a Strange Land*, explained with much enthusiasm that to her the best possible commune would be the one where everybody lived in one large room. Absolutely no private space was necessary. An hour later she was unhappy because she couldn't get rid of her kids in order to be alone for the weekend.

To give another example, at a Fourth of July party

The Master Game, 1968, Dell Publishing Co., pp. 211–212.

given by a community group in Boston, I noticed a friend of mine sitting in a corner, looking quite sad. Sad, he was, amid demonstrations in Hatha Yoga, animated conversations, wild dancing, a great variety of delicious food, good drinks, and even fireworks — a really great party. I couldn't imagine what was wrong, so I asked him. He replied, "Sure, it's a good party, I guess. But we're not getting any closer to the community we want this way!" He was utterly convinced that a community had to be a particular *place* with a particular *kind* of behavior, so that he was unable to enjoy the present. He allowed his ideals to stand in the way of his enjoyment of the unplanned, unexpected pleasures of life.

PLOTTING THE i IN SELF DIRECTION

Back in 1965, before the new experimental community movement had really started, I ended a term paper on Brook Farm and the Hopedale Community (19th-century American utopias) with the statement "When better people are made, the world will be a better place to live in." I came to that conclusion as a result of academic studies up to that point in time. Now, six years later, I have again come to the same conclusion, this time as a result of my personal experiences.

The universal truth inherent in that conclusion does not, however, provide any practical advice in answer to the all-important question: "How?" One possible answer is: Start with oneself in the company of others who also seek self-improvement, keeping in mind that it is absolutely essential to provide opportunities for isolation and privacy. Without such opportunities, one can too easily become totally other-directed and manipulatable rather than self-willed and autonomous. (Happy is the commune that builds into its organizational structure the possibility of periodic leaves of absence.) Nevertheless, it is essential to have others serve as a mirror in order to provide a true reflection of oneself, this mirroring being a major instrument for personal change.

Trying to live a different life style sheds great light on one's own imperfections. One discovers immediately that the problems of life and society are not "out there," anymore than utopia is. One also learns that it becomes necessary to change one's behavior and that that inevitably requires going through some difficult and painful experiences. During the meetings of the Wednesday Night Group we tried to open up to one another and to reveal our real needs and feelings. Many of us became aware of things about ourselves that we had been unwilling and unable to admit in the past. We were forced to see ourselves through the eyes of others. These experiences were sometimes painful and frightening, several married in the group wound up getting divorced. Nevertheless, most of us felt that we had become better people as a result of these difficult experiences.

The Wednesday Night Group did produce positive results, but not without our making considerable effort over a long period of time. So it is with all such endeavors. They demand a great deal of time and labor. There are no miracles, no short cuts. "Perseverance Furthers," as is frequently repeated in the *I Ching*. No wonder that book has lasted two thousand years or so; we can still profit from its wisdom.

Perseverance without perception "wastes" rather than "furthers," so it is essential to couple the use of time with the use of all the senses. And inevitably, persevering perception leads to contemplation about the nature of reality. There are many levels of reality but on the highest and most meaningful level, "You and I are not we, but one." Accepting the idea that we are one (an idea which has to be arrived at through experience rather than logical deduction), then it follows that you are one and all, I am one and all—we are all the same one. It's something like "Thou art that"—"Thou art God" in religious terms. What this signifies is that each of us is *totally responsible* for everything that happens; we are *totally free* to make whatever happens, happen. This particular viewpoint precludes the allocation, dispensation, or fixing of blame in any form or amount. Just as you and I may be totally responsible and totally free, so is everyone else. Genuinely or deliberately forgetting this makes absolutely no difference.

Loading guilt or blame onto ourselves or others is just another excuse that each of us uses to avoid confronting our own responsibilities. It is easy to say: "Let George do it" or "If so and so or such and such had not been like that, then things would be better," or "Why don't *they* behave?" or "I can't do anything right so I'll always be a failure." But such plaintive observations are simply different aspects of the same thing.

Last spring I attended the meeting of a Gurdjieff group in San Francisco. When I entered the room where the meeting was taking place, there were 40 or 50 people sitting in a large circle and being asked by several leaders what they wanted out of life. One young man said the reason he was there was because more than anything he wanted to work out his relationship with his wife. The leaders asked him if he was willing to accept total responsibility for all that happened in the relationship. "Of course not," he responded, "she's wrong sometimes too." But they said, "Forget it. Until you can assume total responsibility you have no chance of working out the relationship. If you assume it, it does not mean that your marriage will stay together, but you will work it out, one way or the other."

I knew what they were talking about, for I had just spent two or three years thinking: "If only my wife weren't like that, everything would be all right."

If we accept this view of total responsibility and freedom, if we concentrate on being one with all, on being open to the universe, then things we want to happen will happen without a great deal of planning and organizing and effort. The more open we are, the less so-called preparation is necessary.

At Starr King School for the Ministry some years ago, I was moaning and groaning in class about the difficulty of preparing a sermon. One student, who was preaching three Sundays a month, said, "It just comes to you, if you're open to it." A lot of help that is, I thought. But he was right. The thing to do is relax and concentrate on being the universe, and—HERE IT IS: *You attract what you seek.*

I needed a typist to work on the magazine, but I hadn't been actively hunting for one. When the need became great, I happened to meet a guy, just a block from my place, who offered to do the typing. Another day, I was talking to my friend Jackie about Lou Gottlieb and Morn-

372

ing Star Ranch and Ramon Sender: 30 minutes later, Ramon and Lou and Rena called and then came over to see me. Then there was the time when, at 3 o'clock in the morning, I wrote a note to remind myself to call Verbie about Sunday's church program and to find a mimeograph machine and typist. Seven hours later, at 10 A.M., I was awakened by a telephone call from Verbie: she knew a typist with a mimeograph machine. Beautiful coincidence, right? But it happens all the time if you're open to it. It is really and simply a matter of connections, interconnections — we are all one. So the vibrations get sent out and, before you know it, zap — it's all there!

Have you ever bought a new or different car? Trade in that Chevrolet for a Volkswagen and then notice the multitude of Volkswagens on the road that you never noticed before. Or the same thing can happen by switching from a VW to a Chevie. Everything is right there before your eyes — just open up and see. Even the negative things that happen to you — open up and you see why *you made them happen.*

Looking on life with a consistently positive viewpoint and a working sense of humor is not too easy in a world full of poverty and many seemingly unresolvable problems. It is one thing to say that there is little you can do about these worldwide problems, but it is quite another matter to evidence an equal degree of gloom and helplessness when confronted with your own situation. It comes down to this: if you don't like your work, don't do it. (Of course, there are aspects of any job that we don't like — I'm talking about the job as a whole.) As Kahlil Gibran said in *The Prophet:* "And if you cannot work with love but only with distaste, it is better that you should leave your work and sit at the gate of the temple and take alms from those who work with joy." You will cause far less unhappiness and discomfort in both yourself and everyone around you if you take such an outlook and action regarding your own life.

We can all try to live positively and joyfully yet at the same time realize there is also a universal rule of thumb that applies as much to us as to molecules: "For every action there is an equal and opposite reaction." That doesn't mean that if we're ecstatic today we'll be depressed tomorrow. And it doesn't mean that we should try to balance our time with positive and negative feelings and actions. Rather, it is a guide to understanding that negative as well as positive levels have a place in our lives, no matter how far along we are on the road of self-improvement and self-awareness. So it is by no means wrong to be negative or to express negative feelings. Sometimes, in fact, expressing negative feelings is essential in order for a person to move on to the positive. For example, a teacher once told me to allow the first ten minutes of a discussion for getting all that negativity out; then to move on to doing positive, creative things. Don't get bogged down in negatives!

This is not just a matter of running around with a great big smile on one's face all the time. It is much more fundamental than that, having to do with understanding the implications of being negative. When I was in Berkeley a while ago, I met an old friend coming out of the bank as I was going in; he looked tired and depressed. I asked him about himself, whereupon he launched into a long diatribe about how BAD other people were. He was so critical of other individuals and groups of individuals that he was unable to enjoy anything about them. His attitude made me aware of how all to easy it is to write off groups or nationalities or ethnic types or individuals: "There are millions of other people in the world to relate to, so to hell with you." But we are one, remember? So who are we writing off?

We need to get to such questions before rather than after the fact of acting first and then considering the consequences. And to do so means developing that vital sense of self-awareness. Total responsibility, total freedom, making things happen, living through ideals rather than mentally toying with them, declaring our sense of right to ourselves and the world, recognizing the interrelatedness of all things, *not* writing off anyone — these are only some of the interacting factors that put and keep us on the road to self-improvement. And it is while on such a road that we develop a true sense of self.

All of this means simply that I must be aware that when I get, I give; when I buy, I pay; when I reach for

one thing, another thing is left farther behind. I have to make sure that what I try to attain does not cost me something I would dread to be without. If I become President, I will never again experience the pleasures of not being President; but if I never become President, I will never experience the special peculiarities of that position. So what exactly do I want?

This leads me to the most important lesson I have learned—the most difficult one to follow through on in my own life: I must know what I want. We Americans have been so conditioned to be obsessively other-directed (needing other people or things to define our personal worth) that we are usually way out of touch with our innermost authentic wants. Each person is unique. Each is one. His wants are unique and universal. "Knowing" in the deepest sense is "being" one with self, total, whole, together.

To get in touch with that uniqueness, that oneness, to become self-directed instead of other-directed—these are the fundamental goals that each individual must set for himself. And although the communes have deficiencies, like any human endeavor, I do not know of any other environment which compares with them as the means for fulfillment of these goals.

APPENDICES

APPENDIX I: GUIDES TO ALTERNATIVE LIFE STYLES

The following publications are community-oriented newsletters, magazines, or newspapers prepared by a variety of individuals and organizations throughout the United States. Quality, content, and frequency of publication vary of course, but all of these publications are devoted to some aspect or other of alternative life styles.

Adventure Trails Survival School, Laughing Coyote Mountain, Black Hawk, Colo. 80422. Philosophical newsletter. Irregular. Donations.

Alternatives Newsmagazine, P. O. Drawer A — Diamond Hgts., Sta., San Francisco, Calif. 94131. (See Appendix II.)

Ann Arbor Sun, 1520 Hill Street, Ann Arbor, Mich. 48104. Rainbow People's Tribe newspaper. Monthly.

The Appalachian South, c/o Council of Southern Mountains, Berea, Kentucky 40403. Monthly magazine. Subscription rate, $5 per year.

Aquarian Research Foundation, 5620 Morton Street, Philadelphia, Pa. 19144. New Age newsletter.

The City of Light, P.O. Box 1451, Scottsdale, Arizona 85252. New Age religious newsletter. Irregular. Donations.

Community Comments. Community Services Inc., Yellow Springs, Ohio, 45387. Newsletter and handbook, papers on small communities. Quarterly. $2 per year.

Community Market, 437 Abbott Rd., East Lansing, Michigan 48823. Catalogue of 36-plus communities whose products are available from this one source. Cost of catalogue: $1 annual.

The Green Revolution, Route 1, Box 129, Freeland, Md. 21053. Community newspaper emphasizing decentralization and rural homesteads. Subscription rate: $4 per year, bi-monthly, free sample.

The Homesteader, Early American Christian Home-steading and Community Movement, Route 2, Oxford, N.Y. 13830. Back-to-the-land community newsletter; correspondence course. Irregular.

Journal of Behavior Technology, c/o B.R.I., 3 Goodwin Place, Boston, Mass. 62114. Skinnerian (Walden Two) psychology approach to establishing communes. Quarterly publication, $10 per year.

Koinonia Partners, Americus, Georgia 31709. Community newsletter, books, records, Christian philosophy, pecan products. Irregular. Donations.

The Leaves of Twin Oaks, Route 4, Box 16, Louisa, Va. A Walden Two community newsletter. Details of how they live and deal with problems. Subscription rate: $3 per year. Bi-monthly.

The Meeting School, 427 Cedar Ave., Minneapolis, Minn. 55416. Communal free-school paper. Irregular. Donations.

The Modern Utopian. P.O. Drawer A—Diamond Hgts. Sta., San Francisco, Calif. 94131. (See appendix II.)

Mother Earth News, P.O. Box 38, Madison, Ohio 44057. It tells you how to do things—the community movement's "Popular Mechanics." Subscription rate: $6 per year. Bi-monthly.

Multilateral Relations Study Project, c/o L. and J. Constantine, 23 Mohegan Road, Acton, Mass. 01720. Papers, research, and counseling services on group marriage. Irregular. $2 for specimens.

Order of Saint Michael, 6914 West 117th Avenue, Crown Point, Ind. 46307. Episcopal community newsletter. Irregular. Donations.

Peacemaker, 10208 Sylvan Avenue, Cincinnati, Ohio 45241. Concerned with the peace movement and communities. Subscription rate, $3 per year. Bi-monthly.

PreForm, P.O. Box 607, Grants Pass, Oregon 97526. Survival techniques, nomadic-living newsletter. Irregular.

The Questors, 37700 Van Fleet, Cathedral City, Calif. 92234. Guide to starting intentional communities, newsletter. Irregular.

Society of Brothers, Westside Road, Norfolk, Conn. 06058. Information on all Bruderhof communities.

Vocations for Social Change, Canyon, Calif. 94516. Lists places needing people and developments in the movement. Donations. Bi-monthly.

Walden Three Communitarian. Box 1152, Annex Station, Providence, R.I. 02901. Skinner's *Walden Two* is the basis for this new magazine. Subscription: $10.

(Last) Whole Earth Catalog, Portola Institute, 558 Santa Cruz, Menlo Park, Calif. 94516. Access information for tools, books, etc. $5.

Win, 339 Lafayette Street, New York, N.Y. 10019. Published by the War Resisters League. Primarily pacifist, antiwar materials. Monthly, $3 per year.

The Futurist, World Future Society, P.O. Box 19285, 20th Street Station, Washington, D.C. 20036. Technologically oriented magazine on the future. Bimonthly, $7.50 per year.

APPENDIX II: THE MODERN UTOPIAN/ ALTERNATIVES FOUNDATION

A long time ago, Dick Fairfield, a student at Tufts University, started a magazine and named it *The Modern Utopian*. In it he set out to gather all the news about present-day man's search for a better world—Utopia, as some call it. The magazine stimulated thought and suggested that people do not have to accept the kind of world they are born into unless they especially like it. A directory of intentional communities and searching groups was issued and people were encouraged to exchange ideas. This was the forerunner of today's urge to discover and try out new ways of living.

Dick Fairfield continued *The Modern Utopian* when he moved to the Starr King School at Berkeley, California, to finish his BD Degree for the Unitarian ministry. Now the magazine has become part of an organization known as Alternatives Foundation, which has as its purpose the publication of information on alternative life styles. The magazine expresses a variety of ideas and reports a wide range of activities. With them all you may not agree, but the essence of Alternatives Foundation is expressed in these lyrics by Sly Stone which appeared in an issue of *The Modern Utopian:*

Stand
In the end you'll still be you
One that's done all the things you set out to do

Stand
There's a cross for you to bear
Things to go through if you're going anywhere

Stand
For the things you know are right
It's the truth that the truth makes them so uptight

Stand
All the things you want are real
You have you to complete and there is no deal

Stand, stand, stand
Stand, stand, stand

Stand
You've been sitting much too long
There's a permanent crease in your right and wrong

Stand
There's a midget standing tall
And the giant beside him about to fall

Stand, stand, stand
Stand, stand, stand

Stand
They will try to make you crawl
And they know what you're saying makes sense
    and all

Stand
Don't you know that you are free
Well at least in your mind if you want to be

Everybody
Stand, stand, stand

> — Sly and The Family Stone (Epic Records)
>   written by Sylvester Stewart

Subscribers to the Alternatives Foundation received the
following publications in 1971:*

Two issues of *The Modern Utopian:* COMMUNES, USA, a
special 188 page description of over 40 existing utopian
communal experiments in America, including a list of

---

*Write to Alternatives Foundation for information on the current avail-
ability of the 1971 publications. 1972 subscribers receive two giant issues of
The Modern Utopian: COMMUNES, EUROPE and UTOPIA, USA as well as the
quarterly *Alternatives Newsmagazine,* etc.

alternative publications and organizations which suggest ways out of the rat race. (As suggested by its title, this special issue represents the forerunner of this Penguin Book.) MODERN MAN IN SEARCH OF UTOPIA, another giant 196 page issue which discusses the ideals of modern utopian writers and presents ideas about how these ideals can be actualized now. Included is a list of free schools, growth centers, and groups organized to bring about meaningful social change, nationwide.

Alternatives Newsletter, three reports on Alternatives Foundation, including letters and responses from subscribers and from communes, free schools and others.

Alternatives Newsmagazine, a magazine which reports extensively on the activities of individuals and groups seeking and practicing new life styles.

People Directory, a quarterly directory for members who wish to exchange a personal description of themselves with other members in order to meet and explore alternatives together.

How to Booklets — three booklets, one on how to buy land, another on ways to make money while living in the country, and the third on how to start a commune.

Subscriptions are $10.00 per year. The organization's address is: Alternatives Foundation, P.O. Drawer A — Diamond Hgts. Sta., San Francisco, California 94131.

BIBLIOGRAPHY

I THE GENERAL BIBLIOGRAPHY*

1. PLANNED COMMUNITIES, COMMUNAL GROUPS, AND UTOPIAN EXPERIMENTS (NON-FICTION)

Alyea, Paul E. and Blanche Alyea. *Fairhope 1894–1954*. University, Alabama: University of Alabama Press, 1956.

Andrews, Edward D. *The People Called Shakers*. New York, N.Y.: Oxford University Press, 1953. Reissued in paperbound edition, New York, N.Y.: Dover Publications, 1963.

Armit, Karl J. R. *George Repp's Harmony Society*, 1785–1847. Philadelphia, Pa.: University of Pennsylvania Press, 1965.

Armytage, W. H. G. *Heavens Below: Utopian Experiments in England, 1560–1960*. Toronto, Ont.: University of Toronto Press, 1961.

Arnold, Emmy. *Torches Together, the Beginning and Early Years of the Bruderhof Communities*. Rifton, N.Y.: Plough Publications, 1964.

Ballou, Adin. *The Hopedale Community*. Lowell, Mass.: Thompson & Hill, 1897.

Beam, Maurice. *Cults of America*. New York, N.Y.: MacFadden-Bartell, 1964.

Berneri, Marie Louise. *Journey Through Utopia*. London, Eng.: Routledge & Kegan Paul, 1950.

Bestor, Arthur E., Jr. *Backwoods Utopias 1663–1829*. Philadelphia, Pa.: 1950.

Bettelheim, Bruno. *The Children of the Dream*. New York, N.Y.: Macmillan, 1969. [An analysis of Israeli kibbutzim.]

Bishop, Claire H. *All Things Common*. New York, N.Y.: Harper & Bros., 1952.

Bole, John A. *The Harmony Society*. Philadelphia, Pa.: American Germanica Press, 1904.

Broome, Isaac. *The Last Days of the Ruskin Co-operative Association*. Chicago, Ill.: Charles H. Kerr and Co., 1902.

Burton, Katherine. *Paradise Planters: The Story of Brook Farm*. London, Eng.: Longmans, Green & Co., 1939.

---

*This general bibliography was furnished by Dr. T. E. Ryther, a sociologist at San Francisco State College. I have taken the liberty of editing this list and adding several other titles — R.F.

Calverton, Victor. *Where Angels Dared to Tread*. New York, N.Y.: Bobbs-Merrill, 1941.

Carmer, Carl. *Listen For a Lonesome Drum*. New York, N.Y.: Farrar & Rinehart, 1936.

Clark, Bertha. "The Hutterian Communities," *Journal of Political Economy*, vol. 32 no. 4 (June 1954).

Clark, Elmer T. *The Small Sects in America*. New York, N.Y.: Abingdon Press, 1937.

Codman, John Thomas. *Brook Farm Memoire*. Boston, Mass.: Arena Publishing Co., 1894.

Conkin, Paul K. *Two Paths to Utopia*. Lincoln, Nebr.: University of Nebraska Press, 1964.

Curtis, Edith Roelker. *A Season in Utopia: The Story of Brook Farm*. Camden, N.J.: Thomas Nelson & Sons, 1961.

Darin-Drabkin, H. *The Other Society*. New York, N.Y.: Harcourt, Brace & World, 1961.

Duss, John S. *The Harmonists*. Harrisburg, Pa.: The Pennsylvania Book Service, 1943.

Eaton, Joseph W. and Saul M. Katz. *Research Guide on Cooperative Group Farming*. New York, N.Y.: 1942.

Edmonds, Walter D. *The First Hundred Years (1848–1948), Oneida Community*. Oneida, N.Y.: Oneida Community, 1948.

Egbert, Donald E. and Stow Persons (eds.), T. D. Seymour Bassett (blbiog.). *Socialism and American Life*. Vol. II. Princeton, N.J.: Princeton University Press, 1952.

Falkner, Robert. *Nauvoo: Kingdom on the Mississippi*. Urbana, Ill.: University of Illinois Press, 1965.

Gide, Charles. *Communist and Cooperative Colonies*. New York, N.Y.: Thomas Y. Crowell, 1928.

Hendricks, Robert J. *Bethel & Aurora: An Experiment in Communism and Practical Christianity*. New York, N.Y.: The Press of the Pioneers, 1933.

Hinds, William A. *American Communities*. Chicago, Ill.: Charles H. Kerr & Co., 1902.

Hine, Robert V. *California's Utopian Communities*. New Haven, Conn.: Yale University Press, 1953.

Holloway, Mark. *Heavens on Earth 1680–1880*. New York, N.Y.: Library Publishers, 1951. Second edition, New York, N.Y.: Dover Publications, 1966.

Hostetler, John A. *Amish Society*. Baltimore, Md.: The Johns Hopkins Press, 1963.

Infield, Henrik (ed.). *Cooperative Group Living*. New York, N.Y.: Henry Koosis, 1950.

Infield, Henrik and Koka Freier. *People in Ejidos*. New York, N.Y.: Frederick A. Praeger, 1954.

Kaplan, Bert and Thomas Plaut. *Personality in a Communal Society*. Lawrence, Kansas: University of Kansas Press, 1956.

Kolaja, Jiri. *Workers' Councils: The Yugoslav Experience*. New York, N.Y.: Frederick A. Praeger, 1965.

Leon, Dan. *The Kibbutz: Portrait From Within*. New York, N.Y.: Pergamon Press, 1969.

Lockwood, George B. *The New Harmony Movement*. New York, N.Y.: D. Appleton & Co., 1905.

_____. *The New Harmony Communities*. Marion, Ind.: The Chronicle Co., 1902.

MacLean, J. P. *Bibliography of Shaker Literature*. Columbus, Ohio: 1905.

McBee, Alice Eaton. *From Utopia to Florence. The Story of a Transcendentalist Community in Northampton, Mass., 1830–1852*. Northampton, Mass.: 1947.

Morse, Flo. *Yankee Communes: Another American Way*. New York, N.Y.: Harcourt, Brace & Jovanovich, Inc., 1971.

Murry, John Middleton. *Community Farm*. London, Eng.: Peter Nevill, 1952.

Nordhoff, Charles. *The Communistic Societies of the United States*. [originally published in 1875] New York, N.Y.: Hillary House Publishers, 1960; New York, N.Y.: Schocken Books, 1965.

Orvis (Dwight), Marianne. *Letters From Brook Farm, 1844–1847*. Poughkeepsie, N.Y.: Vassar College, 1928.

Parker, Robert A. *A Yankee Saint: John H. Noyes and the Oneida Community*. New York, N.Y.: G. P. Putnam's Sons, 1935.

Parrington, Vernon Louis, Jr. *American Dreams: A Study of American Utopias*. Providence, R.I.: Brown University Press, 1947.

Pearlman, Maurice. *Adventures in the Sun: An Informal Account of Communal Settlements of Palestine*. London, Eng.: Gollancz, 1947.

Peters, Victor. *All Things Common: The Hutterian Way of Life*. Minneapolis, Minn.: University of Minnesota Press, 1965.

Ploesch, Donald G. *Centers of Christian Renewal*. Philadelphia, Pa.: United Church Press, 1964.

Podmore, Frank. *Robert Owen: A Biography*. New York, N.Y.: D. Appleton & Co., 1907.

Rabin, A. *Growing Up in the Kibbutz*. New York, N.Y.: Springer Publishing Co., 1965.

Richter, Peyton E., (ed.) *Utopias: Social Ideals and Communal Experiments*. Boston, Mass.: Holbrook Press, 1971.

Sams, Henry W. (ed.). *Autobiography of Brook Farm*. Englewood Cliffs, N.J.: Prentice-Hall, 1958.

Senior, Clarence. *Democracy Comes to a Cotton Kingdom*. New York, N.Y.: League for Industrial Democracy, 1940.

Shalom, Ben. *Deep Furrows*. New York, N.Y.: Hasomer Hatzain Organization, 1937.

Shamburgh, H. *Amana: The Community of True Inspiration*. Iowa City, Iowa: State Historical Society of Iowa, 1908.

Shepperson, Wilbur S. *Retreat to Nevada: A Socialist Colony of World War I*. Reno, Nev.: University of Nevada Press, 1966.

Simpson, Eyler N. *The Ejido: Mexico's Way Out*. Chapel Hill, N.C.: University of North Carolina Press, 1937.

Spiro, Melford E. *Children of the Kibbutz*. Cambridge, Mass.: Harvard University Press, 1958.

_____. *Kibbutz: Venture In Utopia*. Cambridge, Mass.: Harvard University Press, 1956.

Sugihara, Yoshie and David Plath. *Sensei and His People: The Building of a Japanese Commune*. Berkeley, Calif.: University of California Press, 1969.

Swift, Lindsay. *Brook Farm: Its Members, Scholars & Visitors*. New York, N.Y.: The Macmillan Co., 1890.

Thrupp, Sylvia L. *Millennial Dreams in Action: Comparative Studies in Society and History*. The Hague, Netherlands: Mouton, 1962.

Webber, Everett. *Escape to Utopia: The Communal Movement in America*. New York, N.Y.: Hastings House, 1959.

Williams, G. (Stewart Grahame, pseud.). *Where Socialism Failed: An Actual Experiment*. New York, N.Y.: McBride, Nast, & Co., 1912.

Wilson, William E. *The Angel and the Serpent: The Story of New Harmony*. Bloomington, Ind.: University of Indiana Press, 1964.

Wooster, Ernest S. *Communities of the Past & Present*. Newllano, La.: New Llano Community, 1924.

Yarmolinsky, Avraham. *A Russian's American Dream*. Lawrence, Kansas: University of Kansas Press, 1965.

Young, Marguerite. *Angel in the Forest*. New York, N.Y.: Reynal and Hitchcock, 1945. New York, N.Y.: Scribner, 1966.

2. THEORETICAL UTOPIAS AND "UTOPIAN" THOUGHT (FICTION)

Baldry, H. C. *Ancient Utopias*. Southampton, Eng.: University of Southampton, 1956.

Bellamy, Edward. *Looking Backward*. Edited by John L. Thomas. Cambridge, Mass.: Harvard University Press, 1967.

Bharatan, Kumarappa. *Capitalism, Socialism or Villageism*. Madras, India: Shekt, Karyalayan, 1940.

Buber, Martin. *Paths in Utopia*. New York, N.Y.: The Macmillan Co., 1950.

Eaton, J. W. and S. M. Katz. *Research Guide on Cooperative Group Farming*. New York, N.Y.: H. W. Wilson, 1942.

Fromm, Erich. *The Sane Society*. New York, N.Y.: Rinehart, 1955.

Goodman, Paul. *Utopian Essays and Critical Proposals*. New York, N.Y.: Random House, 1962.

Goodman, Paul and Percival Goodman. *Communitas: Means of Livelihood and Ways of Life*. New York, N.Y.: Random House, 1947.

Gray, Donald J. and Allan H. Orrick. *Designs of Famous Utopias*. New York, N.Y.: Rinehart, Winston.

Harrington, James. *The Commonwealth of Oceana*. London, Eng.: George Routledge & Sons, 1887.

Heinlein, Robert A. *Stranger in a Strange Land*. New York, N.Y.: Berkeley Publishing Corp., 1961.

_____. *The Moon is a Harsh Mistress*. New York, N.Y.: Berkeley Publishing Corp., 1968.

Hertzler, Joyce O. *The History of Utopian Thought*. New York, N.Y.: The Macmillan Co., 1923.

Huxley, Aldous. *Island*. New York, N.Y.: Harper & Row, 1962.

Infield, Henrik. *Utopian and Experiment: Essays in the Sociology of Cooperation*. New York, N.Y.: Frederick A. Praeger, 1955.

Kateb, George. *Utopia and Its Enemies*. New York, N.Y.: The Free Press, 1963.

Kautsky, Karl. *Thomas More and His Utopia*. Translated by H. J. Stenning. New York, N.Y.: Russell and Russell, 1959.

Macroby, Michael. "The Social Psychology of Utopia: The Writings of Paul Goodman," *Journal of the American Institute of Planners*, vol. 28, no. 4 (1962).

Mannheim, Karl. *Ideology and Utopia: An Introduction to the Sociology of Knowledge*. New York, N.Y.: Harcourt, Brace & Co., 1936.

Manuel, Frank E. (ed.). *Utopias and Utopian Thought*. Boston, Mass.: Houghton Mifflin, 1966.

Manuel, Frank E. and Fritzie P. (eds.). *French Utopias*. New York, N.Y.: The Free Press, 1966.

Masso, Gildo. *Education in Utopias*. New York, N.Y.: Teachers College Press (Columbia University), 1927.

Morgan, Arthur E. *Nowhere is Somewhere: How History Makes Utopias and How Utopias Make History*. Chapel Hill, N.C.: University of North Carolina Press, 1946.

Morley, Henry (ed.). *Ideal Commonwealths*. The writings of More, Bacon, Campanella, Harrington. New York, N.Y.: Cooperative Publishing Society, 1901.

Mumford, Lewis. *Story of Utopias: Ideal Commonwealths and Social Myths*. New York, N.Y.: Boni, 1923.

Negley, Glenn and J. Max Patrick (eds.). *The Quest for Utopia: An Anthology of Imaginary Societies*. Garden City, N.Y.: Doubleday & Co., 1952.

Polak, Frederik Ldowijk. *The Image of the Future*. Leyden, The Netherlands; Dobbs Ferry, N.Y.: Oceana Publications, 1961.

Rimmer, Robert H. *The Harrad Experiment*. Los Angeles, Calif.: Sherbourne Press, 1966.

————. *Proposition 31*. New York, N.Y.: New American Library, 1968.

————. *The Rebellion of Yale Marrett*. Boston, Mass.: Challenge Press, 1964.

————. *The Zolotov Affair*. Los Angeles, Calif.: Sherbourne Press, 1967.

Russell, Frances T. *Touring Utopia*. New York, N.Y.: The Dial Press, 1932.

Sarnoff, Irving. *Society Without Tears*. New York, N.Y.: Citadel Press, 1965.

Skinner, B.F. *Walden Two*. New York, N.Y.: The Macmillan Co., 1948.

Soklar, Judith. *After Utopia: The Decline of Political Faith*. Princeton, N.J.: Princeton University Press, 1957.

3. THE FOLK COMMUNITY: INTENTIONAL COMMUNITY PROTOTYPE

Arensberg, Conrad M. and Solon T. Kimball. *Culture and Community*. New York, N.Y.: Harcourt, Brace and World, 1956.

Banfield, Edward C. *The Moral Basis of a Backward Society.*
Glencoe, Ill.: The Free Press of Glencoe, 1958.

Borsodi, Ralph. *This Ugly Civilization.* New York, N.Y.: Harper
and Brothers, 1933.

_____. *Flight From the City.* Suffern, N.Y.: School of Living,
1947.

_____. *Education and Living.* Suffern, N.Y.: School of
Living, 1948.

Borsodi, Ralph, Oliver Edwin Baker, and M. L. Wilson, *Agriculture in Modern Life.* New York, N.Y.: Harper and Brothers,
1939.

Dalton, George. *Tribal and Peasant Economics.* New York,
N.Y.: The Natural History Press, 1967.

Daraul, Akron. *A History of Secret Societies.* New York, N.Y.:
Citadel Press, 1962.

Hillery, George A. Jr. *Communal Organizations, A Study of
Local Societies.* Chicago, Ill.: University of Chicago Press,
1968.

Hoebel, E. Adamson. *The Cheyennes.* New York, N.Y.: Holt,
Rinehart & Winston, 1960.

Lee, Dorothy. *Freedom and Culture.* New York, N.Y.: Prentice-Hall, 1959.

Lewis, Oscar. *Tepostlan, Village in Mexico.* New York, N.Y.:
Holt, Rinehart & Winston, 1960.

Neihardt, John G. *Black Elk Speaks.* Lincoln, Nebr.: University
of Nebraska Press, 1950.

Opler, Morris. *Apache Odyssey.* New York, N.Y.: Holt, Rinehart
& Winston, 1969.

Powell, Sumner Chilton. *Puritan Village.* Middletown, Conn.:
Wesleyan University Press, 1963.

Radin, Paul. *The World of Primitive Man.* New York, N.Y.:
Henry Schuman, 1953.

Redfield, Robert. *The Little Community.* Chicago, Ill.: University of Chicago Press, 1955.

Rothenberg, Jerome (ed.). *Technicians of the Sacred.* New York,
N.Y.: Doubleday & Co., 1968.

Sandoz, Mari. *These Were the Sioux.* New York, N.Y.: Hastings
House, 1961.

Trigger, Bruce G. *The Huron.* New York, N.Y.: Holt, Rinehart
& Winston, 1969.

4. GENERAL ESSAYS ON CONTEMPORARY SEARCH FOR SMALL COMMUNITY

Baltzell, E. Digby. *The Search for Community in Modern America*. New York, N.Y.: Harper & Row, 1968.

Boyd, Malcolm. *The Underground Church*. Baltimore, Md.: Penguin Books, Inc., 1969.

Brode, John. *The Process of Modernization: An Annotated Bibliography on Sociocultural Aspects of Development*. Cambridge, Mass.: Harvard University Press, 1969.

Hammerz, Ulf. *Soulside: Inquiries into Ghetto Culture and Community*. New York, N.Y.: Columbia University Press, 1969.

Klapp, Orrin E. *Collective Search for Identity*. New York, N.Y.: Holt, Rinehart & Winston, 1968.

Minar, David W. and Scott Greer. *The Concept of Community*. Chicago, Ill.: Aldine, 1969.

Roszak, Theodore. *The Making of a Counter Culture*. New York, N.Y.: Doubleday & Co., 1969.

Stein, Maurice. *The Eclipse of Community*. New York, N.Y.: Harper and Row, 1964.

Suttles, Gerlad D. *The Social Order of the Slum*. Chicago, Ill.: University of Chicago Press, 1968.

Van der Zee, John. *Canyon*. New York, N.Y.: Harcourt, Brace & Jovanovich, Inc., 1972.

Wilson, R. Jackson. *In Quest of Community: Social Philosophy in the US 1860–1920*. London, Eng.: Oxford University Press, 1968.

5. CONTEMPORARY COMMUNES

Ald, Roy. *The Youth Communes*. New York, N.Y.: Tower Publications, 1971.

Atcheson, Richard. *The Bearded Lady*. New York, N.Y.: The John Day Company, 1971. [Going on the commune trip and beyond.]

Diamond, Stephen. *What the Trees Said: Life on a New Age Farm*. New York, N.Y.: Delacorte Press, 1971; Delta (paper), 1971. [Story of a successful communal farm by one of its founders.]

Gould, Peter. *Burnt Toast*. New York, N.Y.: Alfred Knopf, 1971. [A novel based on the Packer's Corner, Montague communes.]

Hedgepath, William and Dennis Stock. *The Alternative*. New York, N.Y.: Collier, 1971.

Houriet, Robert. *Getting Back Together.* New York, N.Y.: Coward, McCann and Geohegan, Inc., 1971. [A journey of discovery through American communes.]

Katz, Elia. *Armed Love.* New York, N.Y.: Holt, Rinehart & Winston, 1971.

Mungo, Raymond. *Total Loss Farm.* New York, N.Y.: E. P. Dutton & Co., Inc., 1970.

Zablocki, Benjamin. *The Joyful Community.* Baltimore, Md.: Penguin Books, 1971.

II PRIMARY SOURCE BIBLIOGRAPHY OF THE ONEIDA COMMUNITY

Unless otherwise noted, all materials herein were published at Oneida, N.Y. by the Oneida Community.

1. BOOKS AND ARTICLES

Estlake, Allan. *The Oneida Community.* London, Eng.: G. Redway, 1900. [A brief summary of and sermon on the history and practices of Oneida as seen by a former member.]

Noyes, George W. (ed.). *The Putney Community.* 1931. [A "must" in the study of events leading up to the founding of Oneida and the life and struggles of John H. Noyes and his group of Perfectionists.]

_____. *Religious Experiences of John Humphrey Noyes.* New York, N.Y.: The Macmillan Company, 1923. [Another must for understanding the Oneida Community and its roots in the theology of J. H. Noyes. Contains 416 pages of primary source materials, including correspondence of Noyes and others in the Putney Community. This work helps to provide a knowledge of Noyes's Perfectionism and the religious bases on which the community was formed and developed.]

Noyes, John Humphrey. *The Berean,* Putney, Vermont: 1847. [This is the official "canon" of writings by J. H. Noyes, dealing with his theology of Perfectionism.]

_____. *Bible Communism.* Putney, Vt.: Putney Community, 1853. [The theological basis for the social practices of Noyes's Perfectionism is documented and logically supported in this work.]

_____. *Confessions of J. H. Noyes.* Putney, Vt.: Leonard and Company, 1849.

_____. *Dixon and His Copyists.* 1871.

394

———. *History of American Socialism.* 1870. New York, N.Y.: Hillary House Publishers, 1961. New York, N.Y.: Dover Publications, 1966.

———. *Home Talks.* Edited by George W. Noyes. 1875. [The occasional talks—lectures, sermons—presented to the community at its evening meetings. Deals with a wide range of topics, mostly religious.]

———. *Paul's Prize.* Putney, Vt.: Putney Community, 1845.

———. *Way of Holiness.* Putney, Vt.: Putney Community, 1838.

Noyes, Pierrepont. *My Father's House.* New York, N.Y.: Farrar and Rinehart, 1937. [Excellent and readable story of a stirpicultural son of J. H. Noyes and his early life in the community at Oneida, including the break-up period.]

Oneida Community. *Annual Reports, 1850–1851.* Nos. 2 and 3. 1850, 1851.

Oneida Community. *Handbook of the Oneida Community.* 1867 (1st ed.), 1871 (2d ed.), and 1875 (3rd ed.).

Oneida Community. *Male Continence.* 1872.

Oneida Community. *Mutual Criticism.* 1876.

Oneida Community. *Scientific Propagation.* 1877.

Worden, Harriet. Old Mansion House Memories. 1950. [The mother of Pierrepont Noyes gives us a glimpse into the practical, everyday life of the community and its many and varied day-to-day activities.]

2. BOOKLETS AND PAMPHLETS WRITTEN ABOUT AND PUBLISHED BY THE ONEIDA COMMUNITY

Easton, Abel. *The Dissolution of the Oneida Community.* 1886.

———. *From the Roman Church to Christian Communism.* No date.

———. *Synopsis of a New Work on the Oneida Community.* No date.

Gordon, G. A. *The Void Which Oneida Perfectionism Alone Can Fill.* No date.

Non-Communists are Non-Christians. No author or date.

The Oneida Community. [Reprint from the *Encyclopedia Britannica.*]

Oneida Community, Limited. [Reprint from the *National Magazine* (November, 1905).]

The Oneida Community As It Exists At Present. [Reprint from the *Indianapolis Journal* (June 14, 1901).]

The Rise and Progress of the Oneida Community. [Reprint from the Denver Times (August 11, 1901).]

Seymour, Henry J. *The Oneida Community—A Dialogue.* No date.

————. *Oneida Community Confession of Christ.* No date.

Skinner, Harriet H. *New Haven Perfectionism vs. Methodist Sanctification.* No date.

III GROUP MARRIAGE: AN ANNOTATED BIBLIOGRAPHY OF NONFICTION MATERIALS*

Alpenfels, Ethel. "Progressive Monogamy," in Otto, *op. cit.* [see below]. [Considers what is sometimes called sequential polygamy (several partners, one at a time).]

Anderson, Ole Stig. *Rogen om Storfamilia.* Rhodes, Strandgada 36 D., Copenhagen, Denmark: [In Danish. Unavailable in English at present. Included for completeness.]

————. Interviewed in *Communes, Europe.* Richard Fairfield. [To be published by Alternatives Foundation, spring, 1972.]

Anon. "Group Marriage: How It Really Works," *Sexual Freedom*, vol. 1, no. 2 (January 1969), pp. 12–13. [Short piece based on single interview with one working group marriage (Harrad West). Accurate but very shallow, barely penetrating the public image.]

Anon. "Letters on a Group Marriage," *The Modern Utopian*, vol. 4, no. 2 (Spring 1970). [A short realistic picture of the distinct perspectives provided by two participants in the same group-marriage attempt.]

Bernard, Jessie. "Women, Marriage, and the Future," *The Futurist* (April 1970), pp. 41–43. [Explores how technological unemployment, birth control, and women's liberation might influence family structure. Sees need for sex as male chauvinist plot. "Celibacy is honorable state." Rhetoric.]

Buckley, Tom. "Oh Copenhagen," *The New York Times Magazine* (February 8, 1970), pp. 32–46. [Describes, among other things, the "storfamilia" (expanded families) of Denmark.]

Constantine, Larry L. and Joan M. Constantine. "Multilateral

---

*This group-marriage bibliography is excerpted from a more extensive one on multilateral relations prepared by Larry and Joan Constantine (Multilateral Relations Study Project).

Marriage: Alternate Family Structure in Practice." Unpublished plenary address 1970 meeting of the Indiana Council on Family Relations. [Early position paper. Defines multilateral marriage and contrasts it with other forms. Identifies some key problem areas giving early observational results on role of these in practice. Suffers from being too long, too preliminary.]

—————. "Where Is Marriage Going," *The Futurist* (April 1970), pp. 44–46. [Short summary of multilateral marriage, nothing new. Identifies the intimate network (cf. Stoller) as probably more widely practiced in the future.]

—————. "The Ultimate Intimate Group." [Unpublished manuscript for semi-popular article, which we, the authors, killed when the editors insisted on distorting our materials. Similar to "Multilateral Marriage" (see above), but more recent, less formal.]

—————. "Pragmatics of Group Marriage: Year One," *The Modern Utopian*, vol. 4, nos. 3–4 (summer-fall, 1970). [Informal "primer" on realities of group marriage, aimed toward potential participant.]

Constantine, Larry L. "Personal Growth in Multiperson Marriages." [Unpublished manuscript, but has been submitted for publication. Somewhat clumsy analysis of relationship of "growth" to group-marriage participation. Does discuss important pressure-to-grow phenomenon. Group marriage is seen as both demanding and facilitating personal growth.]

—————. "Methodology for the Study of Multilateral Relations." [Manuscript in preparation. Describes development of emerging humanistic methodology for the Multilateral Relations Study Project. Of interest mainly to professionals and those concerned for ethical-humanistic issues in "touchy" research.]

—————. "Group Marriages and Communes: A Definitional Note." [Unpublished paper. Elaborates on distinctions between these frequently confused phenomena.]

Downing, Joseph J. "The Tribal Family and the Society of Awakening," in Otto, *op. cit.* [see below]. [Tribal families are more communes than families, as is clear from Downing's account, most of which is on his favorite fantasy—the "Society of Awakening." His analysis of work roles and sexual differentiation show he is clearly either confused on the ethos of the "society" or confused by confusing more than one faction. Frequent non sequiturs in his effort to present the "society" as praiseworthy.]

Ellis, Albert. "Group Marriage—A Possible Alternative," in Otto, *op. cit.* [see below]. Reviews early literature on group marriage (probably wrong that group marriage has always been around, appears to incorrectly interpret Westermark, cf. Fison). Several of the major difficulties and advantages are correctly identified and discussed. Generally very good. Ellis's most serious shortcoming is his lack of definition and precision. Crashing, promiscuity, mate-swapping, etc.—all at times seem to be treated as "group marriage."]

Fison, L. and A. W. Howitt. *Kamilaroi and Kurnai: Group Marriage and Relationship.* New York, N.Y.: Humanities Press, 1967. [Photochemical reprint of original 1880 edition. 372 pp. Index, citations (not useful). From heart of last century's debate over whether group marriage was ever a reality. It appears that something directly related to "tribal marriage" did actually exist across Australia but was dying out even as it was studied, Westermark, et al., to the contrary. Recommended only for most serious student. (Price, $12.95).]

Gourley, H. Wayne. "Group Marriage: Utopian Ethics," *The Modern Utopian*, vol. 2, no. 1 (Sept. 1967). [Proposes group marriage as necessary and ideal for utopian communities. Narrow in understanding of monogamous marriage. Exclusiveness of Eros is seen to eliminate Agape altogether.]

————. "Walden House and Group Marriage," *The Modern Utopian*, vol. 1, no. 1 (September 1966).

Hammong, Liz. "Family Living—A Radical Solution," *The Modern Utopian*, vol. 4, no. 2 (spring 1970). [Proposes communal living as alternative to nuclear family. No content.]

Harrad West. "Statement from Harrad West," *Sexual Freedom*, vol. 1. no. 2 (January 1970), pp. 10–11. [*Public* policy stance of one extant, successful group marriage.]

————. "Harrad West," *The Modern Utopian*, vol. 4, no. 1 (winter 1970). [Same as in *Sexual Freedom* (above), but with worthwhile commentary by Dick Fairfield on swinging as a route to group marriage (i.e., swinging is not appropriate.)]

Henriksen, Alfred J. N. "An Alternative to Monogamous Marriage." Unpublished address delivered March 8, 1970, at Pacific Unitarian Church, Palos Verdes Peninsula, California. [Based on an informal meeting with members of two group marriages, the Reverend Henriksen presents a fair, realistic picture of group marriage. He was able in a surprisingly short time to isolate a number of the balances, trade-offs, and sacrifices necessary in a group marriage. Non-judgmental approach.]

McKain, Barbara and Michael McKain. "Building Extended Families," *Women: A Journal of Liberation* (winter 1970), pp. 24–25. [A plea for abolishing contractual families, tying women's liberation to group marriage. Rhetoric, little content.]

Neubeck, Gerhard. "Polyandry and Polygyny — Viable Today?" in Otto, *op. cit.* [see below]. [Neubeck erects a straw man, a peculiar form of rotating polygamy — two weeks with one spouse, two with the other — and explores it in fantasy. His structure is antithetical to the ethos of most contemporary group marriages in being built on compartmentalized relationships, virtual denial of the existence of other relationships, and minimal openness. He is patently wrong in his assertion that compartmentalization is essential; it is, to the contrary, what tumbles his straw man.]

Orleans, Myron and Florence Wolfson. "The Future of the Family," *The Futurist* (April 1970), pp. 48–49. [Explores trends from general perspective. Covers communal child-rearing, serial monogamy, group marriage. Predicts triads will predominate (we, the Constantines, concur; true today). Sees home as workplace and more a "community."]

Otto, Herbert A. (ed.). *The Family in Search of a Future.* New York, N.Y.: Appleton-Century-Crofts, 1970. [The only contemporary nonfiction references on alternative marriage structures prior to our work. The most pertinent chapters are listed separately in this annotated bibliography.]

————. "Has Monogamy Failed?" *Saturday Review* (April 25, 1970), pp. 23–25, 62. [Explores some trends: commune, group marriage, intimate networks, emphasis on growth, freedom, and creativity in monogamous marriages, etc. Concludes "No" to title because monogamy is not rigid but evolving. Somewhat non sequitur. Good article for giving to friends, however.]

Rimmer, Robert H. *The Harrad Letters.* The New American Library, 1969. 160 pp. Includes autobiographical notes (good), original introduction to *Harrad Experiment* (too long, but interesting), and letters from fans. The letters have much praise and excitement, little to offer on pragmatics. In a number of cases we know the writers, whose heads are really much elsewhere from their letters.]

————. *You and I Searching for Tomorrow.* New York, N.Y.: The New American Library, 1971.

Roy, Rustum and Della Roy. "Monogamy: Where We Stand

Today," *The Humanist* (March–April 1970). [Builds a strong, systematic case for failure of contemporary monogamy.]

Solis, Gary. "Group Marriage and California Law." Paper for class in family law, University of California, at Davis. [Excellent analysis of legal status of group marriage in one state. Citations to cases (none yet involving a group marriage). Points out peculiar status of (legally) married versus single participants in group marriage. Conclusion: the Man can get you any time he wants (including under the Mann Act).]

Stoller, Frederick H. "The Intimate Network of Families," in Otto, *op. cit.* [Carefully analyzes current family isolation and proposes network of distinct but intimately connected families as a viable structure. The picture of the intimate network is complete except for the factor of sexual intimacy, which Stoller ignores. Good paper otherwise.]

Walley, David. "Getting It Together," *Scenes*, vol. 2, no. 4 (December 1969), pp. 39–41, 58. [Deals with three Boston "urban communes"—one is a short-lived attempt to form a group marriage, another is a group marriage but not called that by its members. Reporting is superficial, the reporter being misled in several cases by the "public image."]

Some other books published by Penguin are described on the following pages.

Benjamin Zablocki

THE JOYFUL COMMUNITY

This is an account of the Bruderhof, an experiment in Christian communal living now in its third generation. The author offers a revealing look at this unique commune — its founding in Germany in 1920, the difficult period of persecution and exile, the years of schism and crisis in America from 1959 to 1962, and its new American prosperity from the manufacture of beautiful toys. Most especially, he emphasizes the Bruderhof's everyday life, showing its members at work, at play, at worship, and in the important problem-solving and decision-making processes of communal life. Benjamin Zablocki, of the Department of Sociology at the University of California, wrote this book because he believes that the Bruderhof experiment is fundamentally related to mankind's eternal quest for brotherhood.

Benjamin DeMott

SURVIVING THE 70'S

A survival manual for the 1970's by one of America's top social critics. In these pages Benjamin DeMott considers the liberated woman, the college dropout, the "ecological summons," the new sexuality, and various other patterns of thought and action that characterize the contemporary scene. He asks: "How can a human being cope with the tilts of assumption and belief now occurring regularly in all corners of the culture? . . . What kinds of order can a mind work out for itself?" In answering such questions, *Surviving the 70's* looks not only at the mixed nature of experience today but also at the opportunities that lie beyond.